We Danced All Night

BARBARA CARTLAND

We Danced All Night

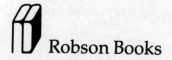
Robson Books

This Robson Paperback edition first published in 1994
by Robson Books Ltd, Bolsover House, 5-6 Clipstone
Street, London W1P 7EB.
First published in hardback in Great Britain in 1970.

British Library Cataloguing in Publication Data.
A catalogue record for this title is available from the
British Library.

ISBN 0 86051 925 2

Printed in Great Britain by WBC Limited, Bridgend,
Mid-Glamorgan.

Illustrations

Author's Acknowledgements

I want to thank my dear friend Mary Lady Delamere for her help in correcting much of the manuscript.

Noël Coward and his agents, Curtis Brown and Chappell and Company Limited, for permission to use his lyrics which are so much part of the period.

Lady Diana Cooper for permission to quote from her enchanting autobiographies: *The Rainbow Comes and Goes*, *The Light of Common Day*, and *Trumpets From the Steep*.

The late Michael Arlen's agents for permission to quote from *Those Charming People*.

Mr. H. E. Bray and his staff at Illustrated Newspapers for their inestimable help with the photographs, and I cannot think how I could have managed without them.

Also Madame Yevonde for permission to use several of her lovely pictures.

Miss Paulin, the County Council Librarian for Hertfordshire, Mr. R. J. Busby of Welwyn Garden City County Library, and Mr. S. Gillam of the London Library, who have been tireless in their efforts to find me the right books of the period.

Chappell and Company Limited of 50 New Bond Street for permission to include: 'Button Up Your Overcoat' by de Sylva, Brown & Henderson; 'The World is Waiting For The Sunrise' by Eugene Lockhart; 'Blue Boy Blues' by Cole Porter; 'Spread A Little Happiness' by Clifford Grey.

I also want to thank Ascherberg, Hopwood and Crew Limited for permission to quote from 'And Her Mother Came Too' by Dion Titheradge.

'Bye, Bye, Blackbird'—Copyright 1926 by Jerome H. Remick & Co., U.S.A. English publisher—Francis Day & Hunter Limited, 138–140 Charing Cross Road, London, W.C.2. Reprinted by permission. 'Don't Bring Lulu'—Copyright 1925 by

The Song of the Twenties

'Ev'ry morning, ev'ry evening,
    Ain't we got fun?
Not much money, oh! but honey!
    Ain't we got fun?
The rent's unpaid, dear,
    We haven't a sou,
But smiles were made, dear,
    For me and for you.
Though there's nothing in the larder,
    Don't we have fun?
Times are hard and getting harder,
    Still we have fun!
There's nothing surer,
The rich get rich and the poor get—children.
In the meantime, in between time,
    Ain't we got fun?'

CHAPTER ONE

I'm just wild about Harry,
And Harry's wild about me.
The Heav'n-ly blisses of his kisses
Fill me with ecstasy.

'DARLING, I love you! Will you marry me? I can't live without you.'

The moon was full. The sky was bright with stars. The waves of the Solent were lapping the beach. Behind me in the Clubhouse a band was playing.

This was living! This was life! This was being alone with a man!

I had left school in July 1919 and my mother had taken me and my two brothers to Bembridge in the Isle of Wight for the holidays. Still terribly depressed, dressed in the deep black of a widow with a floating veil, she had not cared where we went, feeling that her life had come to an end in May 1918 when my father had been killed in France.

She had been told that Bembridge was a gay and amusing place for the young, so she had rented a furnished house there for four guineas for the month. And it was there that I first looked with astonished eyes on a world which contained men. It is difficult today for people to understand how strictly the daughters of what was called 'the gentry' were brought up at the beginning of the century. A schoolgirl was treated as a child. And everything aimed towards a momentous goal when one was told one would 'come out'.

It literally was a 'coming out'. One emerged from the cloistered, sheltered, ignorant world of a child, and it seemed as though suddenly every door was open.

All the time one was still a 'flapper' there were innumerable restrictions and taboos. 'No, you can't go to the races. There would be nothing new for you to do when you "come out".' 'No, you can't go to a ball—or a late party—or a theatre—you must wait for these things until you "come out".'

It was also considered very fast if one talked about, or even thought too much about, men. And as for making oneself attractive, that, too, had to wait until I 'came out'.

At school I had been sent from the dinner-table on several occasions because I had powder on my nose, and told to wash my face. At home I was not expected to push myself forward or talk too much when people were there.

There was in most adults' minds the idea that children should be seen and not heard; and, though I talked nineteen-to-the-dozen when I was alone with my mother, when there were visitors I kept my place as a schoolgirl.

Now the restrictions were ended. I was out! I was grown-up! I was expected overnight to be amusing, gay, and attractive to men. And incredible though it seemed, I was! This was the third proposal I had had in two weeks, since I left school. The third man who had asked me to be his wife.

Men were an unknown but very fascinating species. I had seen few of them during the Great War which had ended on the 11th November the previous year. The boys I had known since child-hood had rushed in for an hour or so while they were on leave and I had been overwhelmed by how grown-up and important they seemed in their khaki uniforms and Sam Browne belts. But even if they had asked me—which they didn't—to go out with them, I should not have been allowed to do so.

There was however, at Bembridge, still talk of being chaperoned.

'If you go to the dance tonight,' my mother said, referring to the dances which took place at the Garland Club, which was the gay centre of Bembridge life, 'Mrs. So-and-so will chaperone you.'

The fact that from the moment I arrived to the moment I left I never saw Mrs. So-and-so again didn't matter. I was chaperoned. I was obeying the conventions.

Surprisingly, during the day, I was allowed to go sailing or for a walk with a young man, and of course at night one slipped away from the crowded dance-floor out into the moonlight to sit on the beach and receive, in that romantic setting, yet another proposal of marriage. I had never drunk champagne, but I felt this heady, bubbling excitement was what champagne must taste like!

I had been brought up to believe that my destiny was to fall in love and get married. That, I knew, was the whole point of being a woman.

'When I am married . . .'

'As soon as I am married.'

'I can't do that until I am married.'

I never for one moment thought that I wouldn't get married. Indeed, there was no other career open to women save that of being a governess or a companion. There had been talk during the war of women being emancipated, a word connected most distastefully with the Suffragettes who had 'made fools of themselves', and who were spoken of most scathingly by all 'sensible' people. But I and my contemporaries at school had realised that because of the war, finding a husband was not going to be as easy as it might have been had we emerged from our chrysalis five years earlier.

A million men who should have been in the right age group to be potential husbands had been killed, and we learned with feelings of anxiety that in consequence there were two million surplus women.

I suppose that because such information was continually drummed into our ears we became instinctively suspicious of every woman of our own age. She was, in fact, a potential enemy.

But in my case such fears were unnecessary. My mother had often quoted my grandmother, who was worldly wise and cynical, as saying: 'If one man wants you, they all do.' Well, she was right! Men wanted me. I had forty-nine proposals before I finally said 'yes'. Of course it wasn't only the marriageable—the eligible —men who went out of their way to seek me out. There was a raffish old baronet at Bembridge who pursued me relentlessly until, as my mother wrote in her diary:

'Had a few sharp words with Sir H. He's one of those tiresome old men who always runs after a pretty girl.'

There were several others like Sir H. In fact, after only a few weeks of leaving school, I began to think I was irresistible.

I think the main attraction was that I was full of gaiety and laughter. I also looked the part. Every man's ideal girl was

Gladys Cooper—fair, blue-eyed, the typical English Rose type—as Lily Elsie, the pin-up girl of the trenches, had been.

There was an air of gentle unsophistication about them both which made a man feel he wanted to cherish and protect them. There was nothing frightening, hard or challenging about their looks. They were essentially feminine, womanly and sweetly pink and white.

I was a pale imitation of such loveliness, but still of the same mould. Fair hair fluffed over the ears, large rather surprised eyes—mine were actually green—red lips, subject of much criticism and many arguments, and a clear skin helped by a chalk-white face powder. There were only three shades obtainable, dead white, yellow and almost brown!

Apart from my face and my youth, I had little to offer. I was certainly incredibly ignorant—not only of the world, of life, of sex, but also of politics, of almost every known subject, and even of the war itself.

My father had been killed in France, which had brought to our house, as to practically every house in the British Isles, an atmosphere of gloom, misery, and deep, unrelenting mourning. But in the last four years I had only seen my father at intermittent intervals when he had come on leave from France. He would arrive home, we his children would greet him with open arms.

He was a hero, we were surprised he hadn't already won the V.C. But almost before he had arrived, he was gone again.

Of course, we talked about him. Everyone we knew had a father in the Forces. In fact, my school at Netley Abbey reduced the fees because I was the daughter of a serving officer. I was, however, rather overshadowed by my best friend whose father was a general, while mine was only a major!

But while we boasted about our fathers we lived in manless homes. We were brought up by women, and Edwardian women at that. We were fenced round with narrow restrictive social customs, nurtured on snobbery, and isolated from any contact with, or knowledge of, people outside our own accepted class.

War had been a break-down of tradition for men, but the schoolgirls like myself had no idea of what war entailed. The nearest I got to it was hearing the soldiers singing in the troopships as they moved down the Solent, and occasionally going to

Netley Hospital to perform for the wounded. As the school plays were incredibly amateurish, they must have been a doubtful entertainment. Except, of course, that the troops had little else to amuse them.

What today seems so incredible is that I never read the newspapers. At home my mother took the *Morning Post*, as my grandfather had done, only his paper was ironed every morning by the butler before he read it. I suppose I could have looked at it in the holidays had I wished to do so. At school we weren't allowed newspapers. In the evening the headmistress would occasionally read us extracts from *The Times*, which were terribly dull. It was considered far too morbid and upsetting for us to follow the course of the war, though we were occasionally told 'a big battle was in progress' or 'the position had improved'. That was all we knew.

This idea of it being unnecessary for children to read newspapers was universal. Lord Rothermere told me the other day that as a child he was forbidden to look at a newspaper of any sort, and it was only when he went to Eton that he was able to order one.

'In fact,' he said, 'I found there was a detective story in one of my father's newspapers and having read a little of it by chance, I used to creep down at night to follow the story. I was caught and severely punished for daring to do anything so outrageous as to read a newspaper!'

When I was quite young I remember seeing a pink paper called *The Pink'un* in my father's study. This had as its motto 'High Toryism, High Churchism, High Farming and Old Port for ever'. There was also a magazine called *The Winning Post*. I used to peep at these occasionally but the jokes were seldom intelligible. A newspaper which came on Sundays was called *The Police Court News*. I was strictly forbidden to touch it, and after my father had finished reading it he put it on the fire.

My knowledge of current affairs was, therefore, nil. I had, however, heard the shocking stories ground out by the official propaganda machine directed by Lord Northcliffe. Like most people in England, I believed that the Germans were extracting fat from human corpses which were tied together in bundles and sent from France in cattle-trucks.

My father had written home that one of his brother officers

had actually seen them. A crucified Canadian, cut down by an advancing regiment, had, we were told, been found to conceal a lethal booby-trap.

I also believed implicitly that Russian soldiers 'with snow on their boots' had been seen in trains all over the country being carried to the Western Front.

Hate for the enemy was something that my contemporaries had grown accustomed to, not only because the Germans had destroyed our fathers, brothers, uncles, cousins and friends, but because they had disregarded the accepted rules of war. The torpedoing of hospital ships, the use of flame-throwers and poison gas shocked and disgusted us, although without television or even radio programmes we had not the slightest conception of what this actually meant in terms of human suffering.

By 1918 there were books published about the war, but I didn't read them. It seems incredible, but at my 'finishing school' there was no library. I read a history book called *Heroes* over and over again. It was the nearest thing I could get to a story.

As I grew older I found that for twopence a time I could borrow books from the local library. At one time, when I was seventeen, I was reading three books a day! But they were only novels, because most lending libraries offered only the popular type of romantic literature—Victoria Cross and Elinor Glyn were strictly forbidden as 'hot stuff'. Ethel M. Dell, Ruby M. Ayres, Ian Hay, Baroness Orczy and, of course, E. M. Hull were my favourites.

'A hard sob broke from him and he kissed her trembling lips fiercely. "I will never let you go now. My God! If you knew how I wanted you. If you knew what it cost me to send you away. Pray God I keep you happy. You know the worst of me, poor child— you will have a devil for a husband."'

This certainly gave me a yearning for romance, and it made men a fascinating, unknown species. Every woman instinctively wants to tame a devil through the purity of her love. I was no exception. Everything was entrancing and exciting, and love and marriage were waiting for me!

To the men returning home alive from the filth, the horror and the terror of the trenches, I and my contemporaries were everything they thought they would never see again. They wanted to get married, they wanted security, they wanted comfort, above all they wanted love. For four years, or for some of them from the moment they had left school, they had been indoctrinated with hate. 'Hate the German, he's your enemy! Kill him! Fight him! Strain every muscle of your being to destroy him and everything he stands for!' It is not surprising that they didn't want to talk of what they'd been through.

Looking back, I can't remember anyone relating to me horrific details of their experiences, or even talking about them. There seemed so many other things to discuss, though they were certainly not academic! We were young, the sun was shining, there was music to dance to. What more could anyone want? Except to marry, to settle and to have a home of one's own.

The songs of the period all harped on marriage.

'I'll give you a golden ring
And my whole heart.
We're hearing a blue bird sing,
We'll never part.
No matter what fate may bring,
What we may have to do,
We'll challenge the world and win,
Now I have you.'

We really believed it!

It was Ragtime all the way, Ragtime to which I had first been introduced in one never-to-be-forgotten, marvellous night in July 1914.

My parents were staying in London and I had come home for the holidays. My father took me to see *Hello, Ragtime* at the Hippodrome. I can remember now the excitement of putting on my best dress. It was white lace and I felt I looked rather childish in it. But to compensate for that, I had an enormous black ribbon bow at the back of my hair—a flapper's bow, to which I was not yet really entitled, but which I wore, this evening of all evenings, like a badge of honour.

I had never been in London before and as soon as I arrived I had been taken to the Zoo. I saw the crowds in the streets, the horse-drawn buses—and had actually travelled on top of one of them. I was entranced by the shops with their glittering windows and by the hansom cabs with their elegant occupants as they looked out over the closed door which seemed to hold them prisoner.

At the Hippodrome I had sat wide-eyed, overwhelmed by the lights, the music, the beauty of the chorus. Miss Shirley Kellogg, the blonde American star of the show, seemed to me like a creature from another world. When she came down a gangplank over the orchestra with a basket of pink roses to distribute amongst the male members of the audience, my father caught one and gave it to me. I felt my cup of happiness overflow with the wonder of it all.

Then war was declared. A week later my father left for France and our home in Worcestershire was closed.

The nearest I got to the dangers of war was in 1915. In fact, I often think of how a fraction of an inch one way or another made the difference between life and death for me. I was in Somerset, where I was having lessons with a friend of my own age and sharing her governess. A jolly middle-aged major, who liked showing off to young girls, came to stay.

He offered to show me his service revolver and brought it into the billiards room. We were alone and he demonstrated how one took one out the clip which contained five bullets. Then he said: 'Now it's empty.'

Jovially he pointed it at me and pulled the trigger. He had forgotten the sixth bullet in the chamber! It whizzed through my hair and with a deafening report buried itself in the wall behind me! I had never before seen a man really go deathly pale.

'Don't tell anyone,' he begged.

I didn't, but I was deaf in my right ear for a week.

All my life people were always telling me 'not to tell'. When I was young they wanted to confide because I would listen; when I became a writer they looked on me as a confessor, adviser, clairvoyant and morale-booster. I can't think why people who practise certain professions like doctors, solicitors, barristers, and apparently authors, loosen the tongues of others, but they do.

In about 1912 I was at a huge Conservative rally arranged by my father for our Member of Parliament. There must have been two thousand people there and the platform was a hay-cart. As the audience were assembling round the cart I walked round the back and found a short, stocky, red-haired man poring over some notes.

I recognised him as Mr. Stanley Baldwin, a newly elected Member of Parliament from an adjacent constituency. He looked up at my approach, and I saw his face was covered with sweat and his hands were trembling. I stared, and he said quickly:

'I'm not ill—just nervous. I'm always like this just before I make a speech. Don't tell anyone.'

I didn't. But even when he was Prime Minister Mr. Baldwin was never to get over his nerves before making a speech.

Bembridge in 1919 gave me four weeks of sailing in little red-wing yachts, dancing, and the incredible experience of learning how to flirt.

'Where do you want to live?' my mother, brave and unselfish, asked.

'London.'

'But why? We know no one there.'

'I shall get to know everyone.'

'You are sure?'

'Quite sure!'

My mother rented a tall, gloomy, furnished house in Neville Street, South Kensington. It cost four guineas a week. She had very little money and two boys to educate, Ronald twelve years old, Tony aged six.

Every public school had a war memorial scheme, for sons of old boys killed in the war. Charterhouse, where my father had been because he was thought to be delicate and it was on a hill, made my mother a grant of £100 a year for Ronald, but even so there were heavy expenses. There had to be a roof over our head, there was Tony's schooling, there were clothes, food, holidays and a war memorial to be paid for, which my mother felt must be erected to my father's memory.

For the first time it was suggested that I should get a job. I had never imagined such a thing might happen and I was completely unskilled at anything which might earn money. What was more, there just weren't jobs to be had.

Men were pouring out of the Services, all wanting employment. They were prepared to take anything, but the work wasn't there. They certainly weren't proud. All the chorus boys in Albert de Courville's review at the London Hippodrome were demobilised officers. And several were D.S.O.s and M.C.s.

My grandmother employed a butler who had been a major

and won the D.S.O. Lord Vivian would only employ ex-Servicemen, and the more limbless and disabled the better. He insisted on their always wearing their service medals.

I was continually finding that taxi-drivers were known to the young man who was escorting me to some dance. 'Oh, hello, sir,' they would say in rather embarrassed tones, as they saw who was driving us. And some of the commissionaires and waiters at the night-clubs we visited had been their brother officers or even of superior rank in the trenches.

In every street in the West End there were pathetic little bands of ex-Servicemen rattling money boxes at the passers-by and singing songs like:

'Where do flies go in the winter-time?'

'You might get a job as a secretary or receptionist to a doctor,' my mother suggested. I think she believed that doctors were not interested in sex. Anyway it sounded safe. And sexual safety was something that mothers were still very concerned about.

Before the war no girl had been considered safe alone with a man. In my mother's day it was unthinkable for an unmarried girl to drive alone with a man in a carriage or a hansom, while to lunch or dine alone with one was to be socially damned! As for a girl going to a man's flat, well there could be one reason he had invited her and one reason only!

It was, therefore, a mother's job to protect her daughter against the virile passions of every man who saw her. The war indeed had broken down a great many barriers—even so, the things nice girls couldn't do were endless.

One thing my mother discovered on our arrival in London was that invitations said simply 'Miss Cartland and partner'. Chaperones had ceased to exist. Hostesses just couldn't afford them.

'No champagne and lobster suppers!' my mother's generation exclaimed regretfully. 'The girls today don't know what they're missing!'

But we didn't care what we ate. We didn't mind whether we ate or drank as long as we could go dancing.

'Can you come in tomorrow evening? I bought some new records.'

'How lovely!'

'It'll be buns and lemonade on the back stairs, and Mother won't let me use the drawing room.'

'What does it matter. I'll be there!'

'Bring a man!'

'Of course!'

The men coming out of the Services were exhilarated with the knowledge that they had escaped death. They wanted a bed with sheets to sleep in and the company of women. But most of them knew all too well that unless they could get a job they faced starvation. So they eked out their money as carefully as they could, which meant that mothers had no part in post-war entertaining—they wanted to take a girl out alone.

The mothers, therefore, evolved a very curious arrangement. You might not dine alone with a man, although you could dine four if you could find another girl and a man to join you. But he could take you out to dance after dinner. This, of course, suited the impoverished male escort. He could have a sandwich or something cheap at his club, pick me up in a taxi after I had dined at home, and we could go dancing.

The most popular place in the last months of 1919 and the beginning of 1920 was the Grafton Galleries. The Prince of Wales was a member. It was an enormous picture gallery, underground in Grafton Street. It was extremely respectable, so much so that when there was an exhibition of nude drawings they were covered at night with pieces of tissue paper.

The refreshments supplied by Gunter's were very simple—sandwiches and iced cakes. Only non-alcoholic drinks were served—iced coffee and a concoction known as 'Turk's Blood', which was bright pink and in which floated small cubes of some unidentified fruit. There were tables all round the gallery and a Negro band.

We one-stepped to:

> 'He's sweet just like choc'late candy,
> And just like honey from the bee.
> Oh, I'm just wild about Harry,
> And he's just wild about,
> Can-not do without,
> He's just wild about me!'

We waltzed to the lovely dreamy waltz 'Love will find a way' from *The Maid of the Mountains* which José Collins' golden voice was to sing for 2,352 performances.

Sometimes the band played 'Destiny', the waltz so popular just before the war which had been the last tune, played on a squeaky gramophone, heard by thousands of young men before they went to their deaths.

As it was music, music all the time, the songs of the day became an inseparable part of our living, and most of them were as gay and tinkling as our restless twinkling feet. They also told us what we wanted to hear: 'Bye, Bye, Black Bird' was later the typical song of the whole era—

'Pack up all your cares and woe
Here I go singing low,
    Bye, Bye, Black Bird.
Where somebody waits for me,
Sugar's sweet and so is she,
    Bye, Bye, Black Bird.'

The men all wore tails and white ties and the greatest achievement at that moment was to see for how long one could twirl round and round and round the room with one's partner—the man's tails flowing out behind like a propeller.

Soon after the New Year of 1920 my partner and I found a more exciting night-club than the Grafton Galleries, or, at least, one to go on to after 'God Save the King' had been played by the Negro band at 2 a.m. This was called 'Rector's', a rather sordid place deep down underground in a cellar in the Tottenham Court Road.

It had a low ceiling and little ventilation. Here a man could get a drink by going to the cloakroom, but the owners were always in fear of a police raid and everyone was inspected through a grid in the door before admittance. I was not supposed to go to Rector's, but who could resist the temptation?

I remember Rector's was the first place where face-powder was free in the ladies' cloakroom. It was dead white and had a very strange, cheap scent, which seemed to pervade not only the cloakroom but the whole premises.

Rector's was extremely gay. The Negro band had one number

where they used to put on firemen's helmets and process round the room, playing noisily on brass trumpets and cornets. And, after all, any place looked gay and glamorous with all the women wearing full evening dresses and the men sporting white ties, tails and carnation buttonholes.

Very short skirts had not yet come in. I wore dresses just above the ankles and the poor, like myself, could buy black or white—there were no other colours on sale—stockings in a coarse shiny art-silk, which ended just where one's skirt began.

'Do be careful, darling, not to cross your legs,' my mother would warn me.

One was very conscious of 'legs'. Women landworkers in the war had worn breeches and gaiters; for:

> 'Dainty skirts and delicate blouses,
> Aren't much use for pigs and cows-es.'

Whether this was sensible or not, country people had still been shocked and disgusted. As our old gardener said:

'Oi reckons if women starts alooking like men, we'll soon have 'em thinkin' like men, and then they'll be abossing us like men.'

How right he was! Because the women, fascinated by wearing 'the trousers', were never going to give them up.

Pictures of the twenties show us with short skirts. But these, like everything else, developed slowly and took some years to rise. Here is the actual rate:

> 1919–23 : Skirt just above the ankles.
> 1924   : Up to the calf.
> 1925   : Just below the knees.
> 1926   : To the knees, but no further!

In 1928 skirts started by dropping at the back in the evenings, and for the daytime slowly came down to below the knee and lower still by the early thirties.

The drop at the back was very becoming. The dress in which I was presented at Court for the second time on my marriage was layer upon layer of white tulle, very full and cascading to the floor at the back but showing my legs in the front. The bodice was embroidered all over in 'diamond' thistles.

In 1919 the length of our skirts did not prevent very spirited dancing. We sprang about the room, full of gaiety and irrepressible high spirits. At private dances there were at first programmes, with their tiny pencils attached.

There was enormous satisfaction in having a full programme, utter misery when there were many blanks. But programmes were soon dispensed with, and the band put up numbers instead. One said:

'I'll dance number eight with you.'

But as the numbers only went up to twelve, it was often:

'The third extra!'

Numbers were easy and at least one could get rid of a boring partner without all the manœuvring which takes place today.

Private parties were gradually increasing as people recovered from the shock and the financial restrictions of the war. Only young people were asked but the hostess usually invited half a dozen of her personal friends to give an impression of chaperonage. Inevitably, after an hour or so, my partner would say:

'Deadly dull—let's push off to the Galleries.'

'I daren't, she'll see us.'

'No she won't! We'll walk outside for some air—then seize a taxi.'

'What about my cloak?'

'Leave it! We'll collect it on the way home.'

We went.

> 'We dance at breakfast,
> We dance at tea,
> The husky moan of the saxophone
> Drew you to me.
> You are my dream girl, my dear delight,
> That's why my darling
> We dance all night.'

Dancing at night wasn't enough. The *thé dansant* had been started in the war, and now as both men and women were unemployed they had plenty of time to dance at the Savoy Hotel for five shillings a head, at the Café de Paris for four shillings, where the price was the same as the Piccadilly Hotel, which was considered rather fast, or the Express Rooms. I was not allowed to go to the Regent Palace or the Astoria Dance Hall where tea with dancing only cost two shillings. But I once went to a supper dance at the Regent Palace, which I considered very dashing. And the price was three shillings and sixpence a head.

Of course, there were plenty of afternoon dances in private houses too. My mother had a friend called Mrs. Kerr Smiley who lived in one of the huge houses in Belgrave Square (now all Embassies or the Institute of Directors). She was American and every Sunday she gave a *thé dansant*. At first my mother was horrified at the idea. She had always been very religious and playing cards and dancing were two things we had never been allowed on a Sunday.

'But I must go,' I pleaded with her. 'All my friends are going. How can I refuse?'

'Very well,' my mother said. 'You can go, but you must teach in Sunday School to make up for it.'

I accepted this compromise with delight and hurried off every Sunday morning to the children's Sunday School, St. Paul's, Knightsbridge.

It seems extraordinary that nobody instructed me what I should teach the children or supervised my lessons. I was given a book with simple Bible stories in it, and after I had asked the children a few questions, I used to tell them a story. My class was quite big but it was the best behaved and best attended in the whole church. For I told them dramatic stories, inventing them as I went along and serialising them, so we started where we left off the previous Sunday.

Then, feeling very virtuous, I would go off to what was known as church parade in Hyde Park. This had been a very important function of the London season before the war. All society paraded at Stanhope Gate, where they sat on green chairs and watched their friends walk or drive by.

Most of the men wore frock-coats and top-hats. But the rendezvous petered out and finally disappeared when motor-cars began to carry the more prosperous out of London into the country. A weekend spent in the country meant that the young no longer went to church and were therefore not seen at Stanhope Gate, the traditional meeting place, in their best clothes.

But until this the most exciting thing that could happen on

Sundays was to be invited to lunch at Claridges with a young man. I used to pray that someone would ask me, and when they did I would sweep proudly into the restaurant, feeling that with my frock-coated escort I was really creating a sensation! And then off to the *thé dansant*!

One of the young men to be seen at Mrs. Kerr Smiley's *thé dansant* was her brother, Ernest Simpson. He was in the Guards and was rather stiff and reserved. He had a very square chin and always looked as if his collar was strangling him. He took me home once in a taxi and tried to kiss me. I refused, knowing he was not seriously interested in me because his sister had reiterated over and over again:

'Ernest has to marry money!'

Ernest didn't! Seventeen years later he brought home an American called Wallis, who was not rich but who was to rock the monarchy and the British constitution as no woman had ever done before.

We all danced and danced. When we were asked to the country to stay for a Hunt Ball we started dancing as soon as we arrived, hurried upstairs to dress, drove ten or fifteen miles to the ball, danced till 5 a.m. and were up for breakfast at least by nine o'clock the next morning. No one breakfasted in bed unless they were ill.

In one house I stayed in, the son, who had invited me, said: 'Please don't be late for prayers. We have them at eight. And Father is furious if everyone doesn't come down.'

I remember getting to bed at 5.30 and crawling downstairs and still half asleep at one minute to eight, to find everyone, including all the staff, assembled in the dining room waiting for me!

In 1920 the better-class restaurants grew anxious to attract the young people. The Berkeley allowed clients they knew to dance from nine o'clock to well after midnight and order nothing but a jug of beer or orangeade. Naturally, with so much exercise on so little food, we became hungry and this necessitated a call at the Hyde Park Corner coffee-stand in the early hours of the morning. There, the taxis drawn up in long rows, we would imbibe very milky, sweet coffee out of thick china cups, sometimes sitting talking until the dawn broke.

I can recall so vividly the musty leathery smell of the high-roofed taxis; the fragrance of the milky coffee in the thick white

26

cups; the sense of being isolated in a tiny world which contained only a man and me. It was cosy, warm and intimate, and aroused a delicious feeling of anticipation. Would he try to kiss me? Would he propose? We would talk until the stars went out, the darkness faded. Then regretfully I'd say: 'I must go home,' and my young man would fetch the cabman from the green wooden shelter known as the 'Junior Turf Club', where he had been sitting waiting with his colleagues.

It was being alone with a man in a taxi and later dining alone which convinced me—then and for ever—that the best party in the world consists of two people. I didn't want huge dinner parties with the hostess in a tiara, I didn't want diplomatic receptions or musical soirées. I wanted a table in a restaurant with a soft shaded light and someone saying in a hoarse voice: 'God! You're wonderful! I'm mad about you!'

Already there was talk about the impropriety of the post-war young women. The older generation were deeply shocked because we powdered our noses and painted our lips. In fact my great-aunts said openly that because I did these things I was fast and improper. After I wrote a novel in which the Duke on page 200 kissed the heroine rather chastely, they said that it proved what they had always suspected, that I was extremely immoral and must have written from experience.

I can only speak for myself. But I was, when I came out, absolutely and completely innocent. I knew, of course, that people who slept in the same bed had babies, but I had no idea what they did. I suppose it was a kind of shyness which kept me from asking.

My mother had always said to me, 'If you want to know anything, do ask me.' But I hadn't liked to ask and though I had been to two high schools, two boarding schools and been educated with another girl and a governess for two years, I honestly had no knowledge at all about sex.

Finally, after my fifth or sixth proposal of marriage and when I had become secretly engaged to a young Irishman in the Life Guards, I asked my mother how one had a baby. I was so shocked and horrified by what she told me that I broke off my engagement immediately. For weeks I walked about, staring at people in the street and thinking, 'Good heavens! They've done that!'

Looking back I am quite certain that most of my contemporaries were as ignorant as I was. At any rate, if they knew, they didn't talk. We would have blushed at discussing such things!

Therefore, when we sat in the rows of taxis at Hyde Park Corner, a gentle kiss was all that 'happened'. I never even contemplated that there might be anything else—nor was there.

In those days there was a very great gulf between the lady and the prostitute. I believed, as my mother's generation had believed, that a prostitute felt passionate about a man and a lady did not. At the time this belief was almost universal. In 1926 a well-known London doctor went to Oxford and lecturing to the undergraduates told them that 'no woman was capable of feeling passion'.

The young men I knew in 1919 and 1920 treated me as if I were made of Dresden china. They never swore in front of me, I was never told a risky story, they made no improper advances. To the men who asked me to dance I was a 'lady' and entitled to respect. They rose to their feet automatically when I came into the room; they walked on the outside of the pavement (a Georgian innovation to save one from being splashed by coach-wheels on the muddy road); they helped me in and out of a car; they asked if they could smoke; they raised their hats to me and to every female they spoke to, whatever her station in life.

These good manners were not confined to one class. Men stood aside to let a woman get on a bus first, the conductor would reach out to help. Inside no man would think of sitting while a woman was standing; tradesmen, such as butchers, bakers and delivery men, touched their forelock or took off their hats to all their customers and addressed them as 'miss' or 'ma'am'.

There was still—despite the women war-workers, who were really only a small proportion of the population—a glamour and a mystery about the respectable woman. She was a thing apart, still to be wooed. before she was won. And how delightfully one was wooed. Men who loved me would stand outside my house late at night on the evenings I did not go out with them in a silent salute. Men who dropped me home in the early hours of the morning, would leave a note a few hours later, for me to find on my breakfast tray. They would write me poems and there would be flowers.

'Good morning, darling,' one note read, 'I want these roses to see you.'

They wrote poetry easily, they felt poetical, they were romantic. One young man when we parted wrote:

> 'Was this our parting to no other end?
> Have I no other harvest of my tears
> Than desolation through the lonely years?
> Yet am I praying that the past may lend
> Lost love, lost joy, one moment to depend
> Time passing from those vain regretful spears.
> I'm asking when this cloud of sorrow clears
> For all I've lost—can time make no amend?'

What no historian seems to record is the mental state of the men returning from the hell of the trenches. Those who had lost a leg or arm received a lot of sympathy, but there was no one in those days to talk of their psychological reaction to what they had been through.

They were all to a certain extent shell-shocked. Boys of eighteen, like my future husband, had gone straight from Sandhurst to the indescribable horrors of Passchendaele, where a subaltern's expectation of life was twenty minutes. Many had seen their friends shot down, often while still alive to drown in the stinking mud or lie out in no-man's-land for days.

Those who returned alive were nervy, tense, abnormally depressed and apprehensive. Some were suffering from venereal disease or the after-effects of the treatment. This was the old-fashioned, extremely painful mercury cure, very little changed from the time of Charles II who had used it.

Of course, I had no idea of this at the time, any more than I knew, as I do now, that the soldiers being demobilised all showed signs of malnutrition in some form or another. The Army in Flanders had certainly not been provided with a balanced diet on bully beef and plum and apple jam. And like us at home—where food was in short supply and expensive—they were, although we had no idea of it, desperately short of vitamins. These had been discovered by E. Funk in 1912 but their value was not yet popular or appreciated.

Was it any wonder that we found ourselves in emotional and dramatic situations, which we could not understand and had no idea how to cope with?

Owing to my mother's revelations regarding sex, I had broken off my secret engagement to Dick, the young Life Guardsman. I had entered into it light-heartedly, as I always found it difficult to say 'no' to anyone pleading with me. Now in my state of shock on learning the truth about sex, I knew I could never marry him.

Two nights later I found myself in a party with Dick at Rector's. He had expected to meet me, while I was surprised to see him. He insisted on my dancing with him and then said he had to see me alone. He was so insistent that I agreed that he should take me home.

We started off in a taxi and stopped at the Hyde Park coffee stall. Dick fetched the customary two cups of coffee; then shutting the taxi door he drew a revolver from his pocket.

'Either you marry me or I will shoot myself!'

I didn't believe him, but it was difficult to know what to do. Ethel M. Dell's and E. M. Hull's strong silent heroes had not prepared me for this. Their men had passion flaming in their eyes, but they exercised an iron control over their feelings. The heroine had only to appeal to their better nature. Dick wouldn't listen to me.

'I'll shoot myself, unless you marry me.'

'But I don't love you.'

'You said you did. You can't offer a man happiness on a plate, then take it away.'

'It's all my fault and I'm sorry—terribly sorry—but I don't love you enough.'

'Enough for what?'

'Enough to marry you.'

'Then I'll shoot myself.'

What did worry me was that the revolver seemed all the time to be pointed at my stomach. I hadn't forgotten the jovial major! We argued as the hours passed, until the dawn came and passers-by could see into the taxi. By this time we were both very tired and some of the aggressiveness seemed to have gone out of Dick's manner.

'I will give you my answer when I get home,' I promised finally.

To my relief he agreed. When I reached the house, I jumped out and opening the front door said:

'No, I can't!'

Dick didn't shoot himself. He arrived next day to see my mother, while his mother, also a widow, asked me to go and see her. I was lectured, pleaded with, but I didn't give in.

Thirteen years later Dick did shoot himself. He had been married in Kenya where he had settled, and was piloting his own aeroplane to South Africa for his honeymoon. The machine got into a bad spin and crashed, killing the bride. Dick was found dead among the wreckage, a revolver in his hand. He had left a note saying:

'I have killed my darling and I no longer wish to live.'

The older generation in the twenties were full of advice about these desperate young men—'A man who says he will kill himself never does,' they said positively.

My greatest girl-friend was pursued by a young man called Angus, who belonged to a distinguished and noble family. Angus, I know now, was suffering on his return from the trenches from shell-shock. He was moody, tense and had frequent headaches. Like most of his friends, he couldn't get a job and he would sit in the Guards Club drinking until my friend would go out to dance with him.

Angus had a great friend, Tim, who had been in the same regiment and was in love with me. We often used to dine as a foursome and we had some happy times together.

Angus became more and more persistent until my friend said finally it was no use, she couldn't marry him. That evening he collected his gun from his home, drove out of London to a golf club near Esher and shot himself.

Unfortunately he left a letter addressed to my friend saying he could go on no longer without her. This meant that she had to attend the coroner's court. Her mother was ill, so desperately upset, she begged me to accompany her. My mother was away, so without asking anyone's permission or advice I agreed.

It was typical of the troubles we got ourselves into through ignorance of the world that when Tim offered to borrow a car from another man-friend to get to Esher we accepted. We were all poor and to hire a car would have cost pounds.

Very few men had cars and the only one Tim could get hold of was an open racing model, driven by the owner. We piled into it.

I remember thinking I must wear black. I had one black hat, but it was very large and made of lace—what was called a 'picture' hat. It couldn't have been more unsuitable, but I wore it.

The case was distressing and the details of how the body was found shot in the head were very gruesome. During a break in the proceedings, while I sat in a small whitewashed room in the police station on a hard chair, Tim informed me dramatically that unless I married him, as he had for some time been asking me to do, he also would shoot himself.

'How can you talk in that way—at this moment?' I asked angrily.

'I mean it,' he replied. 'I swear I will put a bullet through my head. I've lost Angus, the best friend a man ever had, and if I lose you also there's nothing left.'

I wondered desperately what I should do! I had been very fond of Angus. It was ghastly to think of him with his head blown off. I didn't know how to cope with Tim, his threats or the tears running down his face. As we drove back to London, we were all of us shocked into silence.

Next morning, the newspapers carried headlines of the full text of the letter Angus had written to my friend; what his father had said in court; details of his family tree; the coroner's comments; pictures of my friend, and, of course, a description of her and her friends arriving in an open sports car!

It gave the impression of heartlessness and a deliberate disregard for the decencies which should be accorded the dead. The older generation were quite rightly very censorious.

'The young don't care—they are heartless and callous—I expect they went straight out to dance.'

We didn't. I spent the evening with Tim who was in the depths of despair and drinking too much, while my friend, utterly miserable and asking herself over and over again if she could have prevented the tragedy, went away to stay with friends in the country.

But who would believe what had really happened?

Actually, with the elasticity of youth, outwardly we revived quickly, although the scars remained. These were dramas, frightening for the moment, but life was full and exciting. It was only a part of this new, fascinating, unpredictable adventure. Like the men who danced from the sheer joy of being alive, we danced from the sheer excitment of finding out about the world we lived in.

We were like nuns who had never seen over the convent wall until now. Everything was unexpected, fascinating, thrilling and unusual. Many books on the twenties describe us as empty-headed, frivolous, unthinking creatures. We were none of these things—what we really were was ignorant, innocent and continually surprised. It was like finding one's way through an intricate mass, with traps for the unwary but inestimable prizes for those who got through. Not for a moment did we want to stop looking, feeling, learning.

The only difficulty was that there wasn't enough time in the twenty-four hours for everything. But who wanted to sleep? One might miss something, good or bad, which was new!

CHAPTER TWO

I'm for ever blowing bubbles,
Pretty bubbles in the air.
They fly so high,
Nearly reach the sky,
Then like my dreams
They fade and die.

TODAY it is accepted universally that in the twenties we were hard, cynical and without any sentimentality. If we appeared to be so, it was, of course, a tremendous façade, put on at first as a defence against the misery and tears of the older generation.

We had all of us during our most impressionable age been subjected to an almost intolerable tension. There was hardly a house in Great Britain which had not experienced bereavement; but it was not the sudden shock that had been so unbearable, it was the anticipation of what might happen spread out over four long years of war.

We had watched our mothers go pale and fight for control at the sight of a telegraph boy coming to the door. We had watched them open a yellow envelope with trembling fingers, and though there had often been a glad cry of 'How wonderful, Daddy's coming home on leave!' there had also been that inevitable moment when they had either fainted or turned blindly away as they read the telegram which began 'The Secretary of State for War regrets . . .'

But that was not all. In thousands and thousands of homes like my own the male member of the family who was on active service was 'missing'. This was perhaps the worst of all to endure. My father was actually presumed dead, reported missing, then again presumed dead.

We who were growing up could never forget those long-drawn-out days when we waited for the postman, when letters came from friends or comrades of my father saying they thought he was a prisoner, the speculation which went on and on, day after day, week after week, month after month, as we wondered where he might be, what he was doing, whether he was wounded, whether he was being well treated.

Every story we heard of the way the Germans treated their prisoners was another twist of the knife in the wound.

We lived through it all, every moment, every anxiety, every horror of it, until the final memorial service with its rendering of the Last Post. Of course it left its mark upon us: four years is a very long time in the life of a child or an adolescent.

When the war was over we were sick of it all. We couldn't go on living under the dark strain with those tears and miseries, we couldn't bear all those anniversaries: 'the anniversary of the day that Daddy was missing', 'the anniversary of the day that he was reported killed', 'the anniversary of the day he last came home on leave', 'his birthday'.

So we tried to become detached from it all.

But that didn't really mean we were hard, it just meant that we couldn't go on betraying our feelings for the world to see. We had to grow another skin, we had to protect ourselves or break.

So we appeared not to care. But inside we were in fact over-sentimental, vulnerable, and, of course, romantic. Why not?

We had no reason to be bitter or cynical. We had never been disillusioned, we had just seen people being tortured by their feelings, which is a very different thing.

When I watched David Frost, the most brilliant of today's young television interviewers, talking with Noël Coward, now acclaimed as 'the Master'. I thought that David seemed for once a little out of his depth. It was almost as though he didn't understand Noël and wasn't quite certain why.

'Of course, you're not a very emotional person, are you?' he asked.

For a moment Noël didn't answer, and David went on:

'I mean, you're not sentimental, you're not the sort of person to cry into your pillow.'

Again that little pause, and then Noël said positively:

'Oh no, of course not.'

I laughed. I knew it so well, that instinctive reaction to being thought sentimental, that recoil from anything which might make us admit to being emotional.

But did David really believe that anyone could write *Bitter Sweet* or *Cavalcade* without feeling romantic, without being sentimental? Couldn't he understand that the song which Noël had just said was his favourite, 'I'll See You Again', is incurably, ecstatically, romantic—a cry from the heart of someone who understands the whole essence of romance?

'I'll see you again
Whenever Spring breaks through again.
Time may lie heavy between,
But what has been
Is past forgetting.
This sweet memory
Across the years will come to me.
Tho' my world may go awry,
In my heart will ever lie
Just the echo of a sigh,
Goodbye.'

How many memories that song evokes in us all, how many wonderful moments in the spring of our hearts, how many sighs for those who have died, or for a love which went wrong!

In the twenties we gave the older generation exactly what they expected, and so the legend grew up. I was dancing at the Berkeley when I saw a party of my mother's friends sitting at a table. I went over to talk to them, and one of them said:

'I expect you're surprised to see us here amongst all you young people. You think we're too old to enjoy ourselves, don't you?'

I looked at their curious disapproving eyes all turned towards me, and I knew they expected a pert reply. So I gave it to them.

'Of course I think that everyone over forty should be exterminated.'

I swept back on to the dance-floor amidst a gale of laughter, and I had added another brick to the wall which was being steadily built between the young and the old.

'They don't care.'

'They haven't any hearts.'

36

'They're as hard as nails.'

'They are just dancing mad without another thought in their heads.'

Those were the things which were being said about us, and after a time it became easy to give the impression of caring about nothing except the music of Negro bands which were playing the new jazz around the clock.

Noël became the high priest of 'the wicked twenties'.

'I was unwise enough,' he relates, 'to be photographed in bed wearing a Chinese dressing-gown and an expression of advanced degeneracy. This last was accidental and was caused by blinking at the flashlight, but it emblazoned my unquestionable decadence firmly on the minds of all who saw it.'

It actually set the seal on everything everyone believed, and wanted to believe, about the young.

An Armenian Jew called Michael Arlen had also begun to portray the twenties, and his books, which were thought dashing and provocative, described all the emotions and inborn drama which we found around us.

He made us gay and courageous, a combination of dashingly attractive bad and good. All his stories ended with that strange mixture of 'bitter-sweet' which Noël took as the title of his greatest musical operetta. It described only too well our lives and the lives of those around us.

What is so often forgotten is that in 1920 there was still an enormous overlap from the previous generation. One doesn't suddenly become different—the change is very gradual, sometimes almost imperceptible. So Edwardian London was all around us, and we were living with Edwardian people. We had not yet any history or identity of our own.

London in 1919–20 was structurally unchanged from the Edwardian days. Gas-light was still common in the private houses. Piccadilly was a line of dignified mansions and clubs; the great houses, such as Devonshire, Grosvenor, Dorchester, Lansdowne and Londonderry, were all inhabited by their owners.

Devonshire House had magnificent wrought-iron gates tipped in gold facing into Piccadilly. It was from this house that the blonde, lovely Georgina, Duchess of Devonshire, a compulsive gambler, emerged to canvass for Charles James Fox in the Westminster Election of 1784, and bought a vote from a butcher with a kiss. It was here, after her death, that her greatest friend Lady Elizabeth Foster—dearest Bess—having secretly given birth to two children by the Duke, married him.

In my mother's day the Devonshires were spoken of with awe and respect, despite the fact that the Duke was nicknamed 'Harty Tarty' and the Duchess 'Grand Slam'. She wore a yellow-red wig, and was obsessed by the new deviation of whist which was called bridge.

I wasn't interested in people who were dead or too old for me to meet them, but it always seemed to me that the gates of Devonshire House and the great high walls had a special magical quality for stimulating the imagination.

Behind its garden there was Lansdowne House—of perfect Adam design—facing into Berkeley Square, and dividing these two princely mansions was a narrow passage, which was a private right of way. One day every year Lord Lansdowne sent his men to lock and bolt the doors at each end of the passage, but for the other 364 days it was available as a short cut between Curzon Street and Berkeley Street.

Many crimes had taken place in Lansdowne Passage, with its high, sightless walls; but it was not the stabbings, the robberies or the vile assignations that I thought about when I walked through Lansdowne Passage, or the beautiful, passionate Devonshires, but of the ghost which is reputed to haunt it.

'Why,' I asked Michael Arlen, who had written a story about the ghost, 'did you make her an ageing prostitute?'

'There will be too many ghosts of pretty girls like you in this part of London.'

'Must we become ghosts?'

'Alas, it is inevitable.'

'But how sad! I do so enjoy being alive.'

'And I am very glad you are,' Michael Arlen said gallantly.

Londonderry House was the centre of the political world. Great receptions were held there on the eve of Parliament. Political hostesses were said still to exert a considerable influence over leading Ministers.

Lady Londonderry, who always looked like Boadicea in her chariot, carried the fabulous Londonderry diamond tiara as if it was a crown. In fact, it looked not unlike one. I remember being very overawed by her and the glittery, bejewelled and bedecorated company as I climbed from the marble hall up the great winding staircase to where at the top she and Lord Londonderry received their guests.

There was the stentorian announcement of names, the chatter of educated voices, the rustle of silks, the heat of people crowded together, moving very slowly step by step, the fragrance of scent and flowers, and an occasionable whiff of mothballs.

After World War II when the ballroom was let out for parties, we held my daughter Raine's wedding reception there and I found there was no way at all of ventilating the long room with its arched ceiling and windowless walls hung with over-life-size Londonderrys.

The Marchioness in her youth had been very gay and wearing a pork-pie hat would ride a bicycle all over London. Once she and a number of friends were chased by a policeman down the Mall because they were riding after dark without lights.

She was still sprightly in the twenties and had a snake tattooed on one of her ankles. We were always being told about the musical parties she gave every week at Londonderry House to her friends, over whom she had a great influence.

Ironically she made them members of her special 'Ark Club'— a personal zoo where everyone was allotted the name of some animal. She herself was 'Circe', which she had been nicknamed as a child. Lord Londonderry—who was distinguished, handsome, charming and with an irrepressible 'roving eye'—was 'Charlie the Cheetah', Lord Hugh Cecil was 'The Lynx', The Prime Minister in the late twenties, Ramsay MacDonald, was 'The Lion', who because of his attraction to Lady Londonderry was, it was whispered, 'saved' from the worse excesses of Socialism.

The young MacDonald was a cartoonist's dream, with rebellious forelock and indignant black moustache, curling like a pair of bicycle handlebars. But 'Gentleman Mac', as he was called by his colleagues, was soon to be more at home with duchesses than dustmen.

Lady Londonderry could be very frightening. I was at a dance at Londonderry House when a débutante started to stub out a cigarette on the base of one of the marble statues. Lady Londonderry put up her hand and stopped the band.

Controlled and extremely impressive, she walked across the

floor and in an icy voice which could be heard all over the room said to the trembling offender:

'Would you be so kind as to use an ashtray to put out your cigarette!'

In Park Lane Sir Ernest Cassel's mansion was a monument to Edwardian taste and a financier's money. He had bought eight tons of Tuscany marble, and even the kitchens were lined with it. His dining room, with its antique oak panelling and great arched ceiling, could seat more than 100 guests.

After he was dead I went to a committee meeting in Brook House for some charity I was helping. I stared open-mouthed at the magnificent white marble hall. I felt slightly shocked when I was told it was nicknamed 'The Giant's Lavatory'. The Van Dycks hung between lapis-lazuli pilasters, and there were innumerable rooms with very high ceilings.

This, which is something many have forgotten now, was one of the most delightful features of Georgian, Victorian and Edwardian houses. They were spacious, roomy and lofty. Their great halls, their long French windows hung with expensive Genoese velvet curtains tasselled and braided, the Georgian cornices and great crystal chandeliers, all gave an impression of opulence and magnificence. It was inevitable that their occupants should be formal, conventional and somewhat stately, as a reflection of their surroundings.

I remember in the thirties going to lunch in the great block of flats in Park Lane which stood on the site of what had once been Brook House. I was carried up in a lift, which had a few weeks before stuck halfway with Queen Mary in it, to the Mountbattens' penthouse on the top of the building. It was original, modern, low-ceilinged, and, being Lord Mountbatten's, full of gadgets. But it was also, compared with Brook House standards, very informal.

The decorations and furnishings were not yet finished, so we ate off card-tables in a sitting room. One of the guests was the Crown Prince of Sweden. The food was served on odd bits of China because it hadn't all been unpacked, and there were no silver ornaments or flowers on the table. As we talked and laughed, I thought how surprised Sir Ernest Cassel would have been.

The house I most regret never having seen in its glory was Stafford House, where Queen Victoria had said to Harriet,

Duchess of Sutherland: 'I come from my house to your palace.'
The glory of the Edwardian era has been summed up in the words of Victoria Sackville-West in *The Edwardians*:

'Deevy parties at Stafford House always. And Millie looking like a Goddess, with a golden train half way down the stairs. The charm of that woman! Everybody will be there.'

An artist fainted at the Duchess's beauty when he saw her at a fancy-dress ball. During the war she had her own hospital at Calais. She wore a special white uniform with a huge ruby cross on her breast. My husband was taken there desperately wounded, and he told me: 'She was so beautiful, she made dying men, like myself, want to live.'

Tall, with a curved feminine figure, she had perfect bone construction, huge expressive eyes, golden hair, a fabulous white skin, and a smile which made your heart turn over in your breast, it was so entrancing.

Millicent Sutherland was naturally beautiful, but she also took 'trouble' with herself. When she was over eighty she always made up her eyelashes, rouged and powdered her face, and arranged her well-waved hair before she allowed anyone to see her. How can the girls today, with their greasy uncombed rat-tails, sunburnt and neglected skins, fingers stained with nicotine, compete with that?

We followed the Duchess's generation in never letting ourselves be seen until we were 'presentable'. When I woke up in the morning the first thing I did, and still do, was to powder my face and arrange my hair. When I had a baby and later a major operation, as I came out from the anaesthetic I asked for powder and lipstick.

When I also blackened my eyelashes the matron in the nursing home said:

'I've never seen anyone take so much trouble, so soon.'

I was brought up always to make an effort. When I was ill my mother said:

'It is common to lie in your bed dirty and unwashed. Get up, have a bath and change your nightgown. You will feel much better.'

However ill we might be, none of my generation would let a

doctor into their bedroom until they were arranged elegantly against clean pillows!

Today in hospitals women are encouraged to use cosmetics and make themselves attractive as a morale-booster. Doctors say there is no doubt that it does speed their recovery.

In the twenties I came to know the exquisite Duchess Millicent —the Sutherlands always speak of their duchesses by their Christian names—very well and loved her. She used to talk to me of her success as a beauty; of her parties, balls and receptions; of the incredible grandeur and luxury of her life married to a man who was treated as the King of Scotland.

Later, when she was widowed and had married again unhappily, the Duchess wrote a book about her life called *That Fool of a Woman*. But her son disapproved, so he bought up every copy and destroyed them.

'I always loved stupid men,' she confided in me, 'it was such a relief to get away from the clever ones, to relax and take off my kid gloves.'

The Duke of Sutherland, with 1,250,000 acres, was the largest landowner in the British Isles. He had his own private train and railway line and owned a coal-mine. A navvy seeing him set off from Dunrobin, his castle in Sutherland, said:

'There, that's what I call a real dook—there 'e is a-driving 'is own engine, on 'is own train, and a-burning 'is own bloody coals.'

The Duchess told me how she had met her husband.

'It was just chance! How much that counts in all our lives! The Duke came to stay with my father and mother, and, of course, as I was only sixteen and still in the schoolroom it was most unlikely I should ever set eyes on him. But at the last moment it was discovered there would be thirteen at dinner. I was hurriedly dressed in my best frock and sent downstairs.'

'And the Duke fell in love with you?'

'As soon as he saw me! He proposed shortly afterwards, to the consternation of my parents! But we were married on my seventeenth birthday.'

The Duke of Sutherland was one of the first really rich men to sense that the social revolution would slowly undermine his wealth. He could still pin a £1,000 note on his wife's pillow while she slept, but he started to dispose of some of his property and Stafford House in 1912 was the first to go.

The displacement of the wealthy was in full swing in the twenties. The upper middle classes with fixed incomes of £2,000 to £5,000, which had once been thought of as 'extremely well-off', were finished.

Their estates were sold, their London houses converted into flats, their family treasures went to the Americans.

At the beginning of the century my grandfather with £4,000 a year was a very rich man. It was the equivalent today of over £20,000 with income tax at only eleven pence in the pound! He had a fine Georgian house with a large estate in Worcestershire, where he and his six children hunted five days a week.

He took a house in London in the season for his marriageable daughters, and brought up his carriage and horses. He and my grandmother travelled often for six months of the year. They went round the world three times in sailing-ships and were the first Europeans to cross Russia on the Trans-Siberian Railway.

In October 1919 Phillips Oppenheim, who wrote the first thriller-cum-crime-fiction books, calculated the difference in his expenditure on an earned income of £4,000 a year:

	Pre-war	Post-war
Income-tax	£440 per year	£1,620 per year
Chauffeur	£ 1 10s. per week	£ 3 10s. per week
Indoor servant	£ 1 per week	£ 2 per week
Garden boy	9s. per week	15s. per week

On this cost of living there was an 80 per cent increase.

'If I keep up my pre-war style of living,' Phillips told me, 'I shall spend £2,000 a year more than I earn, instead of saving, as I've done in the past, £250.

I wonder what my grandfather's and Phillips's expenses would have been today?

Phillips Oppenheim was the Prince of Storytellers. He wrote some 200 books, published approximately thirteen million words, and was the most popular author of the twenties. He enthralled millions all over the world. His success lay in that, like Edgar Wallace, he gave his readers 'escape', but while Edgar Wallace wrote of burglars, Oppie wrote of millionaires.

Most of his readers lived drab, dull, middle-class lives in economic circumstances which left little margin for luxury. The men were married to nagging, overworked, harassed wives worn out by childbearing. The women were tired of their cramped, ugly, back-breaking houses filled with adenoidal whining children.

To these people Oppie brought a world of suave *maîtres d'hôtel* serving exotic dishes on moonlit terraces overlooking the Mediterranean. There were mysterious countesses draped in sables and diamonds, moving slinkingly like snakes, and dangerously handsome villains being carried in sleek, shining limousines to spy, endanger or destroy.

It was the world Oppie knew and loved himself, for he lived in the South of France. The popping of champagne corks, the whirl and rattle of the little ivory ball in the roulette wheel and the acrid fragrance of a Havana cigar were the background of his life.

Oppie had the reputation on the Riviera of being a Don Juan, which was enhanced when he bought a yacht, which having been built by a Frenchman for his honeymoon was little more than a floating double bed. This occupied almost the entire space in the saloon, and many stories were told of who occupied it with the famous author.

Oppie could afford such extravagances. Once he earned £10,000 in five weeks working half-time. What was more, his titles alone could sell a book—*A Prince of Sinners, The Great Prince Shan,* and *The Million Deposit.*

Oppie said to me once:

'Give them thrills, give them excitement, give them dreams!'

He did not say give them sex because Oppie would have nothing to do with passion or seductive scenes. One of his friends was to write of him:

'The man himself could pull back the sheets and nip into a double bed as quickly as any man living, even at the age when most men are indulging in more sedate pleasures. But in conversation all through his life he was as prim as a geometry mistress with steel-rimmed spectacles and elastic-sided boots.'

But in many middle-class homes there was real, heart-breaking, genteel poverty, just like after the last war, when teachers and other professional men wrote pathetic letters to the newspapers complaining that they couldn't afford a holiday, they never had a new suit, their wives were household slaves. So it was in 1919.

But it was also estimated that there were 346,000 wealthy war-profiteers in England! A number of them edged their way into society by paying for the privilege. So despite crippling economies many social habits still survived which to the older generation brought back moments of nostalgia when they remembered the magnificence and opulence of pre-war days.

As I went out to dance in some night-club, I would see outside one of the famous houses a red carpet leading to the pavement's edge, and footmen waiting to usher in the guests. In Park Lane and around Grosvenor Square there would often be straw on the road, which traditionally had been put down to deaden the noise of the horses' hooves when someone important was ill.

There were still houses with the huge padded and curved-topped hall chair in which the night footman snoozed whilst waiting to open the door for his master and mistress. At Arlington House, at a dinner party at which I was a guest, thirty people were served on gold plates.

In Worcestershire, Earl Beauchamp wore the blue ribbon of the Garter round his portly chest at dinner parties—the local joke was that he went to bed in it—and every night armed 'the ladies' into the dining room.

When I dined at Eaton Hall, the Duke of Westminster's colossal bastard-French pseudo-gothic palace, the dinner-table was covered with a most elaborate arrangement of exotic flowers. They were, I was told, thrown away the next morning and replaced by the gardeners with something different the following night. It was always said that the architect of Eaton Hall mixed up his plans with the design for St. Pancras Station.

At Trent Park, the country home of enigmatical Sir Philip Sassoon, guests were supplied with every published newspaper when they were called in the morning, and at night, when the men went up to dress for dinner, there was a cocktail and the choice of a red carnation or a gardenia buttonhole waiting for them in their bedrooms.

Some rich people had footmen again, and they had polished up the big crested silver buttons on their livery which had lain tarnished and unwanted during the war. Lady Randolph Churchill —Winston's mother—had disliked having parlourmaids when every available man was at the front; so she had transformed her two maidservants into 'footmaids'. They wore black skirts, very

45

smart swallow-tail coats and evening waistcoats, with white shirt-fronts, winged collars and black ties!

There were still horses in the mews behind the houses in Mayfair, although already some of the mews were being converted into garages or living accommodation for the New Poor.

Horse manure was still collected off the streets by small boys with buckets and sold for householders' gardens, for in London one cab in every ten was still horse-drawn. The smell of manure and of leather harness would mingle with the sweet dry fragrance of straw, the scent of flowers from the parks and a whiff of salt from the wind blowing up the Thames. The air of London was not yet polluted with diesel and petrol.

Straw always made me think of how in the country, after church on Sunday, the house party would visit the stables, and the straw edges of the litter, beautifully plaited, were arranged in every stall. Well-washed carrots would be produced by the stable-boy in a basket so that the guests could feed the horses.

'Look well, eh, Abbey?'

'Yes, m'lord.'

'Fetlock quite sound now?'

'Yes, m'lord.'

'Take her easy, Abbey.'

'Yes, m'lord.'

'Good man!'

In country houses there was a lot of ragging—a hangover from the wild ragging of the Edwardians, instituted by the King when he was Prince of Wales. The corridors at Sandringham had echoed with laughter as some unsuspecting guest found a live lobster in his bed, or one of the young Royals dressed up as a ghost to frighten a lady-in-waiting.

In the twenties I was always prepared for an apple-pie bed with a bunch of holly at the foot, or pillows covered with flour. I was, however, extremely shy of being seen going to the bathroom and lavatory, having been brought up to think such places were never mentioned in public.

I therefore went through agonies if there was a squeaky toy under the bath mat or a clockwork mouse in the lavatory, realising that the rest of the party was waiting outside to hear me scream.

46

But, like the other girls, I found it great fun to tease the men until they pursued me with a soda-syphon, or to sew up the bottom of a man's pyjama legs as we imagined him taking hours to unpick them before he could get into bed. It never once crossed my mind that he might sleep without them!

Of course, there were many people to whom house parties and stables and carriages were finished. With the death of their father or their husband, their incomes had vanished too, and instead of a host of well-trained servants they had to manage, as my mother did, with one general servant. This phenomenon cleaned the house, cooked the meals, and waited at table— making a transformation of her appearance at the last moment from the print dress she wore in the kitchen into her best black uniform with its white apron and lace-trimmed cap.

Even so, as far as I was concerned, the rituals which had lasted for centuries still took place. There was time to walk in the park, and even to hire a horse from a riding-stable to emulate our grandfathers, who had brought their best horseflesh up from the country to be shown off in Rotten Row.

I would arrange to meet my friends at the Achilles Statue—a landmark, although I didn't realise it, for centuries. It was where the expensive Victorian prostitutes, like the famous Skittles, had always congregated when they rode in the Row. They were called 'pretty horse-breakers', and the crowds watched them eagerly for something new. When Skittles introduced the round-topped bowler for riding it was copied by all the respectable women who condemned her.

The Achilles Statue had been erected by the Ladies of England to the memory of the Duke of Wellington. The Pope had sent a plaster design of the Pheidlas Statue outside the Quirinal, but some busy British Mrs. Grundys petitioned to have a fig-leaf added!

'Meet me at the Achilles Statue!'

'All right, we'll go and sit at Stanhope Gate and see who's there.'

'Oh, let's go to the Serpentine.'

'It isn't so smart!'

'Never mind, we'll come back by the Row.'

My mother used to tell me how she had seen Lily Langtry driving through the park, but not with King Edward as she had done every morning in her heyday. Nevertheless at the end of the century people had still stood on the chairs to cheer her.

My mother had also seen the Countess of Warwick, whom King Edward had loved to distraction and called 'my dearest little wifie', and who held first place in his affections throughout the eighties, far longer, in fact, than Lily Langtry.

Mrs. Langtry married Sir Hugo de Bathe, always known as 'Suggie', and they lived in the South of France. However, after a while they separated and had their own villas at a different place on the coast. Suggie, who was tall, perfectly dressed and a great character at Cannes in the twenties, was extremely attractive to women, and was always proposing to some pretty girl and then regretting it.

When this happened he would explain he was still a married man, but would 'go and tackle his wife about a divorce'. Lily would be delighted to see him and she always said at once:

'Dear Suggie, are you in trouble again, and have you come to ask for a divorce? I expect you have, and the answer is, of course, *no*!'

Suggie would sigh with relief and say:

'Thank you very much, my dear!'

Then they would settle down to a cosy tea together.

It was these lovely women, like Lily Langtry, Daisy Warwick, Lady Randolph Churchill (Winston's mother), and Lady Helen Vincent who became in the Edwardian days the 'professional beauties', and emerged from their well-bred seclusion into the public eye.

This was the trend, which was revived immediately after the war, for press publicity for 'ladies', while at the beginning of the century it had been reserved exclusively for the demi-mondaine.

The older generation, however, still disapproved of journalism and thought a lady's name should appear in the newspapers only four times in her life—when she was born, when she was married, when she gave birth to a child, when she died.

The fact that I began to be frequently mentioned in magazines like the *Tatler*, the *Sketch*, the *Bystander* and in the gossip columns which were just beginning to appear in the national dailies, gave rise to many caustic comments, the most usual being:

'How much does Barbara pay to be in the *Tatler*?'

But like the 'professional beauties' we in the twenties were delighted to be noticed.

It was, however, haphazard publicity. One was seen by reporters or one wasn't, until about 1933 when Margaret Whigham—the most beautiful girl of the year, and of any year for that matter—came out. She organised her publicity, was charming to journalists and gave what we would now call press conferences. She had in consequence far better and more flattering press coverage than any film star.

But how easy it was in the twenties to be 'sensational'! Paula Gellibrand leaped into fame, not only because she was beautiful but because having been born a 'lady' she became a model—we called it a mannequin in those days. When I wrote my first novel it was given tremendous publicity, not because it was a good book, but because I was a socialite who 'worked'!

It was, however, the beginning of an avalanche. The idea that a 'lady' could actually earn honest money was a fascinating thought. Society women went into trade. Mrs. Dudley Coats, who was in the Prince of Wales's set, started the ball rolling in the twenties with a shop specialising in scent and wedding presents. It was called 'Audrey', and it became the fashion to use one's own Christian name.

Poppy Baring, with a mesmeric voice, who was partnered for a long time by Prince George, opened 'Poppy', a dress shop.

For a very short while I had a hat shop—of course called 'Barbara'. It was a flop because when a customer called I had always 'gone to lunch' wearing one of the best hats myself. I hurriedly sold the shop.

The men in the twenties, whether they were husbands or beaux, were encouraging and congratulating. They did not, like their fathers, want a sweet, gentle creature who could do nothing but look pretty.

The Edwardian gentleman was not particularly intelligent himself, and having a great deal of leisure on his hands he wished to be amused. Those who did work wished to relax in the company of beautiful women and not exert themselves otherwise. Of course there were exceptions, but on the whole, if a woman had a pretty face, it was considered rather tiresome when she exercised her brain, as Lady Warwick had done when she became a Socialist, and tried to argue about it with the King.

There was no doubt at all, however, that the acclaimed 'beauties' really were beautiful. Mary, Lady Howe, the Edwardian English Rose, with her pink-and-white skin, her golden hair, her blue eyes, and what was considered a perfect figure, tall, well bosomed, with a tiny waist, would have been breathtaking at any age and at any time. But in the days without make-up, when even a little powder on the nose was, if it was detected, considered outrageously fast, her strawberries-and-cream complexion sent people into ecstasies.

It was far easier to be attractive, even without make-up, in the swirling skirts, small waists and huge hats of 1910 than it was when I grew up. We all wore jumpers, shapeless and not at all flattering. Women had started knitting in the war. Now it was over they couldn't stop. Eve wrote in the *Tatler* of September 1919:

> 'Aren't we doing the jumper-sweater craze to death, by the way? Short ones, long ones, thick ones . . . blue ones, purple ones, white ones, pink ones, green ones, parti-coloured ones, lemon ones . . . especially lemon ones . . . *All* women wear them, thin and fat, small and tall, dark and fair, rich and poor, good and bad. . . .'

The greatest innovation in 1920 was the backless dress, which was considered incredibly fast. As late as 1923 the London Underground refused to display an advertisement with a woman wearing a very low dress at the back. Mothers who were still insisting on sleeves with dress-preservers sewn in them for dances were appalled at the idea of a dress cut down to the waist. Most of my more dashing friends used to go out demurely hooked up the back, only to go to the cloakroom and pin back their evening dresses with safety pins.

Eve wrote again:

> 'I am glad to read that ostrich fans will be larger. I mean to say, with backless frocks getting more and more backless, we want something protective-like, don't we? But no matter how backless frocks catch on elsewhere, it's a dead snip they won't at Court.'

One of the more revolutionary things the Americans brought us was a new kind of corset. English women in the Edwardian fashion wore stiff whalebone corsets which clipped up the front and were laced at the back. The women wartime workers had abandoned theirs, but in 1919 it was considered very dashing to have anything that was not boned.

'A man could feel your whole body when you danced with him!' our elders exclaimed in shocked tones.

James Laver, the expert on taste and fashion, has said:

'It is a common fact in human history and one well worthy of more attention than it has received from the social psychologists, that the disappearance of corsets is always accompanied by two related phenomena—promiscuity and an inflated currency.'

Modesty was still very important. When I bathed at Bembridge I wore a black bathing suit of a stiff and thick kind of taffeta. It had a small square neck, sleeves to the elbow and a skirt. At first my mother wanted me to wear black stockings, as she had before the war, but reluctantly she conceded I must move with the times.

'When you think,' she said, 'that when your father and I went to the seaside we weren't allowed to bathe together—there was no mixed bathing—it is fantastic that now a man should be allowed to see your bare legs.'

In 1925 *No, No, Nanette* drew crowds at the Palace Theatre, and in one scene the chorus, led by Binnie Hale, wore bathing costumes. When Queen Mary went to a matinée she turned her head away from the stage and would not look at girls so scantily dressed.

When in 1928 I was photographed in a bathing dress without a skirt there were many shocked comments from my mother's friends.

High heels, which had always in the past been associated with the stage, gradually began to be the fashion among the girls like myself. The older generation, who were still wearing very low heels with a strap across the instep, condemned them as causing all sorts of peculiar displacements to the lower part of the body.

'They are a threat to the birth rate,' several doctors reported. 'The future generation will suffer from this ridiculous innovation.'

I hadn't yet been brave enough to cut my hair short. I had chopped at the sides, but there was still a long bit caught into a neat roll at the back and pinned with long hairpins. But the idea of freedom was beginning to be universal and it was not long before I cut off the last remaining tresses of a woman's 'crowning glory'.

Gwen Farrar and Norah Blaney, one of the first cabaret turns, sang:

> 'Shall I have it bobbed or shingled?
> Shall I have it shingled or bobbed?
> Sister Cissie says "Oh have it shorn short, Sue,
> Shingled, shorn and shaven like the smart set do!" '

Men protested. They all thought long hair was feminine and seductive. Elinor Glyn's husband had hired a swimming bath on their honeymoon so that he could watch her swim naked with her long red hair trailing behind her.

No one in 1920 suggested anything so sensational, but men did say rather wistfully:

'A woman's long hair trailing over a pillow is very lovely.'

We never dared reply that to keep our hair fashionably curly we had to go to bed in Hind's curlers or tie our long rats' tails up with 'rags' into tight little rolls. Permanent waving was not yet in existence

Hind's curlers were ugly but effective, but one was always afraid of being seen in them. I remember being terribly ashamed when Lady Queensberry told me that she, Duff Cooper and, I think, Noël Coward, had come to my bedroom at Deauville to ask me to go to the polo with them, and found me asleep. I had put my hair at the sides in Hind's.

'I must have looked awful!'

'Only very young!'

Sometimes lack of sleep caught up with me. In 1922 a young man, because he was a relation of an official at Westminster Abbey, had got me a ticket to Princess Mary's wedding to Viscount Lascelles. We danced all night as usual, I forgot to ask my mother to call me, and when I awoke the wedding was over!

The story of how Princess Mary became engaged was whispered from the Court and talked about in Mayfair drawing rooms, until finally it got into the Press.

Lord Lascelles, who I always thought was rather a dour, unemotional man, was extremely wealthy. He acquired his money by a chance meeting in the street during the war with Ralph

Nevill—an author, expert on the eighteenth and nineteenth centuries and a compulsive gambler of the Edwardian era.

Ralph asked Lord Lascelles to lunch with him at St. James' Club. As they entered the dining room they met the Marquess of Clanricarde, a distant cousin of Lord Lascelles, who sat down with them.

Lord Clanricarde would never speak of the war, but on this occasion he asked his cousin to relate his experiences. That afternoon Lord Clanricarde went home, altered his will, and left the whole of his fortune—about three million pounds—to Lord Lascelles. This made him acceptable as a royal suitor, and he proposed to the Princess, who was very unsophisticated, in the woods at Sandringham. Immediately she exclaimed, 'Oh, I must go and tell Mother!' and flew indoors, only to find the Queen was engaged with an important visitor.

She had to find someone, and finally ran Prince Henry to earth in the garage, tinkering with his car and much too absorbed to notice her at first. However, she seemed so excited and so insistent that he should get hold of the Queen that at last he went indoors and said:

'I don't know what's the matter with Mary, but she seems to want you very badly. Will you come and see her?'

When the Queen heard the news she was almost as excited as the Princess and said:

'Come now, we'll go and tell Father!'

And so the three of them hurried off to tell the King.

Lord Clanricarde had an extraordinary habit of flicking out his tongue and licking his nose. He also enjoyed dipping a banana in his coffee before he ate it. He was a miser and they disliked him at the Café Royal where he would order a cup of coffee and a roll, spreading it with some fish paste he kept in his pocket. It was always said that it was made of the skin and boiled down bones of his breakfast kipper.

Princess Mary remained unsophisticated. In the early thirties her physician in ordinary, Sir Louis Knuthsen, who was also my doctor, asked me to recommend a manicurist as the Princess— now Princess Royal—had never been to one, and the cuticles had grown very high on her nails.

I sent the girl who did my nails to Lord Lascelles' house in Green Street. Afterwards I said to her:

'Were you impressed with the house?'

'Impressed!' she exclaimed. 'I was shown into the lady's maid's bedroom. It had a threadbare carpet and the brass bed was tied up with string!'

When the Princess became a widow she often used to stay with her lady-in-waiting, Lady Paynter, at her lodge on the Helmsdale in Sutherland. She was very shy and it gave her an almost awkwardness which was sometimes disconcerting. But she had a great sense of humour.

The Princess Royal would trudge valiantly over the moors with the guns, but when there was no shooting Lady Paynter would often have to search for things to do which would amuse her guest.

On one occasion they called on Vivien Lockett, the one-time world-famous polo-player, who had rented a tiny lodge for the season. He was not expecting them and they found him watering his flowers. Having no watering can he was using a chamber pot!

The Princess Royal roared with laughter.

When Patrick Balfour was at Oxford in 1923, Elizabeth Ponsonby (daughter of the Under Secretary of State for Foreign Affairs in the Socialist Government) came down to display her shingled head.

'It was the first shingle I had seen,' he said, 'and it induced in me a feeling of astonishment coupled with faint horror. I was, in fact, shocked!'

There was a huge outcry in the Press—'*Shingles Blow to Marriage*', '*Bobbed Hair and Bobbed Love*', *Shingles Leave Girls Single*', '*Is It a Girl or a Boy?*' being some of the headlines. Ten nurses were suspended from a hospital in America until their hair grew again.

I think the reason my generation bobbed and shingled their hair, flattened their bosoms and lowered their waists, was not that we wanted to be masculine, but that we didn't want to be emotional. War widows, many of them still wearing crêpe and widows' weeds in the Victorian tradition, had full bosoms, full skirts and fluffed-out hair. To shingle was to cut loose from the maternal pattern; it was an anti-sentiment symbol, not an anti-feminine one.

The cutting of women's hair was also the last death-knell to the lingering elaboration of the Edwardian toilet. The Merry Widow curls, which Lily Elsie had made the rage, had been replaced by elegantly dressed waves which covered the whole head, and required an enormous amount of work with tongs heated on little stoves burning methylated spirit. It was the women war-workers who had found it impossible to go on fiddling with their hair for hours, and were immediately condemned as looking unfeminine.

The Edwardian vogue, among the demi-mondaine and the stage, had been the ladylike. The King's fancy was for real ladies, chief among them being the fascinating Mrs. George Keppel, whom everyone loved and who unbelievably made no enemies. Lily Elsie, the 'pin-up' of the 1914 War, was another charming, gentle creature, who, despite her tremendous stage success, looked and behaved like a sheltered aristocrat.

She married Mr. Ian Bullough, and they lived in Drury Lane Farm near my grandfather's estate in Redmarley. I often saw her, and she couldn't have been a more unobtrusive, unspectacular person. It was inevitable therefore that the pendulum would swing the other way.

We didn't want to be ladylike in 1920. We wanted to be dashing, we wanted to be gay, and most of all we wanted to be romantic. Of course the really romantic stories we knew were all of the older generation. We hadn't yet had time to live our own histories. So the tales which made us misty-eyed in 1920 were all Edwardian.

One which has always haunted me was the story of one of the loveliest women I have ever seen. Born in the obscurity of a poor country vicarage, her amazing beauty—which Michael Arlen called 'the golden-white beauty of the world's last aristocracy'—had been so overwhelming that at eighteen she had been hastily pushed into marriage with a distinguished and titled cousin.

As a bride she had burst upon the social world, and kings, princes, ambassadors fell at her feet. She was fêted, courted and acclaimed. But the war broke out, and during four whole years her husband saw her for only a few isolated weeks when he was on leave.

After the Armistice she went to Paris to buy clothes and to visit some friends she had not been able to see during hostilities, and there, for the first time in her life, she fell in love. She was ecstatically, completely overwhelmed by it, as only a rather stupid woman can be.

She had never known it possible that she could feel such emotions, and she was prepared to do anything—to throw over her social life, her position in Court circles, her children and her distinguished husband. But Frenchmen, like the Edwardians, did not in 1919 indulge in matrimonial scandals. Love, as they understood it, was not allowed to encroach on everyday life.

She received a letter from her husband. He had been demobilised, and he wrote telling her he was home and asking her to return immediately. She knew there was nothing to do but to go back, and yet she lingered one more week. Her heart and soul cried out at the misery of leaving behind the one romantic, glorious love which had come to her after so many years.

She made the excuse of dressmaker's fittings to be finished, but at last she could prevaricate no longer. She tore herself away and wired the time of her arrival, feeling as she crossed the Channel that she had left half of herself behind.

At Victoria there was the car to meet her, carrying a note of regret from her husband that another engagement had prevented him from being there in person.

When they met he was charming, but uneasily she sensed something was wrong. The days drifted by, she took up her position in the household, began to entertain, and her husband was invariably courteous and considerate, doing in public exactly what might be expected of him. But that was all. He slept in his dressing room. Every morning as he passed through her room on his way to his bath he would say politely: 'Good morning, my darling, have you slept well?'

At last she could bear it no longer.

'What is the matter?' she asked.

He raised his eyebrows and looked surprised.

'Nothing, darling, why should there be?'

She didn't dare question him further, but she was puzzled and not a little frightened.

Soon she heard rumours, the inevitable friend told her tales of other women. They were certainly not in her social class, but always they bore a faint, mocking resemblance to her. There was one woman in particular, she was told, fair-haired, blue-eyed, with a wonderful pink and white complexion!

She felt she could bear this courteous torture no longer. She went to her solicitor and told him that she was desperately worried, and convinced that her husband was being unfaithful to her.

The solicitor, an old man who had known her almost since she was a child, gave her a document.

'I was instructed to hand this to you,' he said quietly, 'in the event of your contemplating any legal action against your husband.'

She opened it and saw with frightened eyes the undeniable evidence of her own infidelity in Paris. Her husband must have known them, all those months ago!

A divorce was inevitable although it took years. By this time her beauty was fading and her lovers were not important, distinguished or brilliant, but rather faded too.

Her last lover was very much her junior, a young man who had taken me out to dance in the early twenties, but found drink a consolation for his own inadequacies. For a short while, as so often happens, her beauty re-blossomed. She was unbelievably lovely as she must have been when she emerged from the obscurity of the country vicarage.

Then he too left her and she had nothing.

As I have said, this story haunted me because it seemed so cruel, so wrong. I wanted life to be as romantic as I had believed it to be, especially for beautiful and famous people. This was the first time I began to see how diverse and tortuous it could be in fact.

There was another story connected with the beauty from the country vicarage, which also seemed to me to be desperately sad.

When she was in her heyday the most handsome, rich, eligible duke in the whole of *Debrett* fell in love with her. He was much younger than her—he was only thirty-three in 1920—but he loved her to distraction and she flirted prettily with him, her heart untouched.

At last his mother, who herself had been a beauty, intervened.

'You can have what love affairs you please,' she said to the Duke, 'but you must get married. In your position in life it is your duty to produce an heir. Find yourself a wife.'

'If I can't have the woman I love,' the Duke replied, 'I don't care whom I marry. You choose one for me, I'm not interested.'

His mother asked three girls to stay. They were all blue-blooded, well mannered, well behaved and pretty enough to carry off the family tiaras. The Duke chose the first one he saw. 'She'll do!' he said, and proposed.

It was a magnificent wedding attended by most of the Royal Family, but after they were married the much desired heir didn't appear. It was then that it was discovered that out of all the girls the Duke might have married, the one he had chosen was barren!

An heir was a constant source of anxiety. The Duke of Westminster's small son died of appendicitis when he was six. The Duke never got over his grief, it twisted and poisoned his life. He married three more wives and gained in consequence a reputation of being a 'Bluebeard'. Mothers said in all sincerity to their daughters:

'I hope, darling, you never meet the Duke of Westminster!'

Lord Hawke and Major Jack Harrison, the tallest and most charming M.F.H. in the country, both had eight daughters.

'I did my best to have a son,' Mrs. Harrison once said to me pathetically.

There was a famous Edwardian doctor who almost guaranteed an heir for £1,000—a fantastic sum, but worth it. Dr. X was known to be almost infallible, and many great families extolled his brilliance.

He used, of course, an early form of artificial insemination. And it was whispered that the reason he never failed was that he himself was extremely healthy and strong!

Long after he was dead two of Britain's most noble and distinguished families were, in the twenties, united in marriage, but there was no heir. It was then remembered by those who knew them well that the bride and bridegroom were both the result of their parents consulting Dr. X.

'Could it be possible they were brother and sister?' people asked.

It was children that the older generation thought was the cure for everything. The whole social pattern demanded that there must be an heir! Every sacrifice was expected so that the title and the estates should be transmitted from father to son.

My generation was also caught up in this frantic desire for an heir. There was a tall, handsome, rich young man, the possessor of a proud title, who was desperately in love with a very beautiful, well-known young married woman. He adored her, he followed her about, white-faced and miserable, wherever she went. Finally his family begged her to send him away, and persuaded her that he must go round the world to forget her. It was, of course, the conventional cure for a love affair.

'He'll soon get over it once he's away,' his relatives said cheerily, 'and then we will find him some nice young girl and he will settle down and have a family.'

The married woman saw that this was the sensible thing to do. She was also too important socially to risk a scandal. She did what was asked of her, and the white-faced young man said goodbye. He went round the world not once but several times. When he came back he ignored the nice girls who were trotted up for him to inspect, and took to himself one mistress after another. Finally, many years later, he married one of them. It was rather a noisy, vulgar wedding, but she became a pleasant chatelaine for his ancestral home. There were no children.

The British insistence on having a son and the fact that once born he was very much more important than his sisters, gave me, and girls like me, an inescapable complex. From the moment we were born all our parents heard was:

'A girl? Never mind, better luck next time.' And we accepted resignedly that we only got the crumbs that fell from the masculine table.

A boy had a better education—we were lucky to get one at all. He went to a university, he had better clothes, better food, a better time and, of course, more money. The British looked incredulously at the American habit of dividing their money equally among their children, whatever the sex.

'Damn it—what do women want with money? They can get a husband to keep them,' was the attitude.

My grandfather left his daughters £100 a year each—they were lucky to get that—all the rest went to his only son. Mothers made no pretence of loving their daughters as much as their sons and the girls accepted without complaint the humiliation of being feminine.

'England is a man's Paradise—America is a woman's,' was a well-known saying. But we had no desire to go to America. We agreed that men were more desirable than women and prayed that when we married we would be fortunate enough to have sons. How awful, how terrible if we only produced daughters!

One of the most attractive young men of the twenties was Dick Curzon. He was the first officer of the Household Cavalry to go into trade after the war. He became a fitter in the Commercial Aircraft Company at Hendon, earning thirty-two shillings and sixpence a week. Later he became managing director of Air Dispatch and Commercial Air Hire, which flew newspapers across the Channel and reporters to and from national events like the Grand National and the launching of the *Queen Mary*. It was one of the few unsubsidised aviation companies to make a profit.

Dick also flew two million pounds' worth of bullion every week to the Continent. He was good-looking, a racing driver, a first-class boxer—a steward of the British Board of Boxing Control—a fisherman, a good game shot, one of the finest pistol shots in the world, a wonderful dancer and a delightful companion. So many girls were in love with him, but he chose to marry Muriel Curzon Dunbar, a very distant cousin who was always called Billie. She was older than Dick and had enjoyed a somewhat 'chequered' career.

Dick was heir presumptive to the estate of his uncle, that redoubtable superior person, George Nathaniel, 1st Marquis Curzon of Kedleston, who desperately wanted a son, since the Marquisate, being of first creation, could pass only in a direct line. He had three daughters by his first wife, and he married for the second time in 1916 a widowed American millionairess, who already had two sons and a daughter.

There was a whispered story of a curse which had been laid on George Nathaniel in India, to the effect that he should never have a son to follow him, nor should his heirs. But this story had no substantiation in fact.

Nevertheless the Marquis died without having a son, and Dick became Viscount Scarsdale. Kedleston is the most beautiful house in Britain. Built by Robert Adam, its perfect proportions, its gold furniture designed for the house, its surroundings, have been the background for so many of my novels because I love it and its beauty haunts me.

To Dick and Billie it was not only a precious heritage, it was something which meant hard, unceasing work. When the Marquis died he had dismantled Kedleston preparatory to doing it up. Furniture was stacked in rooms from floor to ceiling; even to move it was a gigantic task.

Dick and Billie did it themselves, piece by piece, room by room, and at the same time Billie was striving frantically to have an heir.

I stayed with them many times, but I remember particularly being there one lovely hot summer before her third child was born. She had had two daughters, dear little things, but girls! Billie was sick every day and nearly all day. She had been like this with each one of her children. A terrible nausea would sweep over her and she had to go to bed. She struggled gamely against it, but there was nothing she could do but lie down.

'I am so sorry for you,' I said as I helped her into the huge four-poster, with its carved silver posts and exquisite eau-de-nil brocade hangings.

'I don't mind,' she replied. 'It's worth it—so long as it's a boy.

'It must be—this time!'

'Yes, it must be,' she replied, 'Dick wants one so much!'

I felt worried; for vaguely at the back of my mind I remembered an old wives' tale that excessive vomiting foretold that the baby would be a girl. But that, of course, was nonsense—with modern science nobody believed in such things—or did they?

When the baby was born it was another girl. There was to be yet a fourth daughter—but never a son.

But some of the romances of the twenties were all I expected of them and more. The most exciting was between Henry—Viscount Weymouth, now the Marquis of Bath, and the lovely, gay Daphne Vivian.

Daphne was of the new order, a young woman who possessed both brains and beauty. She was tall and slender and she made every other girl in the room seem gawky. Her face would light up and one would find oneself staring speechless at her beauty. While Daphne inevitably was thought to typify all that was casual and indifferent in the Bright Young People, she was incurably romantic.

She fell in love with Henry, and he with her. Henry would have been handsome in any case, but he had broken his nose. This gave him a fascinating raffishness which today still enthralls those who visit Longleat to see the lions, or who watch him on television. He has worn best of all the elegant young men of the dancing years. He is till a Michael Arlen hero.

Daphne's and Henry's parents decided that it would not be a suitable marriage, they were both too young, too wild, and too irresponsible. Henry was told to go round the world and forget Daphne. Daphne was commanded to turn her attentions elsewhere.

This paternal tyranny excited them to immediate rebellion. A month before Henry was due to leave England they made their plans. They took out an ordinary marriage licence and the banns were read three Sundays running at St. Paul's, Knightsbridge.

Henry gave his name as Frederick Thynne, which was of course his family name, and Daphne used her second name, Winifred. The Press must have been blind, deaf and dumb! They were married with two church charladies as witnesses and went to Winchester for the weekend.

Daphne wore her wedding ring on a chain round her neck and Henry went to America. When he returned all opposition to their wedding was surprisingly removed. Conscience-stricken they felt it would be unkind to tell their families how they had been hoodwinked. So they said nothing. They were engaged for five months during which time Daphne suffered agonies thinking someone would denounce them.

They were married for the second time at St. Martin-in-the-Fields. Daphne wore a dress of white net with gold and silver fleurs-de-lis, and was followed by bridesmaids and pages.

'I felt convinced,' she says, in her autobiography, 'that the service would be interrupted by an accusing voice crying out that we were already married.'

But nothing happened and they were very, very happy for a great number of years.

Not for ever—there had to be a twist somewhere.

CHAPTER THREE

I'm seeking love—Where is he hiding?
I'm seeking love—Where can he be?
High in the sky, the rainbow riding
Whispers a promise to me.
Rest assured that love will find you,
Know that he is very near.
I'm seeking love—Is love behind you?
I'm seeking love—Oh is he here?

'I SHALL get married and live happily ever afterwards,' we
each of us said to ourselves and believed it.

I think that the chief reason why, in the twenties, we were so
romantic was that marriage was considered indissoluble. Marriage was the goal, the prize, the grand finale of our hopes and
our aspirations. There was no continuation of the story because
there was no question of there ever being a divorce later.

In 1914 divorce cases were a quarter of one per cent of all cases
heard in the courts of law. It would have been impossible to write
a book with a divorced heroine, or for the hero to have a wife
and family living on alimony. I can remember very vividly the
first time I ever heard the word 'divorce'.

In 1909 my father had become political private secretary to our
local Member of Parliament, Commander Eyres-Monsell. An
exceedingly attractive man, who had been in the Royal Navy, he
had married an extremely rich woman whose family had made a
great fortune manufacturing hooks and eyes.

The union of 'breeding and brass' had become such a fashionable trend since the Industrial Revolution that by the beginning
of the twentieth century the blue-blooded young gentlemen of
England had practically exhausted the home market and were
looking further afield.

American heiresses with huge fortunes from oil, gold and real estate were purchasing the coronets of dukes, marquises and earls. That many of them were both attractive and adaptable was an added bonus to the deal.

In their matrimonial campaigns aspiring bridegrooms by no means lacked allies. Mrs. Vanderbilt was so desperate to secure the Duke of Marlborough for her daughter that she threatened to shoot the man on whom Consuelo had set her affections.

The girl was shut in her room, all letters both from her and for her were intercepted, and she was told that her mother would die of a heart attack if she did not consent to marry the Duke. Helpless, with no one to turn to, she capitulated.

But however unhappy these contrived marriages became, it was not until after the war that couples made any effort to be free. The Eyres-Monsells appeared content with each other. They had a large house and a great many friends, but Mrs. Eyres-Monsell was not a good hostess. She therefore turned to my mother for help in making their parties a success.

'You must come, Polly! You make everything so amusing and gay. I can't do it,' she would say.

Mrs. Eyres-Monsell suffered from that tense stiffness which freezes everyone! Those so afflicted can't help it, but I often think my overpowering grandfather was right when he thundered at his children:

'Stop being shy! Shyness is just conceit. You are thinking about yourself.'

But Mrs. Eyres-Monsell, inarticulate and gauche, seemed to put a damper on her guests so it became inevitable that whenever the Eyres-Monsells had a house party, my father and mother should be there.

Amongst those frequently invited was a tall, good-looking man who had for many years been a close friend of the Commander. His name was Wilfred Ashley, and he was a nephew of the great Lord Shaftesbury. He had married Maud, the only child of Sir Ernest Cassel. Her mother came from an ancient Scots family. She was very lovely and also very delicate and seldom left her home.

My mother and father grew very fond of Wilfred Ashley. He was not a particularly brilliant man, but if I was asked who were the two men in my life who I thought typified the good-looking, elegant, perfect English gentleman I would say Bobby Eyres-Monsell and Wilfred Ashley.

Both over six foot three, both exceedingly handsome, it would have been impossible to imagine either of them doing anything that was not what is best described as 'public school'. They both had an eye for pretty women, but that was a different thing. Where everything else was concerned they behaved with unimpeachable dignity, and had, at the same time, a charm which is almost indescribable.

Maud Ashley died in 1911, and Wilfred Ashley was left a widower with two small daughters. The eldest, aged ten, was called Edwina, and she was to be known later as one of the great women of the century. The other was a little red-haired five-year-old, Mary, who was to mean a great deal in my life in the future.

Another friend that my parents met with the Monsells was the Hon. Mrs. Forbes-Sempill. An exceedingly pretty woman, she was not only well aware of her looks, but had a dozen rather annoying affectations.

She was married to a sailor, Lionel Forbes-Sempill, a delightful, easy-going man with a great number of friends. But not only was she bored when he was constantly at sea, but she found poverty intolerable and she was only happy when she was staying in grand houses. Who could blame her?

Living in an Edwardian country house was the acme of comfort. There were dozens of well-trained servants, the men in their livery with crested silver buttons, the women in black dresses with starched caps and aprons. There were hot-house carnations and lilies scenting the atmosphere. The dining room table, decorated every day with fresh flowers and trailing smilax, was dazzling with its profusion of gold and silver candelabra, ornaments and dishes filled with huge hot-house peaches and purple and white muscat grapes.

Upstairs in each bedroom there was always a day-bed where a lady would rest in the afternoon and a writing-table holding a bewildering variety of materials necessary for the writing of the innumerable letters which was the self-imposed task of every Edwardian.

Lord Curzon made letter-writing almost his principal activity. He would often begin a new missive with the words—'This is my thirty-ninth letter today'. His wife once received a letter over a hundred pages long! Mr. Asquith, when he was Prime Minister, wrote endless letters to Mrs. Venetia Montagu, whom he loved. He revealed to her the Cabinet secrets and even wrote to her during Cabinet meetings.

On the bedroom desk there would be a blotter bearing a huge silver monogram, a letter box for the writing-paper and envelopes, an inkstand in silver, onyx or lapis lazuli, pens, a pen-tray, a pen-wiper, a stamp box, a jewelled or ivory letter-opener, a clock, a calendar, a pin box, a seal, sealing-wax, candle, matches, a framed card showing the times of the post. Besides these, there were numerous photographs of the hostess or the house and a vase of flowers.

At tea-time, when the gentlemen returned from hunting, shooting or riding, the ladies, who had been resting and writing their letters, would descend to the drawing room wearing delectable tea-gowns. These were elaborate creations of pleated chiffon in blended colours very feminine and alluring, being designed by Lady Duff-Gordon—the first society woman ever to open a shop, which she called 'Lucille'.

Molly Forbes-Semphill looked superb in a tea-gown of shaded yellow with gold embroidery. Sometimes she wore with it two provocative little gold tassels in her well-undulated tawny-gold hair.

Occasionally she came to stay with my father and mother when she had nowhere better to go, and as children we disliked her because she said incessantly:

'I don't care for children, I much prefer my pekinese.'

After one of Molly's visits I became aware of whispers. Conversations would cease abruptly when I came into the room; the names Molly and Lionel were repeated on everyone's lips, until the day when I heard a strange new word, 'divorce'.

It took me a long time to understand what was happening. When I did I was frightened—perhaps it was the tone of voice in which my mother spoke of divorce; perhaps it was a premonition of the future. I only know that it seemed something dark and menacing of which I was afraid.

In those days for a woman to divorce a man she had to prove not only adultery but cruelty. Divorce was a long-drawn-out legal action, where the contestants found themselves deserted or

66

cut by their friends, and at the end were involved in an unpleasant amount of unsavoury publicity.

Every word of the case was reported in 'the yellow press', and the society scandals were read avidly by respectable, often envious, women who, however unhappy, could never contemplate and afford a divorce for themselves.

The Forbes-Sempill divorce was heard in Scotland, which had divorce laws different from England and therefore had less newspaper coverage. Nevertheless people shook their heads. The social penalties for having a divorce were very stringent—even the innocent party suffered. There could be no admission to Court or to the Royal Enclosure at Ascot. The greater number of London hostesses closed their doors against both parties who were tainted by the mud of the divorce courts.

The commandments for Edwardian society were very clear. The first was 'Thou shalt not be found out', the second 'There shall be no scandal'.

The men were inevitably forgiven after a short period, but the women were branded however badly neglected or ill-treated they might have been.

It seemed incredible that Molly Forbes-Sempill, who loved balls, parties and all the trappings of society, was prepared to brave all this. Then very shortly after the decree absolute Molly married Wilfred Ashley.

They came to see us at Pershore on their honeymoon. I remember the excitement when their huge open touring-car came down the drive. Molly was looking radiant. She wore a flat motoring hat secured on her head by two large hat-pins, and from it, falling almost to the ground over her thin dust-coat, was a shaded pink chiffon veil framing her face.

She was obviously very happy and very excited. She had not only married a charming, good-looking man, but she had also married Broadlands, the magnificent Regency house which had belonged to Lord Palmerston. Its beautiful pillared exterior, its large reception rooms, its treasures, pictures and gardens were just the background Molly as a poor sailor's wife had craved.

'Aunt Molly,' I said—we called all our parents' friends Uncle and Aunt—'may we get into your big car?'

She checked her animated conversation with my father and mother.

'I suppose so,' she answered a little reluctantly. 'But don't touch anything. Children are so destructive, you can't trust them.'

I remember wondering then how Uncle Wilfred's two little daughters would get on with Aunt Molly. She was now their mother. I couldn't help worrying about them.

That night, when my mother came to kiss me good night, I said in a frightened voice:

'If you and Daddy had a divorce, you could marry another Daddy and Daddy could marry another Mummy. What would become of us?'

It was the cry that thousands of children were to make in the years to come. But my mother only laughed.

'Don't worry, darling,' she said, 'that will never happen. Daddy and I will always be together.'

I put my arms around her.

'We must all be together for ever and ever, mustn't we?' I cried. 'You, Daddy, Ronald, Tony and me.'

'Of course, darling, nothing shall separate us,' my mother promised.

It was not divorce which was to prove her wrong, but two world wars.

After the war the number of divorces rose sharply. The annual average from 1911 to 1913 was only 965, but in 1919–20 it was 4,874, involving a still tiny minority of the population.

The war was responsible for many of the broken marriages; for after the emotional urgency of marrying a man who might be killed within a few weeks of the marriage, the fact that many bridegrooms returned created unexpected problems.

One of my friends married a V.C. before he was demobbed. But he seemed so completely different out of uniform in a worn blue serge suit, she said after she had left him:

'I couldn't believe it was the same man! Oh dear, I'm not really a snob, but he did look awful!'

But even in the thirties most families could still say proudly: 'There has never been a divorce in our family', and the older generation, who had suffered any misery or humiliation rather than create a scandal, were deeply shocked and indignant at any question of 'going to law'.

This meant that when any of us were so unfortunate as to have

68

a divorce, however justified the action might be, it was impossible for us not to feel that we were doing something terribly wrong.

A friend of mine told me that after he was married for the second time he still had 'desperate regrets and conscience' about his first wife. He felt he could never endure another divorce.

That was, of course, the result of the way we had all been brought up. The same sentences were drummed into our ears after every scandal.

'Those whom God has joined together let no man put asunder!'

'You take the vow—"For better, for worse!" How can you repudiate it when things get worse?'

Even more soul-destroying than this was the shame of believing one was a failure. How could two people who had once loved each other reach such an impasse? And who could one blame but oneself?

'Where did I make a mistake?' a desperate wife asked me miserably. 'I loved him and he loved me. But he's found this other woman. What does she give him that I didn't? Where did I fail?'

A society wife has everything to lose and little to gain. If her husband is bored with her and wants to marry someone else, it is usually the wife who must leave the house which has been their home. She must start again in straitened or certainly less affluent circumstances. She may get alimony but can any money compensate her for being uprooted, often in middle age, and having to start her life anew?

A friend of mine in the 20's, who had always been unconventional, fell in love with a married man, older than herself and already notorious for his many love affairs. He was a peer of great social consequence, with vast estates and a wife who moved in Court circles.

He was completely captivated by my friend and, perhaps for the first time in his life, really in love. They went everywhere together, making no effort to hide their infatuation, and being both extremely well known soon the gossip-columns hinted at the association. Finally he asked his wife for a divorce.

Dignified, reserved, an aristocrat to her fingertips, she listened to him in silence. She was hurt, humiliated and unhappy. I think her first instinct was to escape from the sordid degradation of clinging to a husband who no longer wanted her and who was parading his 'paramour' for all the world to see.

Then she looked at the fantastically beautiful house in which generations of her husband's family had lived; she saw the priceless furniture, the pictures, the famous gardens with their fountains and army of gardeners. She also saw her children coming home to find another woman at the head of the dining-table, another woman wearing the family jewels.

She saw all her care of the people on the estate forgotten, her charities neglected, her friends no longer invited. She knew too that her tea parties with Queen Mary would no longer be possible —small intimate occasions which meant a lot to her.

'No,' she said quietly to her husband. 'I will never give you a divorce. This is our children's home and mine. I shall stay here. You must do what you wish.'

Furious, he raged and pleaded, but she was adamant. He and my friend took a villa in the South of France together. People found them gay, amusing and carefree, although they both lived too hard and drank too much. His wife continued to have tea with Queen Mary.

Inevitably, the gay life took its toll. The peer was not young enough to stand the pace. He got ill, my friend found other men more amusing. Finally he went back to his wife. She accepted him without reproach. The great home, the estates, were his and he knew in his heart it was where he belonged.

'How wise you were, dear, not to give Reggie a divorce,' an intimate friend said sometime later.

'Divorce is no cure for unhappiness,' came the wise reply.

It is something too many women forget. They rush into the divorce courts at the first suggestion of adultery, only to find they are left husbandless and lonely with nothing to look forward to. This is especially true when the present-day figures show that a woman over thirty-five has only a fifteen per cent chance of re-marriage. But a man? He can go on marrying new wives indefinitely—and does.

It is not only adultery that wives have to put up with. It is often minor irritations or just boredom which destroys marriage rather than dramatic actions of infidelity.

Consuelo Duchess of Marlborough describes dining with the Duke she had been forced to marry at the end of the century:

'How I learned to dread and hate these dinners,' she says, 'how ominous and wearisome they loomed at the end of a long day. . . . As a rule neither of us spoke a word. I took to knitting in desperation and the butler read detective stories in the hall.'

The most notorious divorce of the twenties was in 1924 between the Hon. John Russell and his wife Christabel. John Russell, who pleaded non-access, won the first hearing when the Court found his wife, who was pregnant, guilty of adultery with an unknown man.

Christabel Russell appealed to the Court of Appeal but her plea was dismissed. Undefeated, she went to the House of Lords alleging that her husband's evidence was inadmissible, and she proved that, although she was having a child, she was, in fact, technically a virgin. She won the case and was said to have 'revolutionised the practice of the divorce courts'.

I grew very fond of Christabel Russell. She started a dress shop and made a success of it. She had great courage and a determination coupled with a reckless disregard of danger, which made her one of the best horse-women of the day.

But I remember in the middle of her long-drawn-out cases, when she badly needed sympathy and friendship, seeing her walk in the Savoy and down the flight of stairs which leads into the restaurant. She was wearing a vivid scarlet dress which was tightly fitted to show off her extremely good figure. On her head a feather rose straight in the air from a cloche hat pulled low over her forehead. She looked lovely, striking, dramatic and what everyone thought was 'very fast'.

It was, I know, an action of defiance, a typical gesture of the twenties against the disapproval of the old brigade who thought we didn't care. But brave though it might be—it wasn't wise or sensible at that particular moment. But none of us were very wise.

It was Sir George Lewis, the first great divorce solicitor, who made his clients 'dress the part'.

'The "twelve good men and true" of the jury,' he said, 'are mostly suburban, middle-class and conformist. They expect the injured wife to appear quiet, sad and respectable and the "other woman" to look a scarlet houri.'

Sir George's petitioning wives wore black and no make-up!

They had a handkerchief handy. You were good or you were bad in the twenties—no murky indecisive grey like today!

A divorced person, innocent or guilty, could not be married in church. The King and Defender of the Faith could not acknowledge divorced persons. Good Christians considered that divorcees had put themselves outside the fold, and were more or less less damned.

'They are living in sin and one can't pretend that is not the truth,' a lady-in-waiting to Queen Mary said. 'A practising Christian cannot think otherwise.'

But the power and authority of the Church of England was crumbling. Before the war its congregations were ready-made. The upper and lower classes went to church because it was their duty. In the villages and small towns the church provided the social centre of the community.

At Knole, Chatsworth, Woburn, and other great houses, everyone employed indoors and outdoors went to church every Sunday by order. At Rangemore—the vast mansion belonging to the Dowager Baroness Burton where King Edward often stayed—they went twice. One side of the church was kept entirely for the Rangemore servants, who numbered over forty all through the war.

The Church of England, unlike the Roman Catholic, had no special form of service or rubric for men dying in battle and the padres, although they did their best, were at a great disadvantage in the holocaust of war.

My father, writing to my mother from France, said:

'On the battle-field we've grown to realise that a man has to be assured that there is something stronger and greater than himself. I have been very impressed by the Roman Catholic priests. After they have heard the Confession of a desperately wounded man and given him their special ministrations, he will die with a smile on his lips. The Church of England padres fumble and fiddle; the only thing they seem to ask is "Shall I write to your parents?" It is not enough. When the war is over I think I shall become a Roman Catholic.'

When peace came in 1918 the Church sank back into a complacent lethargy, expecting the pews to be filled again with respectful worshippers. But the men returning from France were disillusioned and were often without faith. For four years they had seen their comrades blown to bits or blinded with gas. It was hard to believe in a merciful God.

One man said to me years later:

'I remember praying as we went down the line to the trenches that I wouldn't make a fool of myself. I was brought up to go to church, and I suppose you could say I was religious. I went to France straight from Sandhurst—I was eighteen years and two months old. The first day my greatest friend was disembowelled beside me. The next day another boy I had been at school with was caught on the wire as we were driven back. He hung all day about twenty yards from us. His legs were shot away and he was blind, but he was still alive. He called to us to finish him, to put him out of his agony. I could never again believe in a God who allowed that.'

This story had a sequel. When the man who had told me this died of cancer, almost his last words were:

'Tell Barbara I've been praying again.'

Not enough emphasis seems to be laid on the force, power and the efficiency of prayer. Yet it is this 'linking up' of the individual with the Power-House of Faith with its live electrons which has performed all the miracles which have ever happened.

In 1929 the boxer Jack Dempsey, before his championship fight with Jess Willard, had prayed to win. He had also prayed before the bell sounded for the contest.

'I never went to bed in my life and I never ate a meal in my life without saying a prayer,' he said. 'I know my prayers have been answered hundreds of times.'

Prayers are answered, but sometimes we are not sent exactly what we want. The Duke of Rutland once wrote to *The Times* in a season of extreme drought, urging that the prayers for rain in the prayer book should be used in all churches. The rains came, but considerably in excess of what was required, with the result that the farming community clamoured for prayers to save them from the deluge.

Maurice Baring composed the following verse:

'The Duke of Rutland asked *The Times* to pray
For rain: the rain came down the following day.
The pious marvelled; sceptics murmured "Fluke?"
And farmers, late with hay, said "Damn the Duke".'

In 1919 the Church, faced with very depleted congregations, did nothing to bring them in. Instead of contacting those who were desperately in need of spiritual as well as mental and physical help, they merely spent their time denouncing the modern girl and protesting against us enjoying ourselves. The Bishop of London stopped the extension of the closing hours for drinks by declaring dramatically: 'I would rather die on the doorstep of the House of Lords than see this Bill passed.'

It never seemed to strike one single clergyman that dancing was an expression, not only of gaiety, but of a desire to express ourselves to portray something we could not put into words. We danced, while today young people protest.

'The whole purpose of religion is to help to guide and to inspire,' the Bishop of Barking once said to me. He was right; it should not only be a platform for critics. Yet all through the twenties we listened to:

'The use of these dances or any dance as a means of raising money for memorials in honour of the gallant dead who have laid down their lives for the nation and Empire,' said Bishop Weldon, 'is little less than a national humiliation. Is there no sense of propriety or congruity left?'

At the same time, the Bishop of London, in a 'Clean-the-Stage' campaign, said it was 'an outrage on good manners to depict the preliminaries of an outrage on a woman in a public performance'.

Little wonder that young people, restless, curious about life and after-life, just like today, sought a Maharishi or leader. Two of them were Coué, and Dr. Buchman, who had an ever-growing success with his Oxford movement.

Coué was an insignificant-looking little French chemist who became world famous because he said:

'If you clasp your hands together and say "Every day in every way I am getting better and better", you do get better.'

Even so important a patient as Lord Curzon consulted Coué in 1922. There was an amusing epigram written about him:

'This very remarkable man
Commands a most practical plan:
You can do what you want
If you don't think you can't;
So don't think you can't, you can.'

Dr. Frank Buchman, an American Lutheran minister, founded a religious revival movement called 'The Oxford Group'. These who joined affirmed that they had decided to surrender their lives to God and to endeavour to lead a spiritual life.

Their aims were:

Absolute honesty
Absolute purity
Absolute unselfishness
Absolute love.

In 1921 Dr. Buchman first visited Cambridge, then Oxford. So remarkable was the effect he had on a troubled, so-called atheist generation, that he was thanked publicly from a university pulpit 'for the new illumination that had come to Oxford'.

The Marquess of Salisbury—one of the most influential men in Britain—became one of Buchman's supporters. When asked why, he replied:

'It is the Spirit moving on the waters, and I dare not stand aside.'

At this time Lord Salisbury said in the House of Lords:

'If I may use a phrase which is common in a Great Movement which is taking place at this moment in this country and elsewhere, what you want are God-guided personalities which make God-guided nationalities, to make a new world.'

Buchman had many important followers. The Earl of Athlone made a broadcast on 'Moral Rearmament', which the Oxford Movement came to be called; Mahatma Gandhi and Dr. Sun Yat-sen of China became Buchman's friends. While the Bishop of London, Dr. Winnington-Ingram, sent Sir Lynden Macassey, when he was leader of the Parliamentary Bar and later head of Reuters, to examine his work. Both subsequently supported him for the rest of his life.

One of my friends went further afield for inspiration. Rosita Forbes was the first woman explorer of the early twenties. She set off alone to see the remote and dangerous parts of North Africa and the Near East. She visited Kufara, the secret city of the Sahara, and Jizan in Asir, where no white woman had ever been before. Disguised as a Bedouin woman she even tried to get through to Mecca.

'Were you frightened?' I asked, knowing that had she been discovered it could have meant instant death.

'No! Only footsore,' she replied, showing me her feet.

They were cut, bruised, calloused, the heels rough and blistered from walking barefoot. In 1925 a film, *From Red Sea to Blue Nile*, was made from Rosita's stories of her travels.

Rosita was the first person I ever met who really travelled 'light'. She told me that as she was usually moving about on camels or on foot, she had to have a dress that could be whipped out of a bag at the last moment when she arrived at Government House or an Embassy.

'I have one made in lace,' she said, 'which doesn't crease, and I can really get dressed in a few minutes.'

It seemed to me quite sensational at the time because we had inherited the great, bulky, cumbersome luggage of the Edwardians.

After the war there were fewer household servants but there were still railway porters—except when they were on strike. I remember once travelling when there was a porters' strike, and standing helplessly on the station surrounded by three enormous suitcases which I couldn't possibly carry. I looked round for an accommodating young man, who would rush to assist a 'damsel in distress', but the only person I could see was a porter, obviously picketing the platform, and viewing the passengers with a jaundiced eye.

I approached him and said:

'I know you won't help me, but could you please advise me what I am to do. I'm just not strong enough to lift these cases.'

He looked at me, glanced up and down the station to see if anyone was watching, and said:

'I'll take 'em, miss, but don't you tell no one.'

When it became fashionable to travel by ship, the Americans introduced an enormous wardrobe trunk. This was incredibly heavy, in fact it took two or three men to lift it at all as it was really a small wardrobe. When it was opened one had a hanging space on one side covered by a calico curtain, and drawers on the other. It certainly made packing much easier, and if the trunk stood in the cabin, one didn't have to unpack. But it was a ghastly job trying to get anyone to lift it on to a taxi, or even up the gangplank of a ship.

It was not until late in the thirties that manufacturers began to realise that people who were travelling might not only have to pay over-weight, but to carry their own luggage. It was then they began to devise lighter suitcases which were called, quite simply, 'aeroplane-cases'.

Packing had altered a lot with the years. A good lady's maid in the Edwardian days packed with sheet upon sheet of tissue paper. Every sleeve was stuffed, so that it would not crease. Every pleat of a dress was tacked down before it was put in a trunk.

It took hours to pack clothes properly, and equally hours to unpack them, but what did it matter as long as the lady didn't have to do anything for herself?

At the beginning of the twenties we had got so used to the Edwardian manner of having clothes fully lined and stiffened with bones so that they did not require pressing, that it was a long time before we realised our chiffon and crêpe de Chine dresses required pressing every time we wore them. There were, of course, only flat irons, the type that heated in front of the fire. I think one of the greatest blessings that modernisation has brought to women is the electric iron.

But to return to Rosita—I remember she told me once that having travelled for miles across the desert, she arrived in some big town to find an invitation from Government House to dine at eight o'clock. The camel, or whatever had brought her there, had been slower than usual, and she found she only had a few minutes in which to dress.

She pulled open her bag with her lace evening dress in it, and then discovered to her consternation that she had forgotten to pack her stockings. Of course they had to be black—there were only black or dead white stockings in those days—and anyway Rosita's dress was of black lace.

'I had my evening shoes,' she said, 'but there was no time to buy stockings, and as I had never been to this Government House before, I knew no one from whom I could borrow a pair. Besides, there just wasn't time. It would have been unthinkable to keep their Excellencies waiting.'

'What did you do?' I asked.

'Luckily there was a coal fire in my bedroom which had not been lit,' she said. 'I blacked my legs with coal dust. I thought it smelt a little peculiar, so I covered myself with scent and swept downstairs. Nobody noticed, and although I say it myself, I was a success that evening.'

There was no one as daring as Rosita in the early twenties, and she didn't look at all like an intrepid explorer. She was tall, slender and fragile-looking, with an oval face and large slightly protruding eyes.

Needless to say not everyone admired her daring. People were extremely shocked at the idea of a woman going off 'into the blue' on her own. It was 'unfeminine'. But Rosita was seeking something indefinable as we all were.

When the Queen of Egypt, strictly secluded, asked her: 'Why did you want to go to Kufara?' she said afterwards:

'How could I explain? It was certainly not for ambition, I travelled—like Elroy Flecker's Merchants in Hassan—for lust of knowledge and in answer to a deep aching need to learn more about the desert and its life.'

The French Geographical Society gave Rosita their gold medal. The only other woman previously to be accorded this honour was Mme Curie, the discoverer of radium.

Rosita was poised, calm and controlled whether she was in danger of being denounced as a spy or facing death from a Berber knife.

In one pageant that I arranged for the Train Ball at Covent Garden, I asked Rosita to come as 'The Royal Highlander'. She had fifty yards of red velvet train to manipulate—a difficult experience for anyone—but Rosita managed it with the same efficiency as she must have used to control a grumpy camel.

She had before the Second World War a very lovely house in London, but it was one of those destroyed by the Germans, and she decided to leave England and build herself a home on Eleuthera Island, near Nassau. She began by living in a tent, something she was quite used to, while she watched her house being built, brick by brick.

'The hardest part,' she wrote to me, 'is cutting a way through a wilderness of thicket.'

Needless to say, while Rosita went off wandering in the East, I stayed at home, but I studied yoga. I longed to go to Tibet. Later I was to know a white yogi and write in a magazine he started. But without any 'guru' I did the breathing exercises every day and I found they sharpened my sense of hearing and smelling.

I also saw in my mind coloured pictures which sometimes

78

remained clearly to be seen against the darkness of the room when I opened my eyes. But yoga also made me feel very apart from the world and that I thought was a mistake. I wanted to live fully.

Mysticism had always fascinated me. I read every book I could find on the subject. I believed that near us, around us, there was a world beyond and that at special moments we could break through.

Many of my friends were to have revelations of some sort or another. Lady Stonehaven, wife of the Governor General of Australia, saw a blinding light when she was in her bath. It left her with a 'marvellous sensation of peace'. Lord Marchwood, who had sailed in the old windjammers, gone through the Singapore Mutiny and been shipwrecked several times, experienced much the same thing on a golf course.

'A flash of light gave me a sense of unity with all creation.'

My mother very much later, after both of my brothers had been killed at Dunkirk, was in church praying for an unknown Pole who had died in exile when she saw an indescribably vivid light in the chancel. It was there for about three minutes and confirmed her unshakable faith in the survival of those she loved.

Once, in about 1921, I motored out of London after a dance. We drove towards Kingston and turned off the road up a small track which led to a wood of silver birch trees. The moon was full and its beams, shining through the branches, were great shafts of light, blinding, beautiful, mysterious and compelling. I felt I had only to walk into them and I . . . I would hear . . . I would understand . . . I would know. . . .

'You look strange,' my partner said, 'what's the matter?'

'I'm going to find out—to know,' I answered incoherently.

'What do you mean?' he questioned. 'What are you going to know?'

'I'm not certain,' I replied, 'but it's something I've searched for—something I must learn.'

He caught me by the shoulders and turned me round.

'Stop it!' he said. 'You're far away from me and I don't like it.'

He kissed me and drove me back to the main road, but I've never forgotten how very nearly I found out the truth.

It is hard to realise today how we sought for the supernatural in everything. When Suzanne Lenglen arrived at Wimbledon in 1919 and defeated Mrs. Lambert Chambers she became the first woman sports hero. But there was more than hard work and luck in her triumph.

'I was a pale, thin little person,' she said in an interview. 'Father and Mother were afraid I should always be an invalid.'

Father, who had been a champion cyclist, had drilled her to place a ball in any given square of a specially marked court.

'Tennis,' Suzanne continued, 'transformed me magically into a nut-brown maid sparkling with health.'

But the 'match-winning' machine broke down without the expert who had created it. Suzanne went to America without Father, and collapsed at her first encounter with Mrs. Mallory, the American champion.

The importance of Mr. Lenglen's presence on the court was so obvious that it was whispered everywhere that Suzanne actually played in a hypnotic trance. A tennis Trilby to her father's Svengali.

There had been a tremendous interest in Spiritualism during the war when clairvoyants and mediums had been besieged by miserable widows and desperate wives whose husbands were missing. A friend of my mother brought her frequent messages from her husband 'on the other side' that my father was safe in a German hospital.

'I can see him quite clearly,' she said in a trance. 'He is wounded, but not badly, I think it is in the arm. He is worried about his wife. It is important that you tell her that her husband is alive.'

When it was subsequently proved that my father had been pounded to death by the German guns in their last push towards Paris, the clairvoyant admitted there 'must have been a mistake'. But my mother's friend went on talking twice a week to 'her husband' until she married again.

'What happens now?' my mother asked when she heard of the engagement. 'What will you do about Arthur?'

'I shall go on speaking to him, of course,' her friend replied, 'but he seems to have gone so far away. Anyway, he will want me to be happy.'

Those who had been bereaved were greatly comforted and encouraged by Sir Oliver Lodge, who published long conversations with his dead son Raymond. Judge Rutherford, an American, filled the Albert Hall with an eager audience to hear 'Millions Now Living Will Never Die'.

The Rev. Vale Owen, a Lancashire clergyman, announced that the dead 'on the other side' were still alive.

In 1925 Lord Northcliffe, the great newspaper owner, came 'back' to talk to his former secretary and Hannen Swaffer, who with his dirty clothes covered with cigarette ash, shapeless black hat and wide tie was one of the most colourful journalists of the period.

'One is never ill here,' Lord Northcliffe is supposed to have said. 'Never hurt, never depressed . . . We have no money, we work out things in kind. I have worked for my suit . . . I liked the pink flowers you bought me, but don't bother to put any more on my grave . . . Graves, like the earthly body, do not matter.'

It didn't sound much like Lord Northcliffe to me!

A hard-working Irishman, Northcliffe had during his life been a forceful, if temperamental, personality. His 'Hang the Kaiser' campaign of hate against Germany made it impossible for Lloyd George to arrange a just and reasonable Peace Treaty. But he was the first press lord to give the public what they wanted, which was 'yellow press journalism', gossip and what were first called 'dodges', and afterwards stunts.

The *Daily Mail* encouraged anything that was new, inventive and interesting. It pioneered almost everything from wireless to flying, from sand competitions to paper-bag cookery. Its influence was immense and progressive.

According to his brilliant, unpredictable, frank-speaking nephew, Cecil King, Lord Northcliffe had many love affairs, a number of illegitimate children, and died insane.

In our insecurity, we, the young, clutched at straws. We were searching for something beyond ourselves, but we didn't know what it was. I went to many séances where mediums spoke in strange voices, apported flowers and precious stones, gave messages, warnings, predictions. I longed to be—but I never was —very impressed.

When Ronald, my brother, who was as close to me as any twin, was killed at Dunkirk, I was taken by one of the high priestesses of spiritualism to nearly every clairvoyant and medium in London. Some, like Estelle Roberts, who had been amazingly accurate with my mother, were interesting; but I could not be convinced that they were really communicating with Ronald. If they were, then he had become an incredible bore. There was none of the strong, vivid positiveness about his conversations which had made him so outstanding in Parliament.

Had nothing survived, I asked, of his hatred of injustice, his visionary ideas of sweeping reforms, his brilliant sparkling oratory? I could not believe the sender of such dull, drab, commonplace messages was Ronald.

'What are you doing?' I would ask.

'He says he is very busy.'

'Doing what?'

'Helping others. He has a desk.'

'In what way is he helping people?'

'He says he is very busy.'

I remembered almost the same conversations with my father when he was killed. If the million men killed in World War I had really been helping those on earth, why had we become embroiled in World War II? It didn't seem as if their efforts had been very successful!

'He says he is often with you.'

'Neither my mother nor I are aware of it, and we have tried to contact him. Ask him where he has tried to get in touch with us.'

'He says in the home.'

'In my home or my mother's? And where in the home?'

'He just says in the home.'

It was all frustrating, imponderable, inconclusive.

I think it is idiotic to suppose as soon as people die they know —if there is survival—all the secrets of the universe. I think they know as little or as much as they knew on earth. But since Ronald had been brilliant while he was alive, how could these commonplace mutterings be his?

That is not to say that a medium is deliberately trying to deceive those who seek to communicate. She may in all sincerity believe she is in touch with those who are dead. And when people are unhappy and emotionally unbalanced, it is very easy to believe their loved one is present.

Of course, there are those who 'coin-in' on the credulity of the bereaved. There are also the show-offs and exhibitionists. I remember one séance in the twenties at Mrs. Richards' house, who was the mother of the Marchioness of Queensberry.

There was present a mixture of young and old. The first medium, we were told, was the incarnation of an Egyptian princess (they are always royalty, I notice). When I arrived she was demanding brandy.

'I can't loosen up without it.'

When she had drunk a good deal, she danced—dressed in a chiffon scarf wrapped round her breasts and folded between her legs.

'She must be controlled by an Egyptian!'

'Wonderful! Like a frieze in Luxor!'

'I can feel the spirits round her!'

Personally I thought it a pathetic performance brought on by alcohol.

The Egyptian angle was very popular, especially after Tutankhamen's tomb was discovered in 1924 by Howard Carter and Lord Carnarvon. Lady Howard de Walden, who did so much for music in the twenties, used to tell a story of being taken down to dine by Lord Tyrell. As soon as they were seated he said:

'Do please tell me, do you believe in reincarnation, and if so were you perhaps Cleopatra?'

'Perhaps and perhaps not, I'm not sure,' Lady Howard de Walden replied, 'but I am quite positive that I was not Cleopatra.'

'Thank goodness!' Sir Arthur exclaimed, 'for, would you believe it, the last three ladies I have taken in to dinner were equally sure that they had been Queen Cleopatra in their last lives.'

I knew one of the three women to whom Lord Tyrell was referring. She was the mother of one of my friends. She made herself up Egyptian fashion, wore dresses reminiscent of the Pharaohs, and had mosquito nets over the windows of her home in Mayfair.

Lord Carnarvon died from a mosquito bite, and everyone said it was 'the curse of the Pharaohs'. When the tomb was first discovered the brother of King Fuad of Egypt, who was often in England, said to Mrs. Meyrick at the '43':

'It is ill work. The dead must not be disturbed, only evil can come of it. Those who desecrate the resting places of the ancient dead do so at their own peril. You will see.'

Two weeks later his prophecy received its terrible fulfilment. Lord Kitchener's death was attributed solely to the same curse.

Winston Churchill had criticised his action in permitting the sacred shrine of the Mahdi in the Sudan to be destroyed. In the East he who desecrates the graves of religious leaders is supposed to perish through water floods, and the place of his sepulchre 'never to be known'. This certainly happened when Lord Kitchener went down with *The Hampshire*.

'I told you so!' retired colonial colonels said from Cheltenham to Harrogate.

Count Hamon, who was the famous astrologer Cheiro, told Lord Kitchener that his death would be sudden but that he need not anticipate death in battle. Just before Lord Kitchener went aboard *The Hampshire* he told Cheiro that if anything happened to him he would give him a sign.

Cheiro was in the music room of his house abroad when a large hatchment (a coat of arms used when there was a death in the house) fell with a crash and split in two. Cheiro guessed something had happened to Lord Kitchener and found out later it had fallen at the very hour *The Hampshire* went down.

We were intensely superstitious. The death of the Marchioness Curzon, was, we believed, because she had a dress entirely embroidered in peacock feathers for the Durbar when her husband was Viceroy. She certainly became ill immediately afterwards, had one miscarriage after another and died. I've been afraid of peacocks' feathers ever since.

There was a celebrated palmist called Mrs. Robinson, whom everyone visited in her tiny flat up flights of stone steps near Olympia. When she told Winston Churchill's hand in 1898 she 'saw' such an exciting and brilliant future ahead of him that, while praising her 'strange skill in palmistry', he asked her not to publish it.

Her prophetic picture of him was, she said:

'Of a man holding back a pair of iron gates against a mob of millions with arms outstretched.'

Among Mrs. Robinson's clients were Lily Langtry, who took Edward VII to her, Oscar Wilde, Lord Roberts and Shane Leslie. She told me the initials of the man I should marry when I was in love with someone quite different, so it was certainly not thought-reading.

The next turn at the séance of which I was speaking was a girl who we were told had been examined in another room to see if she had anything hidden on her body. She went into a trance, heaved and wriggled about the floor and finally produced a bunch of rather crumpled roses.

'They still have the dew of Paradise on them!' a woman cried hysterically.

I thought that, if tested, it would be suspiciously like London water.

'I'm sure she had those flowers with her,' I whispered to my hostess. 'She is a fake.'

'Hush,' Mrs. Richards exclaimed. 'Don't upset them, it would be too cruel.'

I looked round at the other guests, who all, old and young, had the rapt expression of unquestioning faith. They wanted to believe, they longed to—they did.

I wanted to go to a séance where the medium apported precious stones. We were always being told that not only flowers, but diamonds, turquoises, rubies and emeralds appeared in the sitter's hands. I thought this would be a really good test, because what 'charlatan' could afford such expensive props?

The nearest I got to it, however, was in South Kensington, when, after hours of holding a hot hand on either side of me, the male medium produced one very small stone which could have been concealed anywhere.

'It's a meterorite from another planet!' I was told. I thought such a stone could be found anywhere in the gravel paths of Hyde Park.

On the other hand, Lady Comyn-Pratt, mother of David Niven the film star, had communications with her dead husband which were written in an Egyptian script, so ancient that it could only be deciphered at the British Museum.

Sir Philip Sassoon had a message through a direct-voice medium recommended by Sir Oliver Lodge. This was from a young airman killed in the war who had often piloted his private aeroplane. Sir Philip recognised the voice and 'the airman' said:

'I hope you find my flying-boots useful.'

The medium could not have known that Sir Philip had bought the airman's boots after his death.

Another story which always intrigued me was of Lady Glenconner, who took her own plates to a spirit photographer—an ordinary working man—hoping for a portrait of her dearly loved son killed in action. Fraud would have been easy because the young man's photograph had appeared in all the illustrated papers at the time of his death. A portrait did appear: it was not of Lady Glenconner's son, but of an obscure and unimportant man to whom she had once been engaged and who had loved her deeply until his death a year earlier.

Recently, the dynamic and outspoken Bishop of Southwark, who is conducting an investigation of psychic phenomena, took me to meet the most famous medium of today—Mrs. Twigg. We sat in a tiny room in her home in Acton.

She was undoubtedly absolutely sincere. She was right in many things she said and she told me things she could not have known except by very exceptional clairvoyance. But I am still not convinced that one can talk with the dead, or that, if one can, it is really a help except as a palliative for the sense of loss.

No message has ever said anything nationally or politically constructive. No medium has given warning of train disasters, crashes in the air, or children being burnt to death. People's personal intuitions have often warned them about this sort of thing, but that is very different.

This is not to say I do not believe in survival after death. My husband was one of the young men wounded at the Battle of Passchendaele by a sniper's dum-dum bullet which passed through his lung and out through his back. He lay out for forty-eight hours in no-man's-land and when finally he reached the base hospital he was put in a tent to die. He lived because he was young, but his expectation of life was short.

'When you were so near to death,' I asked him, 'did you hear voices or see angels?'

'No,' he answered, 'I just felt very tired and very far away from everything.'

My husband, like so many of his contemporaries, believed there was no after-life. James Elroy Flecker explained their feelings when he wrote:

'I am no coward who would seek in fear
A folklore solace or sweet Indian tales.
I know dead men are deaf and cannot hear
The singing of a thousand nightingales.'

Yet when my husband died of his war wounds in 1963—the scar tissue touched his heart—I received a message or rather a manifestation so unexpected, so personal, so completely convincing, that I knew he was trying to tell me he was wrong—we do survive the death of our outworn bodies.

But how limp and unhelpful the Church was in the twenties to those bereft of faith who were groping blindly for reassurance and hope. Instead the bishops went on thundering against birth control, Oxford bags, short skirts, cosmetics, speed and the weekend.

What was wrong with the weekend? Our new way of life completed the process of emptying the churches because we had discovered the country and the means of getting there in a Baby Austin!

CHAPTER FOUR

Your headlights like two golden moons
Shine in the silver way.
The wind is whispering faery tunes,
Drive on till you find the day.

CARS were the rage, motoring a craze, the joy of having a young man with a car was indescribable. The Morris production in 1919 was only 387 cars, but I was to know its rival producer, Sir Herbert Austin, very well, when Ronald was the Member of Parliament for King's Norton and the Austin works were in his constituency. Sir Herbert in 1922 designed a car unlike anything in the world—the Austin Seven.

'I sketched it on the billiards table at home,' he told me. 'I was determined to produce a car which could be stored in the side entrance of any ordinary suburban villa and yet could carry four passengers!'

He did it and it only cost £125!

The Baby Austin got a lot of laughs. The first time I went out in one a bus-driver leant out and shouted:

'Jump it in behind, lady, I'll give you a lift!'

It made cars no longer a rich man's toy—it meant motoring for millions. But it was not only Morris and Austin who were designing cars. Thousands of other young men thought they would have a try. They hammered away in small garages, in sheds, in old army huts. Some of the cars they produced were fantastic and dangerous, but some at least could be driven on the road.

An extraordinary car made from an old aeroplane engine was created by George Henderson, the famous flying ace and the first pilot to fly under Tower Bridge. His face had been burnt in the war and he was somewhat disfigured. Because I was sorry for him

I was nicer to him than I might have been otherwise, with the result that he fell in love with me.

He used to follow me wherever I went in his ugly, open, noisy car, which he called 'Barbed Arrow', a somewhat obscure play on my name. Christening it, he gave me a tiny diamond arrow, which was then the latest craze in jewellery.

I tried to be fond of George, but somehow, maybe because of his war experiences, he was one of those people who were touchy and difficult, and always rubbed one up the wrong way. He used to arrive without warning in his enormous car which was just an engine covered with iron plate and mounted on a chassis with two bucket seats taken from an aeroplane. I had to manufacture explanations of his arrival uninvited. As he was very jealous of any other man I knew, it created endless difficulties, which, although embarrassing, were at the same time rather flattering.

George had learnt to fly in 1915 and by the end of the war became a lieutenant-colonel in the Royal Air Force, which in those days used army rank. He flew for Daimler Airways and in 1924 joined the De Havilland Aircraft Company. Then he formed the Henderson School of Flying at Brooklands and started 'joy-riding' which operated at aviation meetings. He opened several flying schools in South Africa and inaugurated the passenger service from Cape Town to Johannesburg.

In 1930 he was the pilot in the tragic Meopham air disaster when an aeroplane fell to pieces in the air over Kent for no reason that has ever been discovered. It is one of those great flying mysteries which has never been solved.

George had arrived at Croydon from Le Touquet in a large Junker monoplane and the machine was then overhauled by engineers who declared it in perfect order. But when he set off again after eight minutes George returned saying he was worried by an unusual noise in the engine.

'A washer in the exhaust has begun to blow,' the chief engineer explained. 'Shall I replace it, sir?'

'Oh no,' George replied, 'that's all right. So long as I know what it is it doesn't matter.'

He reached Le Touquet where he picked up the Marquess of Dufferin and Ava, Viscountess Ednam, Sir Edward Ward and Mrs. Henrik Loeffler, whose husband had owned *The Albion*, the largest steam yacht in the world, which he sold to Sir Thomas Lipton.

They reached Kent, then in the pouring rain the aeroplane fell from the sky—the wreckage being strewn over an area of five miles. There was no explosion, the petrol tanks were intact, the aeroplane as new, having only done 100 hours' flying. All the vital parts of the engine were in order. The cylinder uncracked. No one will ever know why the accident happened.

The whole nation was shocked. The Marquess of Dufferin and Ava was the first speaker of the Senate of Northern Ireland. Viscountess Ednam, who had taken a vacant seat in the aeroplane, given up at the last moment by Lord Victor Paget, was the daughter of Millicent, Duchess of Sutherland. Lovely, sensitive and sympathetic, she was like the fey princess of a fairy tale. She had visited me the previous year in Orkney with her brother the Duke in his yacht *The Sans Peur*.

Everyone loved Rosemary Ednam. She had been a V.A.D. nurse in the war and had done inestimable work in helping crippled children. Duff Cooper in a poem he wrote about her said:

'We shall remember you, Rosemary, always;
Life will be lonelier, sadder than before,
But not less lovely because we shall remember,
Sadder and holier for evermore.
If years be given us which were denied you,
Age may dim eyes that today are blind with tears,
Yet shall we see that smile and hear that laughter,
Echoing for ever through the empty years.'

Rosemary was buried beside her little son of seven who had been killed six months earlier in an accident. She had made for him a 'Garden of Memory' in the grounds of Himley Hall, her home near Wolverhampton.

£65,000 pounds' worth of jewellery was lost from the aeroplane. When the bodies hurtled 1,800 feet to the ground, the priceless necklaces worn by the women broke and the loose pearls were scattered. A farm labourer picked up what he thought was a piece of glass and discovered it to be a diamond worth thousands of pounds.

After the Meopham disaster there was much anxiety about the

risks taken in the air by the Prince of Wales and Prince George. But it was explained that:

'There is no need for perturbation because the Princes fly in two-seater planes which are easier to manipulate than the big airliners. The dangerous moment is when a machine gets out of a spin.'

What is extraordinary now is to see how few people were killed in the airliner disasters of the twenties. They were, of course, very small machines in comparison with their modern counterparts:

1921: London–Brussels airmail crashed in Channel. Two killed.

1922: London and Paris planes collided near Beauvais. Six killed.

1923: French liner crashed over Folkestone. Three killed.

1923: London–Manchester Air Express crashed at Ivinghoe. Five killed.

1929: Imperial Airways Lina 'City of Ottawa' wrecked in Channel. Seven killed.

Something strangely prophetic was found in the decoration of the house in Cheyne Walk owned by Lord and Lady Ednam until their son was killed on the Embankment. The frieze in one room was a terra-cotta painting of the Thames shipping. Following Sir Alan Cobham's dramatic seaplane descent on the river at the House of Commons, an artist had painted in an aeroplane. After the disaster at Meopham, the Ednams' friends wondered whether it had been an omen.

Another friend, a bluff blue-eyed sailor, Commander Dennistoun Burney, M.P., invented the Burney Streamline Car. This had its engine at the back instead of the front, which was a revolutionary idea. It was also before the days of heating and it made the car extremely cold in winter.

Dennis Burney, always wildly enthusiastic about his inventions, was naturally thrilled when the Prince of Wales bought the Streamliner. But His Royal Highness found the Burney was not a good hill-climber and had an inconvenient habit of stalling.

One day when the Prince was driving from Windsor it stopped suddenly in the middle of the traffic on the outskirts of London.

'Its curious appearance,' the Prince said, 'attracted considerable attention, especially when the crowd saw I was inside it. Since it obstinately refused to start up again, I was obliged to send my driver to telephone for one of my other cars before I could continue my journey.'

Dennis Burney was more successful with the paravane which he invented for mine-sweeping. I remember moving down the St. Lawrence River in 1940 in a snow storm with the paravane working on the bows of *The Duchess of Richmond*. I felt it really kept us safe and was deeply grateful to its inventor.

Men with a car in the 20's had a special appeal all of their own. I now had a list of priorities where young men were concerned:

1. The most exciting young man of the moment took me out to dinner and on to dance. As we seldom got home before 6 a.m. this meant I had over nine hours of his company!

2. The next in the list took me out to lunch.

3. Finally came those who took me to tea at Gunter's in Berkeley Square, where we ate finger sponge cakes covered in pink or white icing and very rich real cream ice-creams.

But a man with a car topped all these categories because he could take me away for the weekend—not as young people go away today, of course, but to house parties of my friends or his. No one was surprised when one said:

'May I bring Hugo with me? He will drive me down in his car.'

'He has a car? How exciting! Of course bring him. We might pop over to the Xs' on Sunday. They've been asking us for ages, but we've had no way of getting to them.'

There was one very faithful admirer, who had a car but nothing else to recommend him. He was allowed to fetch me from Eaton Terrace and drive me out to lunch at the Ritz. He was grateful for this small mercy!

Cars were filled from petrol cans which one carried in the back, the driver mended punctured tyres by the roadside, and there were often far more complicated difficulties.

After the war, because young men had cars, the last autocratic paternal authority was broken. How could any father keep 'tabs' on a daughter who could get into a car and vanish into the blue? It had been impossible to go far in a horse-drawn carriage. My mother used to have secret assignations with her young men out hunting or by cycling to an arranged rendezvous, but cars meant a new and exhilarating freedom which left strict parents spluttering helplessly.

Of course, there were innumerable stories of pretended breakdowns, compromising nights spent under haystacks or of girls 'preferring' to walk home.

A rich and attractive girl was pursued by a penniless and dissolute but determined peer. She was amused by him but had no intention of allowing him to marry her for her money. The peer had a fast but unpredictable car, and late one afternoon they broke down miles from home in an isolated part of the country.

They walked a short distance and found a small but attractive inn, where they had dinner while the peer arranged to have the car mended. As the hours passed she believed the breakdown was genuine, and even when the peer told her it was impossible for them to get away that night he was so apologetic that she was not suspicious.

The landlady took her up to an old-fashioned but comfortable oak-beam bedroom with a four-poster bed and a fire burning in the grate.

'How nice to have a fire even though it is summer,' the girl said.

'That's what his Lordship always says!' was the answer.

Quite suddenly the girl saw the trap into which she had fallen. Not surprisingly there was no key in the door. She climbed out of the window and down a drainpipe, found her way to the outhouse into which the car had been towed and with the rugs made herself comfortable for the night.

Early in the morning a baker's cart drove into the yard. She bribed the man to take her to the nearest station. The peer returned to London rather sheepishly. He did not talk about what had happened because it made him look a fool, but he married another heiress the following year.

The worst hazard at that time was driving at night, for the car headlamps were very feeble. I was in an accident owing to this, but I was not in a car. I had been back to Bembridge in August 1920. More sure of myself than I had been the previous year, I had a marvellous time, sailing, bathing and, of course, dancing.

One of the dances was fancy-dress and I made myself a dress of some cheap black material, put a red scarf round my neck and a red handkerchief on my head and looked, I hoped, a cross between a gypsy and a pirate. As it was such a simple idea, I made loose black jumpers and red head-scarves and neckpieces for the men who wanted to go with me to the dance.

It is easy to imagine the fury of the other girls when I arrived with an escort of five men, all dressed like me.

That evening I became engaged to an Irishman nicknamed Pingo. When I left Bembridge he followed me to Tewkesbury in Gloucestershire where my mother had taken a house for the school holidays.

Pingo arrived on a motor-cycle which he had borrowed. It had a side-car but it was noisy, rather dirty and obviously put together from a lot of old parts. But the side-car was an improvement on riding pillion (sitting sideways, of course), which was considered extremely unladylike and very much frowned on.

I was asked to a dance in Bredon and off we went, driving dashingly down the dusty country lanes and arriving safely. During the dance Pingo and I quarrelled. He insisted we go home and I got into the side-car in a haughty silence. Outside Bredon there was a sharp corner; I knew it well, but as I was determined not to speak until Pingo apologised I made no effort to warn him.

In the one pale flickery headlight on the motor-cycle he didn't see the danger until it was too late. The road curved left, Pingo drove straight on. I remember the motor-cycle seeming to leap into the air, then I knew nothing more.

Pingo found himself thrown clear of the motor-cycle. He saw it upside down, half buried in a deep ditch. Then, with mingled horror and relief, he saw me crawl out, my head only an inch from the exhaust which was belching out flames. I survived with a sprained wrist and many scratches, but I still have a mark on my arm as a souvenir.

I was to become very fond of the most popular motorist of the twenties, Dehane Segrave. He won the Grand Prix de France in 1923 and the world speed record in 1929 in his ice-cooled 1,000 h.p. 'Golden Arrow', doing 231 miles per hour on Daytona Beach, Florida.

Dehane's first experiments were with model railways and he built a special house for his elaborate railway system with everything perfectly to scale. I always felt that he must have been deprived of toys in his childhood just as Lord Howard de Walden,

94

of an older generation, had been. Victorians and Edwardians all seem to have neglected their children or been actively unkind to them.

Lord Howard de Walden's parents were separated and he spent most of his holidays with his nurse in France. He was miserable at his preparatory school and during his first years at Eton. The first thing he did when he returned from South Africa and found he was a millionaire was to go to a shop in High Holborn and buy model boats and engines and boxes of tin soldiers. All the toys he had longed for and never had!

Dehane had a rather lazy manner, very unlike the quick, energetic vitality of Stirling Moss. One evening when he came to dinner he had just been summonsed for driving slowly and causing an obstruction in Bond Street.

'I was looking at a very good pair of legs,' he laughed.

Legs were still a novelty, a mini-skirt would have stopped the traffic!

I was told that when Dehane was at Cambridge his great friends were all mechanically minded. There was 'Tommy' Sopwith, later President of the Hawker Siddeley Group; one of the Bentleys who helped produce the first sports car of that name, and William Rhodes Moorhouse who was the first to fly in a plane across the Channel, but it crashed on arrival. He won a posthumous V.C. in the Air Force during the war.

In the early motoring days these young men, forerunners of the 'Bentley Boys', used to play hide-and-seek about the streets of London, skidding full circle or speeding round island lamp-posts!

Dehane was killed in 1930 when the propeller blades of his speed boat *Miss England II* caught some small drifting object and snapped at over 101 miles an hour. Dehane was rescued with several ribs smashed. He asked 'Did we do it?' saw his rescuers nod, and died.

We were, of course, fascinated by motor-racing stars like Dehane Segrave and Malcolm Campbell, both were creators of the twentieth-century records for speed. Malcolm was the son of a diamond merchant and achieved fantastic speeds on land and sea—raising the land speed record to 301 from 129 m.p.h., and the water speed to 141 from 74 m.p.h. He also searched for buried treasure—unsuccessfully—and built aeroplanes.

He hated trespassers and discouraged them by setting traps

in his garden with blank cartridges. Unfortunately causing one of his employees to lose a leg. Malcolm wouldn't wear a crash helmet and spoke proudly of having 'lived a man's life'. His wife Dorothy became after his death an ardent spiritualist. His son Donald was to inherit his father's passion to go faster than anyone else.

Malcolm Campbell helped me by acting as a judge when the Marquess of Donegall and I got up the first charity motor rally. It was an overwhelming success because everyone wanted to show off their precious cars!

Few women at that time drove except, of course, Lady Diana Cooper, who was the exception to everything and had her own two-seater in 1921. But even ten years later when I was asked to organise a women's race at Brooklands, all driving super-charged M.G.s, it was very difficult to collect enough women competitors. In the early twenties we were content to be driven by our young men in Austin Sevens or old hobbledehoy cars, which was before the era of the 'Bentley Boys'. This was the name given to the smart and gay drivers of the first racing Bentley cars.

There was Tim Birkin, Jack Dunfee, Dr. Benjafield, Glen Kidston and 'Babe' Barnato, a broad-shouldered, dark South African with eyes like betel-nuts. It was Babe who first suggested there should be traffic-lights in London, starting in Oxford Street. He was immensely wealthy, but he was never actively interested in his family's diamond mines.

Babe was the original Bentley Boy and won the Le Mans twenty-four-hour race three years in succession. He also played cricket for Surrey from 1928 to 1931 and was scratch at golf. All the Bentley Boys were dashing, attractive and fun to be with.

The first Bentley made its début in 1919. It was the brain child of Walter Owen Bentley, known as W.O., who had won a number of medals early in the century on Rex and Indian motorcycles. Just before the war he and his brother became agents for the French D.F.P. car, which W.O. made into a competition model with special aluminium pistons of his own design.

In 1914 W.O. joined the R.N.A.S. and soon introduced his aluminium piston to the aircraft manufacturers as a fitting for their engines. Next Bentley Rotary engines were produced and made the B.R.I. one of the most successful of the fighter aircraft units.

Captain J. F. Duff entered his own three-litre Bentley in the first Le Mans race of 1923.

96

'I think the whole thing is crazy,' W.O. said. 'Nobody will finish; cars aren't designed to stand that sort of strain for twenty-four hours.'

However he took the night boat to see 'the stupid race'

After a few hours in the pits he became excited.

'By midnight,' he said, 'when the cars were pounding past the stands with their lights on—my first sight of racing in the dark—I was certain that this was the best race I had ever seen!'

Duff, in his Bentley, broke the lap record at 66·69 m.p.h., although he had trouble with broken lamp-glasses and punctures! But the following year he won the race.

The Bentley Boys, of course, got their prize money. They could make £4,000 to £5,000 for breaking a record. Even in the long-distance classes they could get £2,000 to £2,500. There was a great deal of expense, as a team of mechanics was required to look after their cars, and there was always the risk of injury or death.

Jack Dunfee, who was a brilliant and fearless driver besides being extremely good-looking, had a delightful brother called Clive. He married Jane Baxter, a pretty gifted actress whom everyone admired.

Clive was killed instantaneously when he was thrown from his car at 140 m.p.h. on the track at Brooklands. It is well known that in these high-speed accidents the driver's shoes are sucked off, just as if he had removed them himself. Clive's shoes were found neatly placed behind the pedals, which somehow made his death more poignant.

Jack Dunfee became the director of a famous firm of film and theatrical agents. When he gave up racing he took to yachting. He always had a reputation for being charmingly witty, without being malicious or unkind. This virtue has increased with the years and has made him deservedly popular.

Even with unemployment figures rising in 1920 people sang:

> 'Give yourself a pat on the back
> A pat on the back,
> A pat on the back,
> Say to yourself,
> Here's jolly good health!
> I've had a good day today!'

Those seeking jobs were helped to look smart by the 'Fifty Shilling Tailors', where a man could buy a good suit for fifty shillings. Millions of men purchased a 'Mallaby Deeley' suit, named after a Member of Parliament who started the cheaper suits campaign after the war by buying up supplies of government-surplus clothing.

On the music halls they sang:

> 'In my Mallaby Deeley suit,
> I fell into the sea!
> The missus grabbed a boat-hook
> And began to fish for me. . . .'

But cars had to be paid for, as had the night-clubs, the drinks, and the white ties which were already getting a little frayed at the edges. It is easy to write of the twenties as a 'madly gay period', but it was also a period of strikes, extreme poverty and ever-increasing unemployment.

In July 1921 unemployment was to reach its highest peak yet, when the figure was 2,508,000. At the end of 1920 many men without private incomes had grown desperate. They tried everything—chicken farms, mushroom-growing and rabbit-breeding. There was a spate of self-taught decorators, all competing at cut prices; there were bicycle-repairers, window-cleaners, and carpet-beaters. Nearly all of them ex-officers, not being business men they lost money and in some cases it was not only money they lost.

Pingo, the young man to whom I was engaged, was unemployed. He was six years older than I, had been through the trenches, and, like so many of his friends, he wanted to settle down. But he seemed to me to typify everything that was gay, exciting and fun.

I can see now, looking back, how unsophisticated I was, how little I knew about life. Pingo liked me that way and did nothing to disturb or change my innocence, he just loved me.

We would go out dancing and he would bring me home when it was already dawn. Yet when I awoke later in the morning there would be a letter on my breakfast tray: 'I love you, I love you, I love you', he would write, perhaps down three or four pages.

He gave me a diamond engagement ring which consisted of

nine diamonds, family ones, which were old and very beautiful. He showed me pictures of his castle in Ireland. Our engagement was announced in *The Times* and the *Morning Post*, and the presents began to arrive. They were nearly all silver. Regardless of staff problems silver was still the correct wedding present for a bride.

As I had no father, it was my mother who first asked Pingo in a rather embarrassed manner what he thought we were going to live on. Pingo told her that something would 'turn up'.

'You can't live on air,' my mother protested. 'I've been poor, I know how hard it is to struggle without enough money. I can't allow Barbara to marry you until you have a job of some sort.'

Finding a job was as difficult at that time as swimming the Channel. Everywhere one went one saw men with fear on their faces—fear not now of dying but of starving. Pingo besieged his friends and his business acquaintances. He was always slipping off to see 'a man who might be useful', but without any success.

Some of his interviewers were rude and disagreeable because lots of unpleasant people had got into executive positions during the war. But a great many were very like the one Michael Arlen reported—he was not inventing—in *Those Charming People*. Men did talk like Hugo Cypress—who was wanting a job—and Major-General Sir Tobias Blast, K.C.M.G., D.S.O., M.V.O. . . .

'What do you want?' asked Sir Toby.

'Job of work, sir. . . .'

Sir Toby poised, pencil over paper.

'Education?'

'None, sir.'

'Where were you educated?'

'Nowhere, sir.'

'Idiot! Where were you at school?'

'Eton, sir.'

'Shake,' said Sir Toby.

They shook. . . .

'What qualifications for this job in Iraq? Think before you answer.'

Hugo thought.

'Can't think of any, sir,' he said at last.

'Languages? French?'

'Very guarded, sir.'

'Can you live on your pay?'

'Live on anything, sir.'

'Hm! Any private means?'

'Very private, sir. Never seen them.'

'How d'you live in London, then?'

'Pretty well, sir.'

I had a girl-friend called Millicent Orr Ewing. She was tall and thin, and had a greyhound look about her, very like one of Michael Arlen's heroines. He might have been describing Millicent when he wrote:

'She was dark, or rather her hair was dark, but her face was fair—English fair—and many generations have gone into the establishing of her complexion and the exquisite shaping of her delicate, aquiline nose.'

Millicent was the grand-daughter of the Duke of Roxburghe. Her widowed mother, like mine, was not well off, and led a quiet life filled with her religion.

Millicent was religious too, because she was a Catholic. She was warm-hearted and impulsive. I can see her now dancing very close to her partner, her head thrown back, her eyes looking up into his. Her clothes were very ladylike, but Millicent pinned back her evening dress with safety pins as soon as she left home, and was at the back dashingly naked to the waist, despite the fact that her dress had sleeves to the elbow, and would, on anyone else, have looked dowdy.

It was Teddy Gerard, looking like a panther, who had first innovated backless dresses when in *Bric-à-Brac* she sang in her husky, sexy voice:

'We're so glad to see you're back, dear lady.'

Millicent fell wildly in love with Peter Amies, a tall, good-looking young man who was in the Brigade of Guards. One only had to see them together to realise how much in love they were. I always remember finding them sitting on the doorstep of Millicent's house in Hill Street in the early hours of the morning. They just couldn't leave each other.

Millicent became officially engaged and it was not much comfort to find that her fiancé was in the same position as mine—looking for work. After endless refusals, rebuffs and disappointments, Pingo told me that he and Peter had joined an organisation which was being sent to Ireland.

Ireland and England throughout the nineteenth century had, between them, produced a tragic situation of cruelty, stupidity and misunderstanding. Shortly before war broke out my father had been asked to make arrangements to bring over and house ten thousand women and children from Ulster as they were expecting revolution. It had been learnt that thirty-five thousand rifles and three million cartridges had been distributed by motor-lorries throughout Protestant Ulster, the arms being imported from Germany.

War had prevented the conflagration then, but in 1916 a rebellion broke out in Dublin which, savagely and stupidly suppressed, gave birth to a fierce and burning nationalism. The Sinn Fein Republican Government came into active opposition to the British administration, and a special police force, called the 'Black-and-Tans', showed great savagery to the Irish rebels, whom they considered traitors. Ireland was smouldering, and more and more men were being sent out to fight in what was really a new and bitter war.

It had been decided, Pingo told me, that there would be a small supplement of men sent from England as a Special Police Force.

'It means I shall be away six months,' he said.

'Oh, but you can't go away as long as that,' I cried. 'Six months! It's a lifetime!'

'I shall be earning £600 a year,' Pingo replied. 'I will save every penny of it and then we can get married. Besides, this may lead to other things. I can't get a job here, and I can't go on waiting. I want to marry you, you know that.'

I did know it, his love for me was deep and tender. Despite his unquenchable good spirits, he could, now we were engaged, be a serious person, planning and thinking for the future.

We said goodbye.

'Ireland will be lucky for me, you'll see,' Pingo promised me. 'This is a break. We'll be married next year.'

We danced our last dance to:

> 'All the world is waiting for the sunrise,
> Every rose is heavy with dew,
> The thrush on high
> His sleepy mate is calling,
> And my heart is calling you.'

Millicent and I were left behind in England to feel that six months was an eternity and we should never live through it.

Of course, we went dancing—there was no point in sitting at home and moping—but our hearts were in Ireland, confident that the men we loved would soon clear up the mess. After all, it couldn't be really important. A few rebellious Irishmen! How could one feel it was dangerous as the war had been?

Pingo wrote to me every day. They were usually letters scribbled in a hurry.

'Just missed catching Michael Collins. The tea in the pot was still hot on the table, he had left a few moments before we arrived.'

'Had rather a rough night, quite a lot of shooting, but I'm thinking about you. Write and tell me exactly what you are doing.'

'Peter and I are very homesick. Instead of writing this we might be taking you and Millicent to the Grafton Galleries. Oh God, what a bore money is!'

Then two months after they had left my mother called up the stairs.

'There's a telegram for you, Babs darling.'

'A telegram?' I exclaimed. 'It must be from Pingo, perhaps he is coming home on leave!'

I ran down the stairs eagerly and snatched up the telegram. I was no longer frightened of the orange envelopes. The war was over and I had forgotten the tension in one's fingers, that sudden feeling of breathlessness as one pulled out the telegram form.

'It will be wonderful if he's back in time for . . .' I chattered, and stopped suddenly. With a kind of sick horror I read the words that were written on the form and read them again.

'Peter killed this morning. Tell Millicent. Love Pingo'.

It was not until later that I was to know what happened. On 21st November, which for ever afterwards was to be called 'Bloody Sunday', ten officers and four other ranks serving in the Special Police Force had been murdered in their beds.

Peter had been still asleep at 11.10 a.m. He had been out late the night before, and as it was Sunday they had arranged to have a long lie-in and catch up with some of the sleep they had missed while hunting Michael Collins from place to place.

Twenty armed men were let in by the maidservant to the house in Upper Mount Street, Dublin. They asked her where the men were sleeping. Unwillingly, but because she was afraid, without making too much objection, she pointed out the rooms occupied by Peter and a lieutenant of the R.A.C.S. motor transport. Then as the unmasked men moved in she rushed upstairs to awaken an officer sleeping on the upper floor.

'There's murder happening downstairs!' she cried in her broad Irish accent.

The officer sprang out of bed and woke another male lodger. But before they could move a fusillade of shots rang out and a few seconds later they heard the murderers leaving the house.

When they rushed downstairs they found the two bodies in a pool of blood in Peter's bedroom. The lieutenant had evidently been dragged from his bed, in his night-clothes, into Peter's room, and they had both been shot together.

With only the bare news of Peter's death in the telegram I knew none of these horrifying details, but I was numb with shock.

'How can I tell Millicent?' I asked my mother, but she knew that it was something I had to do alone and she couldn't help me.

I took a bus from Sloane Square along Piccadilly. I remember walking down Berkeley Street and through Berkeley Square, my footsteps getting slower and slower as I approached Hill Street. I can still see the railings of the houses: they seemed like prison bars, as I walked down the street, and I can still remember that feeling that it couldn't be true! Peter couldn't be dead! It was just a bad dream, it was all part of the horror and tension of the war, which I believed was over for ever.

A maid opened the door. I asked for Millicent.

'She's upstairs, miss, you know the way.'

I nodded. I knew the way only too well to Millicent's own little sitting room on the top landing. It was a room where she had planned her future with Peter, a room where we had sat so often together talking eagerly of our marriages, our happiness and of the men we loved.

I can't now remember what I said or how I told her, I can only remember the sudden agony in her eyes, the stricken look on her face as though a light had gone out.

Three weeks later the bodies of nine of the murdered officers were brought to London. The coffins were escorted through the streets by four battalions of Guards and two regiments of

Household Cavalry. I went to the Requiem Mass in Westminster Cathedral which was sung for Peter and the other Catholic victims. Soldiers with inverted arms guarded his unusually long coffin which lay in state under a Union Jack.

My mother went with me and we were both dressed conventionally, as was everyone in the congregation, in deepest black. It seemed to me I was back in the darkness of the war. I had been through this type of service so often before and, though I didn't know it then, I was to go through many, many more of them. There was that frustrated feeling that a young life had been wasted, that something beautiful had quite wrongly come to an irretrievable full-stop.

I knew that the service, bringing back memories of my father, upset my mother. Millicent's mother felt the same. They had cried for so long, and it had brought them nothing but a pointless, aching agony of loneliness.

When we got home my mother kissed me.

'I'm sorry, darling,' she said, 'you've had to go through this. It was a very beautiful service, you must write to Pingo and tell him about it.'

'I'm going to write to him,' I answered, 'to tell him I won't marry him.'

I knew then I was running away, but I couldn't bear being involved in death and murder, tears and unhappiness. It had already affected my childhood and I had a horror of anything connected with violence.

I wrote to Pingo.

'It's no use,' I said, 'I don't love you enough.'

That was untrue: it wasn't that I didn't love him, it was just that I was afraid of my own emotions. I couldn't be torn in pieces as my mother, Millicent, almost everybody I knew, had been. I went out to dance!

Two days later I received a telegram from Ireland.

'Retract your decision immediately or I shall go out and get shot.'

It was signed 'Pingo', but somehow it meant nothing to me. I didn't believe he would deliberately lose his life on my account. I couldn't even feel afraid that he might do so.

Pingo got compassionate leave and arrived in London, but I wouldn't see him.

'I can't marry him, I hate Ireland. How can I ever live there?' I said to my mother. 'You must explain it to him, you must get me out of my engagement.'

Pingo was only one of the many young men that my mother had to comfort or to persuade as kindly as she could that it was no use marrying anyone unless one was sure it would be a success. At the moment I had no wish to be married! I didn't want to love anybody. I just wanted to dance, to forget wars and anything to do with them.

It should have been easy. London was busy being repainted, and having what later we would describe as a face-lift. Sugar rationing was finally disposed of in the winter of 1920, and although there had been rationing in the war, the real curb on people buying things had been that many commodities simply were not on the market. It was not only a question of price, the food was not there.

We always seemed to have enough to eat at home, but during the war I had at school often been hungry. I used to think how nice it would be to have a really large meal, to feel one simply couldn't eat any more. There never was enough, and what there was was mostly starch and bread, with far too little meat, eggs and fish which were either expensive or unobtainable.

Despite restrictions, despite unemployment, London began to resume the look and the feel of a gay and carefree city. It seemed to me in those days that London was very beautiful; the dignity of grey buildings, the sudden glimpse of spires or towers, the green of the parks, while the soft, gentle light of street-lamps, still switched on and off by hand, made the streets at night mysterious and lovely.

Yet the papers were already beginning their campaign of decrying the young people for seeking only the smoke-filled, vicious atmosphere of underground cellars where they could dance. The 'shimmy' and the 'twinkle', which had been so much a feature of 1919, had by the end of 1921 almost been abandoned for dances in which you clung closely to your partner described by the newspapers as a 'mere sexual closeness of embrace'.

The modern girl after the war had at first enjoyed a kind of a vogue. She was called a 'flapper', although this before 1914 had meant an adolescent who was old enough to wear her hair tied with a large bow at the back. The war changed this, and in 1919 and 1920 a flapper was a high-spirited girl who typified the Modern Miss.

The new-found freedom inevitably went to some girls' heads, and the men, still old-fashioned in many ways, found their dreams of a sweet, gentle, clinging wife needed adjusting. 'Don't Bring Lulu' was really a masculine protest against wild, excitable, noisy young women who actually did break up some of the parties:

'You can bring Pearl, she's a darn nice girl,
But don't bring Lulu!
You can bring Rose, with the turned-up nose,
But don't bring Lulu!
Lulu always wants to do
What we boys don't want her to.
Every time she starts around
London Bridge is falling down.
You can bring cake, or fillets of steak,
But don't bring Lulu!
Lulu gets blue, and she goes 'cuckoo',
Like the clock upon the shelf.
She's the kind of smarty
Who breaks up every party.
Hull-a-ba-loo-loo, don't bring Lulu,
I'll bring her myself.'

Flag-days were one of the things which shocked the older generation and which brought the flapper girl into disrepute. To raise money, flags, flowers, or any other decoration which could be worn in the lapel, were sold for every conceivable charity. 'The refugees', 'the blind', 'the seamen', 'the benevolent societies', 'unwanted babies' . . . there was no end to them.

Since the war had impoverished so many people, it became more difficult than ever to collect money, and so attractive ex-debs were recruited by some distinguished patron of the charity into taking part in the flag-days.

We started in hotels, most of the large ones allowing flag-sellers to be stationed in the lounge, but we soon emerged on to the streets. At first two girls always sold together, for the fact that one was accosting a strange man by speaking to him and asking him to buy something was considered extremely bold and brazen.

'Will you buy a flag?' I would ask shyly.

'Of course,' the man would reply; 'who could refuse a pretty girl like you?'

He would fumble in his pocket, ogling me at the same time. I would hold out the flag.

'Won't you pin it on?' he would ask.

It was an excuse to get nearer to me and I soon learnt to evade it.

'I'm sorry, I've got so many more flags to sell!'

I would move away nervously. Sometimes he would try to continue the conversation and I wondered why I had ever promised to help.

Later the people who had first criticised the flag-sellers were more or less justified in their contentions. Women used the occasion as a chance to get to know men, and girls who by no stretch of imagination could be labelled 'society' cashed in on the flag-days. So it was no longer 'smart' to sell flags.

It was the small things like this which brought girls out of the seclusion of the home and gradually changed the whole pattern of English life. Then the Americans, pouring into the country for 'the pickings', changed the social scene far more effectively than the war had done.

Britain was forced to welcome the American tourists, at the same time resenting them. She felt that the Americans had entered the war at the eleventh hour, and had exaggerated their service to civilisation at the expense of those who had borne the brunt of the initial fighting. It was true that their casualties had been very slight in proportion to their population, with only a fraction of our losses.

What I think we minded more than anything else was that, far from being impoverished by the war, as we and the French had been, the Americans were now richer than ever before. Yet they were not prepared to cancel the war debts, as Britain and France had proposed.

The position was that Britain owed the United States about £900,000,000, and it is strange to think that in 1940, when I crossed the Atlantic for the first time, the Americans were still talking about the debts we owed them from the First

World War. I remember writing home to my husband and saying:

'I'm sick to death of hearing about the debt we owe the U.S.A., I'd pay it myself if I had the money.'

The Americans, on the other hand, quite reasonably, took up the attitude that American help had saved the Allies from losing the war. They also added, and made it quite clear to us, that they thought Britain was finished anyway, and she never would regain her position of power and prominence in the world. There was a strong dollar and a weak pound, and the Americans swarmed into Britain and Europe in search of bargains.

I remember seeing the Duke of Westminster's 'Blue Boy' just before it left for America, having been sold for £157,000.

Nellie Taylor—who married dapper little Captain Buckmaster, the founder of Bucks Club and one-time husband of Gladys Cooper—dressed as a Blue Boy, sang a song by Cole Porter:

'For I'm the Blue Boy—the beautiful Blue Boy,
And I am bound to admit
I'm feeling a bit depressed,
The American dollar
Bought me and my collar
To show all those cowboys
Just how boys
In England used to be dressed . . .'

'It's criminal,' one of the Duke's relatives complained to me. 'The picture shouldn't be allowed to go out of the country. It belongs to us! Those Yanks won't appreciate it, and this sort of English treasure can never be replaced.'

Of course, she was right, but the once rich landlords were feeling the pinch and they also felt they should cash in on a good thing.

Lady Desborough sold Raphael's 'Madonna and Child' for £170,000, and Mr. William Randolph Hearst, who was called the world's greatest spender, began to accumulate a fabulous treasure store at St. Donat's Castle in Wales.

He had bought the castle after seeing it advertised in a British magazine. Having installed sixty bathrooms and spent £250,000, he paid his first visit to the castle two years later. When I met

108

Mr. Hearst I thought he was without any artistic appreciation except for a pretty woman.

Ancient houses—like the Great Lodge in Essex—were taken down brick by brick and shipped across the Atlantic and rebuilt in the United States, while the new poor, like my mother, parted with their few remaining pieces of silver, or a picture of an ancestor that had been handed down from generation to generation.

It is pathetic to think now of how little people got for goods which today would fetch a fortune. But at least the sales kept going homes which might otherwise have crumbled, or gave the owners what they wanted so very much at the time!

The first antique sharks began to creep around. A man called on my grandmother and offered her forty pounds for the breakfast service she had used for years.

'Forty pounds!' she exclaimed. 'That seems a lot of money!'

It was Chamberlain's Worcester especially made for my grandfather, with large butterflies instead of handles to the cups, and two urns hand-painted with pictures of the Down House. It was in St. James Street the next week priced at £300. It would be worth over £5,000 today.

I could kick myself when I remember that I sold the few diamonds that had been left me by my father's mother. They consisted of a diamond star, a crescent brooch and a ring, all entailed to me as the only grandchild when she was alive.

It had become the fashion to wear a long string of pearls: everyone had them, and cultured or synthetic pearls were still thought rather common. I wanted above all things to have a string of real pearls round my neck.

In a shop in the Brompton Road I saw some strangely shaped baroque ones. They were real but cheap. I persuaded my mother to let me sell the diamonds and buy the pearls.

When I think what diamonds are worth today, while that long string of baroque pearls is unsaleable and unwearable, I realise what a fool I was. But at the time I felt 'in the swim' and that was something we all wanted to be.

Ciro pearls, extensively advertised in the twenties, were responsible for a great romance. During the Great Wembley Exhibition in 1924, Jean, an attractive girl, was put in charge of the Ciro Pearls stall. On the next stall, which exhibited tobacco, there was a red-haired, large-nosed young man called Arthur Elvin.

Jean had little time for Arthur as she had been promised twenty pounds if she could persuade Queen Mary, who was a constant visitor to Wembley, to stop and look at the pearls.

Queen Mary obliged and inspected the pearls, and no sooner had she left than Arthur popped in to congratulate Jean. He suggested they should open a bottle of champagne.

'Thank you, Ginger, I can pay for my own drinks,' Jean answered crushingly.

Arthur disliked being called 'Ginger', but he persevered.

'What about a little drink in the West End?'

'No,' Jean replied, 'not until you learn to dress properly.'

Arthur was astonished, he usually wore very natty suits in green or mustard colour.

'What's wrong with my suit?' he demanded.

'Try blue!' Jean suggested, turning her back.

Arthur did try blue. The following year he assisted in the demolition of the Exhibition. He bought one small building, sold it at a profit and bought another. He resold the sites and later paid Jimmy White £122,000 for the stadium, which he sold the same day for £150,000.

For a year or two the whole property hung fire. Then owing to Arthur Elvin's enterprise there came a resurrected Wembley, the new home of the greyhound racing and international sport.

Nearly £90,000 was spent on the greyhound track; there was a car-park for four thousand vehicles and covered seating for thirty thousand spectators.

I was one of the original privileged guests to sample the restaurant, where one could bet, watch and eat. There was also a dance-floor. 'Going to the dogs' became smart as well as being a national pastime.

Arthur Elvin over the years was responsible for football cup finals, speedway and car racing, horse shows, indoor lawn-tennis tournaments, swimming and ice-skating championships, basket-ball, hockey, water carnivals, ice pantomines, and a magnificent Torchlight Tattoo—the forerunner of those presented later at Aldershot.

I wore my real pearls proudly at every party after I bought

them in 1920, and parties, while getting more numerous, were also becoming more varied. The first rush of spending had begun to subside, and now bottle-parties were invented for those who couldn't afford to entertain expensively. The hostess who was giving the party provided the house, a gramophone (it had to be wound up after every record) and sandwiches, the guests each brought a bottle of drink.

The first I ever went to was given by Christabel Russell. I was taken to her house in Curzon Street by some friends. Although I never drank alcohol, I added my contribution with a small, cheap half-bottle of Graves. I remember the men at the party collecting all the bottles and mixing them together in a huge china jug, the kind which, in those days, was found on the marble wash-stands in any bedroom.

'What a cocktail!' someone exclaimed.

'Well, I shan't drink it,' a man replied. 'Another of those damn Yankie innovations which rots your guts. We should ban them and drink like gentlemen.'

The Americans had undertaken the fantastic experiment of prohibition. 'Pussyfoot' was the catch-word of the comic papers and the music hall. It had been made topical by the evangelising visit of Mr. 'Pussyfoot' Johnson.

He was to feel the full force of British resentment of a 'foreign' conspiracy against our liberties. He was so severely handled in a London students' 'rag' that he lost the sight of one eye. Yes, we had student trouble in the twenties!

The Americans might be decried for introducing cocktails, but actually they were only reviving, or making fashionable, something which England had known for many years.

In the middle of the Victorian era there had been a salon in Leicester Square, kept by a notorious character known as Kate Hamilton, at which cocktails were sold under the names of 'Corpse Revivers', 'Gum Ticklers', 'Eye Openers' and many others.

But English drinking habits had been very conventional for a long time. No drinks were ever offered before meals. If a man wanted a whisky and soda before dinner, he went to the smoking room, or sought out the butler in the pantry. It was unthinkable for a woman to drink at such a time. Even in 1937, in my father-in-law's house, if I wanted a glass of sherry before dinner my husband had to fetch it for me up to my bedroom. There was no question of my being offered one downstairs.

It was therefore not surprising that cocktails being drunk in night-clubs was all part of the atmosphere of sin now being played up by the newspapers until it rose into an angry denunciation of 'flaming youth'.

Another Kate was the Queen of London Night Life and no book about the twenties could omit reference to Mrs. Meyrick, the widow of an Irish doctor. She was a wispy little woman who always had holes in her stockings, but she made the '43' and the 'Silver Slipper' the focus of London life after dark. Mrs. Meyrick served many prison sentences for selling drinks in forbidden hours. No magistrate could surpress her. The '43' was disqualified for being used as a club—it was immediately reopened as an unregistered club! The heaviest fines were not as heavy as the profits.

'Champagne, on the average, cost me 12s. 6d. a bottle,' Mrs. Meyrick admitted later. 'I sold it during licensed hours from 22s. 6d. to 30s., after legal hours at 30s. to £2 a bottle.'

She estimated that she sold £50,000 worth of champagne. 'Door money' brought in £10,000. No wonder the '43's supporters sang:

> 'Come all you birds
> And sing a roundelay
> Now Mrs. Meyrick's
> Out of Holloway.'

Kate Meyrick's two sons had gone to Harrow, her four daughters to Roedean, but when their mother was left with only £50 on which to support herself and them, the girls became dance instructresses.

They all married into the peerage. I knew Dorothy Meyrick quite well, because nineteen-year-old Lord de Clifford, who was a friend of my brothers, was supposed to be dining with us when we received a telegram saying:

'Terribly sorry, owing to unavoidable circumstances, unable to dine.'

The circumstances were his secret marriage to Dorothy, who had been acting as a hostess at another of her mother's clubs, 'The Manhattan'.

When Ted took his bride to his home in the country, most of the county called out of sheer curiosity. They were very disappointed. Dorothy was quiet, ladylike and, quite frankly, rather dull. They expected fireworks and got a little firefly.

Other clubs run by 'Ma' Meyrick were 'The New Follies', 'The Little Club' and 'The Silver Slipper'. To these, especially the '43', went a very mixed procession of prominent people—King Carol of Rumania, Prince Christopher of Greece, the Dukes of Leeds and Manchester, Rudolf Valentino (the heart-throb of the twenties), Joseph Conrad, Tallulah Bankhead, Steve Donoghue, Augustus John and almost the whole of the Brigade of Guards and the youth of *Debrett*.

Why Mrs. Meyrick was such a success no one knew. She had warmth and originality and called all the men 'her boys'. She had a little office near the door where the girls sat who took the entrance fees. From there she would watch everything which went on. Small, dark and full of vitality, her stockings awry, a piece of old green velvet draped round her shoulders, she made everyone feel welcome.

The '43' really was gay. Steve Donoghue, the leading jockey, always went there after the Derby. Greeted with a thunderous shout of welcome, he would be lifted up and carried round the room, everyone singing: 'For he's a jolly good fellow'.

Once they called on Steve for a speech and hoisted him on the piano, but the flap on which he stood gave way and he was thrown violently to the floor—luckily without injury. Two American millionaires who that day had watched their first Derby ordered champagne for everyone and soon the '43' was so packed they had to close the doors.

Most people stayed for 'breakfast' and as the staff were overworked with orders many of the tail-coated young gentlemen, including peers, volunteered to serve the bacon and eggs, kippers and sausages. The Americans ended up by giving each dance-hostess a £5 note.

Yet when Kate Meyrick died she left only £58.

The lure of the night-clubs was firstly that one could be 'alone' with the person one was with, and this incorporated unhappy married people, who could not go home to bed. Secondly, they were both gay and dangerous.

'There was a kind of feverish gaiety which burned high then

low', Sir Philip Gibbs wrote, and night-clubs were dangerous because one never knew when there would be a police raid.

By the end of 1928 some sixty-five clubs had been prosecuted since 1924 and sixty struck off the register. The 'Kit-Kat', where the Prince of Wales went night after night, was raided, while to get into 'The Quadrant' was as difficult as getting out of Sing-Sing. It had three bolted doors, the third of which had a wicket. In the bureau was a push-button which could be worked by a man's foot, and this rang a buzzer in the bar and another in the lounge.

One would have thought this would have ensured that the drinks were whipped away before the police could get inside, but undetected they peeped through a skylight, decided there was illegality and raided the club! Could anything be more absurd? So slowly, but surely, the gaiety of the night-clubs vanished.

The first person who took me to 'The Quadrant' was Laddie Sandford, the handsome, blond polo-playing American, much fêted when he arrived in England. Polo had become smart because the Prince of Wales had taken it up enthusiastically when he was in India.

To me, night-clubs were irresistible—there was that blue haze of smoke across the dim lights, the air of expectant mystery, the deep note of drums like a heart beat, the secrecy of low voices, the thrill of dancing close . . . close . . . to someone with whom, for that evening at any rate, one was almost in love.

CHAPTER FIVE

Twiddle the knob, put on the phones,
There's a shriek which seems to curdle your bones.
Turn it again—there's a moan and a crack
As if some poor devil was stretched on the rack.
Kick the machine! It's broken you know!
No, listen! It's wonderful 2LO!

DURING 1921 we had headphones on our ears and spent
hours of our time twiddling knobs and muttering:

'I've got . . . no . . . bother! It's gone again . . . no, there it . . .
ough! What a screech! It hurt my ears—must be a ship or something!'

At Cowes I met a shy, quiet Italian with a glass eye, whose
yachting cap, square on his head, looked too big for him.

'How does your wireless work?' I asked ingenuously.

'I don't know,' he replied, 'I only know it does.'

Marconi could never explain his inventions! In 1898 he transmitted Morse signals across the English Channel. In 1920 the
Marconi Company Experimental Station at Chelmsford was
opened. By the end of 1921 there were regular programmes. I
spoke myself on these once or twice, and then in 1929 did a series
of six talks on 'How to make the best of oneself'.

After one broadcast I gave on New Year's Day I received a
letter from the Rev. T. H. Jones, a Liverpool pastor, who,
although totally blind, still conducted services in his Presbyterian
church. He wrote:

'This is to thank you for your splendid, sanctified, common-sense
talk on the "wireless" this morning. My angel-guide and myself
enjoyed it to the brim and often responded with an enthusiastic
"Amen".'

'I heard you!' people in shops would say to me excitedly. It was a forerunner of the days of television, when perfect strangers would come up to me and say:

'You were quite right, I agreed with everything you said last night,' or:

'You took that fellow down a peg or two, good for you! These interviewers think they're God Almighty!'

How little we thought in those days of very limited listening how television later would rule our lives.

'Sorry, dear, I can't dine on Wednesday, I must see No. 9 of the Mountbatten series,' or:

'I *can't* miss Peyton Place.'

No one could visualise executives, foremen, workmen and shop girls arguing animately about last night's programme, or being thrown into a deep despondency because their 'telly' had gone wrong.

I might have guessed this would happen when I remember the excitement in 1921 over Dame Nellie Melba's broadcast from Chelmsford, sponsored by the *Daily Mail*.

'I couldn't believe it possible that her voice—like that of an angel—could come to me over the air!' Roland Jackson, himself a singer who worshipped her, cried. 'She was heard over a radius of a thousand miles. Think what that means to the future, it is the opening of the universe!'

I had no idea then that I should one day own the house where Melba was to spend three months in the summer. She was old and tired, but just before she came to Camfield her voice came back because she was in love.

'She was like a girl,' Roland Jackson, who lived nearby, told me years later. 'She blushed, she was coy, flirtatious and fascinating as she had been in her youth. And her voice was as glorious as it had ever been—a divine sound!'

But the young man left her, and with him went her voice. It was a sad little episode!

Incidentally, the title 'Dame' had been a wartime innovation, so it sounded comic to us. The only Dames we knew were the pantomime sort—Aladdin's and Dick Whittington's mother. I still think it is an ugly ageing word.

In May 1922, 2LO broadcast a commentary on a boxing match between Kid Lewis and the handsome heart-throb Georges

Carpentier at Olympia. Of course, the *Daily Mail* was behind the enterprise, which I didn't see as I disliked boxing; but I was present at the three-minute Carpentier-Beckett fight at the Holborn Stadium in 1919, when the gate money of £30,000 broke all records.

When Eamonn Andrews interviewed me in the programme 'This Is Your Life' in 1958 the B.B.C. flew Georges Carpentier from France to meet me, Eamonn said to him:

'Wasn't it quite a new thing in 1919 for ladies to watch boxing?'

'In those days perhaps it was,' Carpentier replied, 'but it was always evening dress at the ringside, you know, and boxing had become a fashionable sport.'

'You were something of a social lion too, Georges.'

'People were very kind,' Carpentier smiled, 'and I enjoyed myself. I met many charming people over here, and I think of my visits with great affection. Ladies like Miss Cartland made me realise that, despite the war, England still retained something of the old elegance.'

'We were all in love with you,' I told him as he kissed my hand.

Harry Preston sat next to the Prince of Wales in the Holborn Stadium. The Prince thought Beckett would win, but Harry said:

'It's easy, sir, to underestimate brain and overestimate brawn.'

Harry Preston, who was called 'the Prince of friends and the friend of Princes', was small, bald, pink, astigmatic and flowery, and owned two hotels in Brighton—the Royal York and the Royal Albion. He literally knew everyone—pugilists, politicians, princes, players and playboys.

He talked in an exaggerated manner in a soft, excited voice. When I was introduced to him he said:

'What a privilege, what a joy to meet a beautiful young lady like yourself! God bless you, dear—we must celebrate! Waiter, a bottle of champagne for this distinguished lady who—God bless her—has honoured my hotel.'

It was Harry Preston who raised the status of boxing. He was of inestimable value to promoters. The Prince of Wales, the Duke of York and Prince George were, on many occasions, his guests at the ringside.

All sorts of celebrities dined with him before the big fights, and their tail-coats and dinner-jackets, like their reputations, gave a new air of distinction to prize fights.

The Carpentier-Beckett fight is the only one I ever attended. Three minutes was enough, expensive though it was. One bright boy put over a clever bit of scally-waggery that night. As soon as he saw Beckett knocked out he rushed out of the building, holding his hand over his eyes.

'Oh, the blood—ugh!' he gasped in horror. 'Horrible, terrible slaughter! Blood everywhere. Anyone can have my fifteen guinea ticket for three pounds!'

There was a rush of willing takers, and the brainy lad disappeared before the word went round that the fight was over.

Broadcasting was immediately given an upper-class image by making the announcers—although, of course, we couldn't see them—wear dinner-jackets. The Hon. David Tennant read the news at one time. He himself was very often in the news. A leader of the Bright Young People, he married Hermione Baddeley—a clever comedienne—and started the Gargoyle Club, which, while considered dashing, had the most respectable committee.

Among them was Lord Glenconner—very good-looking—Lord Henry Cavendish-Bentinck, an M.P., and A. P. Herbert, who was to fight for so many forlorn causes, like better conditions for gypsies and more money for authors, and is still doing it!

The first broadcast by a member of the Royal Family was made by the Prince of Wales on 2LO in October 1922.

The first studio at 2LO was a dingy room about twenty-foot square, with a faded green carpet, a grand piano and a worn-out settee with horse-hair breaking out of it.

At the time I was having singing lessons and asked the B.B.C., who had started daily programmes in November 1922, for an audition. They were so short of performers that they gave me a time to present myself the very next day.

I couldn't get hold of my singing teacher at such short notice, so a friend played for me without any rehearsal. She obviously thought it important to play fortissmo, as it had 'to carry so far', and crashed down on the chords. To make myself heard at all above the accompaniment I had to bellow into the microphone, which was on a stand.

I always remember a man dashing into the room, snatching

away the microphone from in front of me, and putting it against the wall on the other side of the room.

'For God's sake,' he muttered, 'you've broken my eardrums!'

I was not engaged to sing!

As the girls of my age did not read newspapers until they left school it took some time for us to become interested in the news, and the majority of us hadn't yet the independence to take a newspaper on our own. In most houses therefore the reading material was the *Morning Post* or *The Times*, with the *Tatler*, *Sketch* and *Bystander* once a week.

After an exclusive diet of society chit-chat, I was astounded to learn from the radio of the industrial troubles, of the defeat of Lloyd George as Prime Minister, and the appointment of Bonar Law.

I think I must have been rather like the old lady living in the Welsh mountains, who after she had the wireless said:

'I have no doubt Queen Mary is a fine lady, but I can't say I hold with this habit she has of going backwards and forwards all the time to America.'

But it was mostly men who delighted in the wireless, since women were too impatient to struggle with the endless adjustments necessary to get the right sound.

My mother, aged ninety-two, is continually surprised by the wonders of television.

'If anyone had told me when I was young that one day I would see in my drawing room what was happening in Paris and New York, I would have thought them crazy,' she says.

My grandfather had to go out and discover the world for himself; today one can sit at home and television brings it to you. In the twenties the wireless broke through our very narrow provincial outlook and gradually supplied us with a new education.

Sir William Armstrong, who is head of the Civil Service, told me that he was brought up in a very strict household as his father was a Salvation Army officer.

'It was a very restricted existence because we knew nothing beyond the difficulties and problems of "the Army".'

Like me, Sir William was not allowed to read any newspapers, except an occasional glance at the *Morning Post*.

'On Sunday,' he said, 'no newspaper was taken, and we were

only allowed to read *The Pilgrim's Progress*. We didn't have a wireless until years after everyone else had one, but when we did . . . !'

I understood what he was trying to say: it was as if the walls by which we had all been confined had slowly subsided. The world outside was so much bigger and more complex than we ever dreamt.

Sir William told me that today every broadcast on every wavelength in every language is monitored in the B.B.C. They have the only machine in the world which can do this.

'The next step,' Sir William said, 'will be that news and pictures will arrive simultaneously. That is what we will have in the future.'

A long step from the flickering Morse of young Marconi! But, of course, there were critics.

'It's a lot of damn nonsense! I don't want to hear a woman caterwauling out of thin air and coming right into one's own house. It's a blasted intrusion! If I want a conversation, I go to the club.'

I heard this said in more or less the same words hundreds of times. And note the inference that there was no conversation at home with 'the little woman'. How could there be? Her life was bounded by the rise in food and the shortage of servants.

The critics, and this time they were mainly women, also had a lot to say about flying, the most usual being:

'If God had meant us to fly He would have given us wings.'

It was to be a long time before social events were reported on the wireless, and 1921 was a bumper year for these, despite industrial troubles.

'*A Bold Buccaneer's Son and his Bride*', the society papers screamed, when Molly Lascelles, who had 'come out' the same time as I had, married the Earl of Dalkeith, son of the Duke of Buccleuch, watched by a posse of royalty and all the aristocracy. All pink and white and gold with blue eyes and two irresistible dimples, I had seen her at a race meeting a short time before, looking radiant, gay and glowing in the cold wind and rain.

'She *is* pretty!' I exclaimed.

'She is like a melody,' one of the men I was with contributed.

We laughed and started to hum the 'hit' of the moment to which we danced day and night:

'A pretty girl is like a melody.'

One of the young men with me wrote a poem about Molly
Lascelles, which started:

'She is so lovely,
Her face is a dream.
Her lips are like cherries,
Her skin is like cream.'

As we were still rationed, love and food were indivisibly
mixed in our minds.

It was always said that just as George IV had secretly married
Mrs. Fitzherbert when he was Prince of Wales, so Charles II
had legally married his first love Lucy Walters. The result of this
union was the Duke of Monmouth, from whom the Dukes of
Buccleuch are directly descended.

This meant that had the marriage been proved the Duke of
Buccleuch would today be the rightful King of Great Britain.
It was not until the thirties that Lord George Scott was to collect
all the evidence supporting this contention.

I attended a lot of race meetings in the early twenties, was
proposed to on Newmarket Heath in a north-east wind and saw
the Grand National in 1920 run in a snowstorm when only five
horses finished the course.

One delightful racing story of the time added to the many tales
of fantastic escapes by aristocrats from the Russian Revolution
which had taken place in 1917.

In 1920 when the British Military Mission was being evacuated
from Novorossiisk a little man in Russian uniform walked up to
the embarkation officer and said:

'Beg pardon, sir, got any room for me 'orses? I got Minoru
and Aboyeur!'

The cockney stud groom had learnt that the revolutionaries
were killing off pedigree stock and was determined to save the
two great Derby winners. He had harnessed them to an old cart
and driven them from Moscow to Novorossiisk. The only time
a couple of Derby winners have ever pulled a cart together in
double harness!

Minoru and Aboyeur reached Serbia in safety where they
ended their days.

Isadora Duncan was giving matinées the summer of 1921 and
The Times said:

'She plays with human emotions as a pianist plays with the keys of a piano.'

All through the twenties people talked of her immorality and her fluid, beautiful dancing. But she could also be very down-to-earth. Once at Juan les Pins, where her friends were talking about spiritualism, Isadora said:

'If, at some séance, a voice comes through to you after I am dead, and says "For God sake give me a whisky and soda!" then you may be certain that it's mine.'

She died in 1927 when her trailing chiffon scarf caught in the wheel of her car and strangled her.

The newspapers of 1921 reported that the Hon. Lionel Tennyson had become captain of the English team for the Test match at the last moment as C. B. Fry was ill. He made 74 not out. His wife Clare, sister of Lord Glenconner, was one of the most beautiful women I have ever seen. She used to put honey on her face every afternoon when she lay down. It was the beginning of my passion for this food, medicine and cosmetic of the Gods!

C. B. Fry was the most extraordinary athlete of the century. He made 30,886 runs at cricket, averaging 50 an innings. He got first-class honours in classics, established a world long-jump record, represented England at soccer, ran a boys' training ship, was a first-class fisherman and game shot, edited his own magazine and declined an offer to be King of Albania!

When he was over seventy he told a friend he was longing for new worlds to conquer and proposed to take up racing.

'In what capacity, Charles?' his friend asked, 'trainer, jockey or horse?'

Mrs. Asquith in gold brocade was in the gossip columns as being at a dinner party at Crewe House, 'doubtless with great opportunities for adding to her diary, though people are naturally a little stilted in their flow of words in her presence now'.

To me Mrs. Asquith—afterwards Lady Oxford—with her big nose, coarse grey hair brushed upwards from her sharp-angled face, her dark eyes, spindly legs and bony shoulders, looked like a witch in modern dress.

She had a quick wit, but was very superior in her attitude. She was also impatient and intolerant of stupidity, and this often prevented her from appreciating those who were not fools but merely shy.

Margot Asquith's autobiography had shocked all the older generation. She had not only revealed intimacies about her friends, 'the Souls', she had also said that several distinguished men were in love with her! This was considered very indiscreet. Lytton Strachey, the literary giant, disliked the book so much he refused to review it.

Margot Asquith liked to be outrageous, provocative, and permanently in the limelight. She was witty and one of the great personalities of the period, but she had to attract attention. During the war it had been rumoured she was in the pay of the Germans and she was booed in the streets.

Extraordinary stories were circulated about the Asquiths; such as that they had shares in Krupps. As Margot related:

'It was said openly that from attic to basement my household, my friends and my family were pro-German. When Lord Kitchener was drowned I was inundated with anonymous and insulting letters accusing me of having signalled from some secret place in the North Sea to a German submarine that was supposed to have sunk *The Hampshire*.'

She would recount this experience dramatically, but one could not help feeling from the glint in her eye that she had enjoyed the excitement of being a martyr.

Mr. Asquith, the ex-Prime Minister who always seemed in the twenties rather dull to the outside public in comparison with the flamboyant Lloyd George, the 'Wizard of Wales', was, however, described by one of his friends as 'a small man with the beatific smile of one who has seen the heavens open'.

What I admired about him was his serenity in adversity, and the calm manner in which he refused to be disturbed by gossip, rumour and personal attack. He continually quoted the aphorism on a mantelpiece at Blenheim Palace:

'They say. What say they? Let them say!'

It is a maxim I have often said to myself when unkind and untrue things have been said about me.

Lytton Strachey—the most brilliant literary lion of the period, who emerged upon the social scene after the unexpected success of his book *Eminent Victorians* brought him fame, like Byron, overnight—found Margot Asquith 'faintly civilised', but he decided that like so many society people she was unsympathetic.

'Her *mauvais ton* is remarkable,' he wrote in 1918 of her appearance at the Opera. 'She thinks she's the very tip-top, the *grande dame par excellence* and all the rest of it—and every other moment behaving like a kitchen maid—giggling, looking round and nudging Elizabeth (her daughter). As for music, of course it's never occurred to her such a thing exists. Yet, as one looks at her small weather-beaten (perhaps one should say life-beaten) countenance one wonders—there does seem a suggestion of something going on underneath.'

Although Lytton Strachey was so scathing, he began to enjoy being 'lionised' and was continually appearing at luncheon and dinner parties, believing, like so many intellectuals, that so long as he abused society and decried his hostess, he was preserving his integrity!

Margot Asquith had an amusing and original way of saying things about people which, of course, were repeated from the moment she said them.

'She told enough white lies to ice a cake.'

'He's an imitation rough diamond.'

'She's a woman without a roof or rafter in her mouth.'

Asked if she believed in ghosts, Margot replied:

'Appearance are in their favour!'

Margot Asquith made life amusing for her friends, even while they lived on a razor's edge of what she would say next. Oswald Mosley remembers that at his first dinner party in her house, when he had just made his maiden speech in the House of Commons, Margot seized his hand with a claw-like grip and said:

'Your speech reminded me in some ways of my old friend Lord Randolph Churchill. But, dear boy, do not share his vices, never live with six women at once, it is so weakening!'

Margot's importance in the political world is yet to be written, but two extracts from *Whitehall Diary*, by Thomas Jones, who was in the Cabinet Secretariat, show her power:

'November 12th, 1922.
This came as a great surprise to Asquith, who has been kept in a false paradise by Mrs. Asquith, despite Reading's attempts to make him understand that his term as Prime Minister was at an end.'

'October 26th, 1923.
Will Lloyd George and Asquith draw closer together, or will Sir John Simon and Margot Asquith block any approach?'

Elsa Maxwell tells a very strange story about Margot.

'She was intensely jealous of anyone who she felt encroached on her personal glory,' she relates.

The property adjoining the Asquiths' house—The Wharf—belonged to the much-loved Mrs. Norah Lindsay, the famous landscape gardener, who really was a great authority on flowers.

'Margot,' Elsa says, 'pooh-poohed this, saying she knew more about flowers than Norah had ever begun to learn.'

Norah Lindsay developed a Siberian blue poppy, the first in England. She was thrilled and delighted at her achievement. Elsa, who was staying with the Asquiths, called her on Sunday morning, only to find her in tears.

'Someone has stolen my blue poppy,' Norah sobbed, 'my most precious possession. I was so proud to have grown it. Who could want to do anything like that? After all, it's of no value except to me—look!'

She pointed to the flower-bed where the poppy had been.

'Do you see that mark?' she cried. 'It's the imprint of a high-heeled shoe. The thief must have been a woman!'

Later at lunch at The Wharf Elsa related Norah's loss. Margot Asquith sniffed:

'Norah always has these tales of woe,' she said. 'Quite obviously it must have been some animal.'

'It's a curious animal that wears high-heeled shoes,' Elsa retorted.

Margot darted a startled glance at her.

'She knew I knew!' Elsa relates.

I didn't meet Norah Lindsay until World War II, then she was staying in Bedfordshire with Mrs. Sam Whitbread, who was very regal and craved for royalty as other people crave chocolates. Norah was lonely and rather lost because no one wanted her to 'lay out' their gardens, and she had relied on this as a source of income.

But one could still see what a beauty she must have been, still hear evidence of her Irish gift of wit in her conversation.

Eddie Marsh, once secretary to Winston Churchill, had a letter from her describing her first country-house visit to England after being in Italy all the winter.

'It's extraordinary,' she wrote, 'to be here again among all these women with real hair, real busts and real husbands—

so different from those boy-dowagers in Rome and Venice.'

It was also to Eddie Marsh that she made her delightful remark about riding:

'I hate sitting on the back of a great big horse that keeps throwing meringues in my face.'

Once when Betty Bowes-Lyon and I were talking about snobs and social climbers, she told me that her mother-in-law, Lady Strathmore, used to say gently:

'Some people, dear, have to be fed royalty like sea-lions with fish.'

I can never see people sidling up to royalty, with faces eager for recognition and their hands half outstretched, without seeing their resemblance to sea-lions and starting to giggle.

To return to the gossip columns of 1921, Baba d'Erlanger, the daughter of Baroness d'Erlanger, gave up trying to look 'pretty', which she wasn't, painted her large mouth brilliant red, which was sensational, and became *chic* and *jolie-laide* overnight.

She was responsible for introducing an exotic note into the twenties. Delighted with her first success she put black paint under her eyes. She grew her nails long and wore dark red nail-varnish.

'Her fingers look as if they were dropped in blood!' my mother's generation said in horror.

Baba's mother, Baroness d'Erlanger, who had scarlet hair, was almost the first of the society interior decorators. They lived in a house in Piccadilly which had once belonged to Lord Byron which was full of witch balls, shell flowers and mother-of-pearl furniture.

'Irrepressible Jane' in the *Sketch* wrote:

> 'Now that our beloved King and Queen—God bless them—are safely back from Ireland, we breathe again. When the news came at tea-time that they were safe on board *The Victoria and Albert*, the very newsboys' voices vibrated with excitement . . . certainly it was one of the secrets of the great success of the Lansdowne House Ball. The sudden absence of worry affected the spirits of the Heir to the Throne until he surpassed even himself.'

King George and Queen Mary had been to Belfast to open the Parliament of the newly partitioned Northern Ireland. In his speech the King said:

'I appeal to all Irishmen to pause, to stretch out the hand of forbearance and conciliation, to forgive and forget, and to join in making for the land they love a new era of peace, contentment and goodwill.'

This speech coming from the King had an enormous impact. A fortnight later hostilities ceased. The rebel leaders from the South came to London for negotiations, to which Lloyd George brought all his wizardry of persuasiveness. Before the year's end a treaty was signed—the Irish Free State came into being.

One of the people who helped to fashion the Irish Treaty was fascinating Lady Lavery. All soft velvet, sables, scent and big bunches of parma violets, she was irresistibly feminine. She brought Michael Collins and Winston Churchill together, and one day the history books will show once again the power of the petticoat.

Sir John Lavery painted the leaders of both sides—Lord Carson and John Redmond—who remarked that they always expected 'to hang together'.

Lady Lavery gave a dinner party for Winston Churchill to meet Michael Collins, the terrorist leader, whom Pingo had hunted in 1920. He was very attractive, and as one lady present said afterwards:

'No wonder he was never caught, all the women must have been glad to hide him.'

A guest at this unique party said to Michael Collins:

'Don't you think Winston wonderful? He has such imagination!'

'Yes indeed,' Collins replied, 'and that is what we lack in Ireland. They are all dreamers and have no imagination to do the practical thing.'

It was to the Laverys' studio that Michael Collins came after the signing of the Treaty, white and haggard from lack of sleep.

'I have signed some kind of oath,' he explained, and added: 'Well, I've signed my death warrant!'

He prophesied truly. He was ambushed and killed by irregulars in 1922.

Besides being beautiful, Hazel Lavery was kind, sympathetic, charming and adored by many diverse personalities. Tim Healy, Lord Londonderry, James Dunn, Winston Churchill, Ramsay MacDonald and Bernard Shaw were all captivated by her.

Sir John Lavery, who was short and stout, always wore a ribbon four inches wide round his neck as a tie, and a tall top-hat square on his square head. He often stayed with Lord and Lady Londonderry at Mount Stewart, and it was through them he was made a Freeman of Belfast. But he was afraid that his close contacts with Southern Ireland might embarrass them and assured them that he always remembered them in his prayers.

'A form of repayment,' he used to say, 'which I have often found economic and sometimes impressive.'

Sir John faithfully painted his wife every year for the Academy. Lady Lavery was also depicted on the Irish Free State Party notes in 1926 as a colleen with a shawl thrown over her head leaning on a harp.

She was the first person to teach Winston Churchill to paint. He was miserable and unhappy, having lost office during the First World War, and he bought a canvas, but really didn't know what to do with it. Lady Lavery took his brush, mixed the paints, and showed him how to apply them.

Lady Lavery was an artist in her own right, and she gave a joint exhibition with Augustus John. But it is as a charmer she will always be remembered. So many men were in love with her, and women were naturally jealous. She encouraged this by never asking husbands and wives together to her parties.

'Men are never at their best when their wives are there,' I heard her say once, 'and what woman isn't restricted by the possessive eye of a husband who thinks he is being deceived? No! No! I ask them separately.'

But to judge from some of the complaints it was obvious that the wives received unequal portions of fascinating Hazel's hospitality.

In 1921, when the Irish trouble broke out again, Shane Leslie gives a graphic picture of Hazel Lavery at Sir Philip Sassoon's house in Park Lane, compelling Lloyd George to listen for half an hour to her immediate plans for settling the difficulties.

'The Welsh Wizard,' he says, 'could not have been more polite. She really whistled to men, and they obeyed as if it were a Whip fashioned of her eyelashes.'

I was friends at the end of the twenties with a remarkable man who had been Viceroy of Ireland from 1915 to 1918. The Viscount Wimborne and his wife were to play a vital part in the

128

General Strike, and were two of the most outstanding social figures of post-war society.

Lady Wimborne was beautiful, musical, artistic, Irish and unpredictable. One moment, covered with jewels, she would be more regal than royalty itself, the next she would be mimicking a cockney accent with her Bohemian friends.

Osbert Sitwell says of her:

'Her beauty, subtle skill of glamour though it was, and the fact that she was the wife of one of the richest men in England, were apt to blind people equally to her political intelligence, intent and experience.'

Certainly the young like myself were dazzled by the daring of her fashionable appearance, the glitter of her jewels, and the exotic luxury in which she lived.

When I met Lord Wimborne—introduced to him by Lady Castlerosse—I found it hard at first to find the man beneath the trappings. Ivor Wimborne had been frustrated in his political ambitions by falling out with the Liberal Party to which he belonged.

He was a first-class polo player, noted in the hunting field, a great shot (he fired thirty-three thousand cartridges one year), an aristocrat with a natural appetite for travel and diplomacy. He was also flamboyant, and in his elegant frock-coats and high collars, or flowing tweed capes and sportsman's fore-and-aft caps, looked exactly the foreign idea of an English 'm'lord'.

Diana Cooper describes Viceregal Lodge in 1917 when Lord Wimborne was Viceroy:

'Forty to dinner—Convention men, Labour men and Peers— red ties, diamond studs and stars. The Laverys,[1] McEvoy,[2] Leonie Leslie,[3] 'AE'[4]—in fact a court as we would choose one. Her Excellency clotted and weighed down with jewels. Ivor flashy but very graceful—flashy from being unlike *the* King, but not unlike a King. The table and its pleasures a treat—all gold and wine and choicest fruit. One Conventioner said he had never tasted a peach before (I didn't believe him). The footmen, such beauties, battling with their silver cords, blinded by powder.'

[1] Sir John and Lady Lavery.
[2] Ambrose McEvoy, the artist.
[3] Lady Leslie, sister of Lady Randolph Churchill.
[4] 'AE'—G. W. Russell, the Irish poet and Nationalist.

Wimborne House in Arlington Street had a two-pedimented front set back behind railings, and Lord Wimborne had planned it for entertainment on the grand scale. The rooms, opening one out of another, were decorated with fabulous French furniture, and there was a blue and gold parrot chained to a perch in the pillared hall.

Every evening an opened bottle of champagne was left in a silver crested ice-bucket beside a plate of pâté-de-foie sandwiches. Ivor told me he never drank champagne.

'Then who is this for?' I asked.

He shrugged his shoulders.

'Someone might need a drink!'

He was incurably romantic, to him love must always be *'une grande passion'*, otherwise it was not interesting. He always sent bunches of tuberoses (believed by the Edwardians to incite desire) to any woman he fancied.

But he also had a penetrating, exploratory brain, and independent views both on politics and life. The sadness was that his position did not extend him intellectually, and there was apparently no part for him to play in post-war politics.

Of course Lord Wimborne had his enemies.

Hilaire Belloc wrote:

'I must suppose the Lord knew best
When he created Ivor Guest.'

Another rhyme—I don't know the author—went:

'Grant, O Lord, eternal rest
To thy servant Ivor Guest.
Never mind the where or how,
Only, Lord, let it be now.'

Back to the gossip-columns.

The Dolly Sisters entertained audiences in *The League of Notions*, and tycoon Gordon Selfridge, who had brought American business methods to Oxford Street, was infatuated with Jenny. Thelma, Lady Furness, described her jewellery at Monte Carlo:

'My eyes popped,' she says. 'I have never seen so many jewels on any one person in my life as on Jenny Dolly, and every one of them an emerald. The magnificent necklace she wore round her neck must have cost a king's ransom. Her bracelets reached almost to the elbows. The solitaire ring she wore on her right hand must have been the size of a small ice-cube.'

Jenny and Rosie impinged on the political world when Lord Birkenhead, in the House of Lords, scathingly referred to Lord Salisbury and Lord Selborne as 'the Dolly Sisters'.

Gordon Selfridge fell in love with Jenny Dolly when he saw her in a cabaret at the 'Kit Kat' night-club. He was to love her for twenty-four years and to spend two million pounds between 1924 and 1931, the vast bulk of it on Jenny.

The Dolly Sisters were Hungarians and their real names were Janzieska and Roszieska Deutch. With their black hair and fringes they looked like two fragile little Dutch dolls. Gordon Selfridge tried to educate them by giving them books as well as diamond bracelets and orchids. He was also ambitious for them and used to say:

'Push and hard work are all you need to get ahead.'

He bought an interest in the Le Touquet Casino and Jenny and Rosie had unlimited credit there and at Deauville. Anton Dolin told a story of how one night when he was staying with the Dollys at Deauville, Rosie lost all her money.

'Gordon Selfridge had left early for London,' Anton Dolin relates. 'The Dollys invited me to dine with them at ten o'clock in the Casino. Halfway through dinner two white boxes beautifully done up were brought to the table. There was a lovely diamond bracelet for Jenny and a string of pearls for Rosie. With it was a brief note from Gordon—"I hope this will make up for your losses last night, darling". *Your* losses indeed! It was all Selfridge money!'

Gordon Selfridge had given Jenny Dolly, as he had given Gaby Deslys, the run of the store and all its contents. He always appeared in his office wearing a top-hat, morning coat and striped trousers but this did not create confidence in his business ability when it was known, besides owing his company £155,000, he had acquired gambling debts, on behalf of the Dollys, of £8,000 at Le Touquet, and £80,000 owed to Zographos, the most brilliant member of the world-famous Greek gambling syndicate.

One night at Deauville Jenny won £40,000, then lost it and £40,000 more. When the game ended Rosie said:

'Actually I won forty thousand pounds—all my sister lost. Anyway, it is all in the family.'

Jenny lost her money and all she had been given. Gordon Selfridge could no longer help her and she had to sell her jewellery at knock-down prices as well as her château at Fontainebleau. She eventually committed suicide. Gordon Selfridge, having had an income of £90,000 a year, died at eighty-three leaving less than £2,000.

Rosie married as her third husband Irving Netcher. He was short, stocky, forceful and intelligent. Rosie said:

'If this marriage doesn't take, I will go into a nunnery.'

'And I will go into a monastery,' her husband added.

Mary Cunningham-Reid and I went out in their fast speed-boat at Cannes in the early thirties. Rosie kept saying:

'I am so 'appy. It is marvellous, yes?'

What was marvellous was that the marriage did 'take'.

In 1921 Vasco offered the 'wonderful attraction of the permanent wave'. This was something which was gradually to be adopted by practically every woman in the land, but at that time it was controversial. I had my sides done and thought myself very dashing. But some men were shocked by permanent waves as they were by lipstick and rouge. When my aunt had her hair permanently waved, my uncle, Sir John Scobell, was so incensed that he wouldn't speak to her for three weeks.

The London Glove Company sold the best quality French suède gloves for 7s. 11d, and real black kid at 4s. 11d. Pure crêpe-de-Chine nightgowns were 29s. 11d. A moleskin shawl cape was nine guineas, the muff to match six guineas. Large stoles of black cross fox with a muff were only two guineas each. No lady would, of course, leave the house without hat and gloves. My mother had been given a silk nightgown just before the war by a woman with a bad reputation.

'I felt very fast and wicked in it,' she told me. 'Before then I, like my friends, had nightgowns made of fine lawn with long sleeves.'

We all wore large shawl-capes of fur which were really wide stoles. Mine was completely unidentifiable, and although I longed for a muff I couldn't afford one.

In August 1921, at Hawkinge Aerodrome, the 25th Squadron of the Royal Air Force gave an aerial training display. 'Irrepressible Jane' was there and wrote:

'The idea of a passenger flight in single or multi-engined machines all the afternoon at respectively one guinea and half a guinea!

And as though that were not enough in order to give the public the opportunity of viewing at close quarters the latest invention in the art and craft of aeronautical engineering, there is exhibited the "Meteorite".

The inventors of this aerofoil are confident that they have discovered a means of revolutionising the art of flying—their ambition is to establish communication between this and other planets. . . .

It is all very thrilling—scouts, anti-aircraft guns—finally a Handley Page machine is set on fire and an observer made a parachute descent. It was a woman—Miss Marshall! Mercifully her "Guardian Angel" worked admirably, and she came down without adventure. But for some reason she kept hold of the ropes after touching the ground, and was dragged a considerable distance over the rough, hard field before the mechanics reached her.

One last look at Flight Lieutenant Longton (who had made our hearts stop with his upside down flying, his slow rolling and his rolling off loop), and I left to meditate on the wonder that is man.'

The first air service between London and Paris, carrying only two or three passengers daily, started in 1919. The fare was £25, and the fee for an animal was 2s. 6d.

After various unsuccessful attempts the Atlantic had been crossed on 14th June 1919 by Captain Alcock and Lieutenant A. Whitten-Brown, both of the R.A.F. They flew 1,880 miles in 15 hours and 57 minutes and landed in a bog in Ireland. The flyers were knighted and shared a *Daily Mail* prize of £10,000.

It's easy to forget the incredible discomfort in which they flew. Sir Arthur Whitten-Brown said afterwards:

'It wasn't a pleasant trip over the Atlantic, we had no radio to guide us. We had fog nearly all the way across. I saw the sky once for long enough to fix our position by the stars. We sat in an open cockpit with the sleet driving against and obscuring the windscreen.'

But Sir John Alcock lost his life the following year and, as both he and his co-pilot disliked publicity, their exploit was soon forgotten. When Charles Lindbergh made his west to east solo flight in 1927, taking 33⅓ hours, and winning £5,000, most people in America, and a large number in Britain, believed it was the first time the Atlantic had been conquered from the air.

Young Lindbergh was the hero of the world. He received many decorations, and when he flew to England an enormous crowd cheered him at Croydon, and the King awarded him the Air Force Cross.

One sensational aspect of Lindbergh's flight was that when his take-off in America was shown on the newsreels we *heard* the sound of his aeroplane engine. There was no commentary, but this was a fantastic innovation.

Cloche hats, which were then fashionable, became closer and more helmet-like, and were named 'Lindbergh', 'Aviator' and 'Crusader'. Mine was green and called 'Crusader'—was it prophetic of all the crusades I was to undertake?

In the front of our cloche hats we always wore a brooch. The fashion for this decoration had started in the war when the wives of serving soldiers wore their husbands' regimental badges in diamonds. We sported race-horses, the Yacht Squadron flag, or a diamond arrow.

A new fashion was born when Millicent Rogers, daughter of a Standard Oil pioneer, who had a face like a lotus flower, picked a leaf, stuck a pin through it and gave it to Boivin to copy in gold and diamonds.

I met the Lindberghs, but it was after their small son had been kidnapped and killed, so I found them silent and seemingly half-afraid to speak. The whole world sorrowed with them in this terrible tragedy, which in those days could only have happened in America.

What is forgotten when we speak of the flying craze of the twenties and thirties, the speed records broken and the new marvels achieved by the 'heavier-than-air machines', is the number of now unknown men and women who assisted the development of flying.

One friend of mine was Claude Graham-White, who was the first Englishman to gain an aviator's certificate of proficiency. He was educated at Bedford, where he studied engineering. He owned the first petrol-driven motor-car in England and, having taken up flying in 1909, the following year he entered for flying races both in England and America, where he won the Gordon Bennett Cup.

He also founded the first British flying school at Pau in France, and formed a company to run the Hendon Flying Club in London. He wrote many treatises on aircraft, its technical development and its use in war.

Claude, who was dark, thick-set, and looked rather like a prosperous actor, had a charm which women found irresistible. When I knew him he was married to Ethel Levey, an American artiste with an aquiline nose, who I had first seen in *Hello Ragtime*, which my father had taken me to that never-to-be-forgotten evening in 1914. In that show Ethel sang—in a deep, husky, passionate voice—with a sense of rhythm which has never been superseded, even by Negroes.

Ethel was always called 'The Woman Who Fed Mayfair'. She was the first American before the war to entertain with the lavishness which was echoed later by Mrs. Corrigan. It was said that several Americans went broke trying 'to out-Ethel Ethel', and, of course, a great many people disliked her.

Eddie Marsh, social scrutiniser *par excellence*, wrote in 1913:

'You will probably sympathise with me when I say that for me the lid was put on it by finding Ethel Levey, whom I had seen kicking the chandelier at the Hippodrome, dancing and supping as a guest at Lady Wenlock's. Seen at close quarters she is terribly coarse and flashy, and her singing, in a room where some subtlety is required, seemed hopelessly inartistic. I'm getting rather sick of ragtime. . . . Ethel Levey throws rhythm to the winds, and uses the songs merely to exploit her great big enormous bass voice.'

Ethel inaugurated many new fashions, including costume jewellery. Her 'trademark' was a large slave bangle round her ankle, and I never saw her without half a dozen golden bracelets hung with coins and charms. These were copied by women all over the world.

Claude Graham-White had been married to another American before Ethel. She was Dorothy Taylor, who had inherited $15,000,000 from her father's leather business. After their marriage had only lasted three years, Dorothy became the Contessa di Frasso, and her witty tongue and wild escapades made her adored by the gossip-writers of Europe until her death.

Dorothy said once:

'I married England's greatest aviator and then the greatest gentleman in Europe. It's a toss-up which jerk took me for more dough.'

Dorothy had Claude and Ethel (who was her greatest friend) watched by a detective. She then dined out for weeks on the information that Ethel's bedroom ceiling was painted sky blue with a picture of an aeroplane coming through the clouds, as if preparing for a forced landing on the bed!

Dorothy died on a train leaving Las Vegas. She had been to see the famous Flamingo Hotel which, designed by her husband, was to put Las Vegas on the map as a gamblers' paradise.

I was fascinated by flying, as we all were. I was at the Derby in 1922 when a single-seater biplane over Epsom Downs wrote the words 'Daily Mail' in the sky. We were astonished! This, we felt, was progress.

I was not to take part personally in any spectacular flying until after Amy Johnson, who was a friend of mine, had made her brilliant flight to Australia alone in 1930. Amy had incredible adventures and was justifiably fêted and acclaimed, but she remained unassuming and modest. She was killed over the Thames Estuary in 1940, when she was a wartime ferry pilot.

In 1931 I and two young R.A.F. pilots, Flight Lieutenant E. L. Mole and Flight Lieutenant Wanliss, thought up the idea of gliders being towed by aeroplanes.

We developed the idea of building a glider called 'The Barbara Cartland', and carried the first 'aeroplane-towed glider airmail'. It was not until World War II that the Germans showed how much they had profited from our idea, and the Allies used aeroplane-gliders with great effect on D-Day.

The first person who ever took me 'up' was a young man called Geoffrey Rodd. He was in the Navy, and the gayest, happiest person I've ever known. He was a midshipman when we met, the same age as myself, and had therefore not suffered in the war. He loved life, he loved dancing, he loved people.

When he was on leave we would dance all the afternoon and evening, and once I went down with his mother when his ship was in Portsmouth, and danced in the wardroom. What girl could ask more than all a ship's officers for partners?

I remember being swung round to:

'Ev'ry morning, ev'ry evening,
  Ain't we got fun?
  Not much money, oh! but honey!
  Ain't we got fun?'

It was such wonderful, unbelievable fun for me!

Geoffrey was the first young man I knew to have his own private aeroplane—a Pussmoth. He was continually in touch with the firm who built it, and designed several improvements which were incorporated in all future machines.

He flew everywhere, to Scotland, to house parties, to France. A story which always delighted me about Scotland concerned Geoffrey's flying up to stay at Dunrobin Castle with the Duke and Duchess of Sutherland. He took with him Champkin, his personal pilot, mechanic, valet, a delightful man who amused us all.

The morning after they arrived at Dunrobin, Champkin asked:

'Did you have a good evening, sir?'

'So-so,' Geoffrey answered. 'Rather dull people staying, not a very good dinner and I didn't think much of the wine.'

'I am sorry, sir,' Champkin said. 'We had a splendid time downstairs. It was very gay, dancing and masses of the best champagne. You should have been with us, sir!'

Mary Ashley—the sad little red-haired daughter of Wilfred Ashley—was now a titian-haired beauty, and married to Alec Cunningham-Reid. She asked Geoffrey to smuggle her adored dachshund over from Deauville so as to avoid the long months of quarantine.

It was easy in those days to smuggle anything, when there was no radar, and as aeroplanes were new there were few restrictions or difficulties in getting in or out of the country unobserved.

Mary's dog arrived at Six Mile Bottom when I was there for the weekend. Geoffrey landed in a small field and after lunch took me back to London.

I remember that as we took off the telegraph wires loomed right in our path, and I thought:

'This is it! Here's where we crash!'

But we cleared them with an inch or so to spare, and we laughed and talked all the way to London. We passed directly over Camfield Place and I saw the lakes below us. How little did I think then what the future held.

Geoffrey was killed flying over the frozen skating-rink at St. Moritz. His aeroplane got into an air-pocket and crashed, and he was killed instantly. It seemed such a waste of a young life, but his devotion to flying, and that of other rich young men, contributed a great deal to the aeroplane industry in its infancy.

A woman who contributed much to flying was the Duchess of Bedford. Towards the end of the twenties the Press was excited by the exploits of the 'Flying Duchess'. At a reception given for important people of the time I was introduced to a plain, elderly woman, drably dressed, who had that strained look of the very deaf. She was obviously not interested in me until I told her—yelling to make her hear—that I had a house in Orkney. Then her face lit up with almost fanatical interest.

'Have you seen the Northern Divers?'

'Yes, often.'

'I saw a White-Tailed Eagle there—single bird—I think they now are or will be extinct.'

I knew the Duchess was a keen ornithologist, spending two or three months every year on Fair Isle, a barren treeless island between Orkney and Shetland. Not only deaf, she suffered from a continual buzzing in her ears.

In 1926 she flew from Croydon to Woburn. It transformed her life because she found the change in atmospheric pressure brought her a miraculous relief. For two years she flew only as a passenger in her hired D.M. Moth, piloted by Captain C. D. Barnard. Then in 1928 at the age of sixty-two she learnt to fly herself.

Inspired by Barnard's ambition to set up records, they started for India in a Fokker aeroplane. They had engine trouble in Persia and only reached Karachi after six weeks' delay. The Duchess returned by sea.

'The Flying Duchess Does It', screamed the Press a year later when she and Captain Barnard did the same return journey in eight days, a milestone in the history of aviation.

The Flying Duchess was to make many more records and to be acclaimed and respected as a flyer until, striving to complete her two hundred hours' solo flying, in 1937 she disappeared into the air. Neither she nor even the wreckage of the aeroplane was ever found.

Geoffrey Rodd had a very varied collection of friends. He had been shipmates with Prince George and was always 'popping' into Buckingham or St. James's Palaces, where the Prince stayed with his elder brother. This impressed me enormously. The King and Queen and the Royal Family were looked on with awe and respect, one couldn't quite think of them as human beings. In fact, until the Abdication one didn't realise they were torn and disturbed with emotions as we were.

Another friend of Geoffrey's was 'Baby June', a lovely plump little dancer with a round baby face, who sang and danced at the London Pavilion, and was always to be remembered singing:

'Whose baby are you, dear?'

Baby songs had a great vogue at the time.

'Rosebud mouth and little nose,
Naughty eyes and Baby knows,
That I like to count her toes.
My Baby has ten toes!'

I thought it very daring that I could be friends with June. Some years later she married Lord Inverclyde, a great friend of mine who because he spoke such good English I had persuaded to correct my novels.

Lord Inverclyde had inherited an estate of over £2,000,000. His grandfather had been chairman of the Cunard Line, and his great-grandfather had carried the first mail that had ever crossed the Atlantic by steamer. He was charming to meet, attractive, and for a very short time I fancied myself in love with him. But his mother belonged to the old school of snobbery, which was, fortunately, rapidly dying out.

Lord Inverclyde's sister once said to the Dowager:

'I do think, Mother, that Alan ought to get something to do.'

The Dowager looked at her in surprise.

'But he has a very important job,' she replied.

Her daughter raised her eyebrows.

'Has he?' she asked. 'I haven't heard about it! What is it?'

The Dowager looked at her scathingly.

'You forget, dear,' she said, 'that he is Lord Inverclyde.'

It was this sort of attitude, June was to tell us later, that made their life together impossible, and it was not surprising that their marriage was a very short one.

Geoffrey also introduced me to an Edwardian hostess who figures in almost every history of Edwardian times as one of the King's friends.

Mrs. Hwfa Williams was one of the first people I ever met who laughed at everything. She made her reputation, I found out later, by just laughing. She thus created an impression of being gay and responsive. Looking back I think it may have started as almost a nervous habit, but she realised, in the days when people had to have something particular to recommend them, that it was an asset.

A verse of 'The Ballad to Mrs. Keppel' went:

'In the parlour Cassel's counting money,
Mrs. Hwfa can't be always funny.
Send for Mrs. Keppel.'

To be a success in Edwardian society one had to be a blue-blood aristocrat there by right of birth, enormously rich, or to have a gimmick. Mrs. Hwfa Williams' gimmick was her laugh. I was told that it made her parties before the war the most successful in London.

She had been the first hostess—and was later copied by Lady Colefax, Lady Cunard, and the so-called great hostesses of the twenties and thirties—to mix her guests.

Prince Christopher of Greece wrote:

'She was the only hostess in London who could put a dancer next to a Duchess, and a Bishop beside a popular jockey, and get away with it.'

It was, of course, an achievement in the days when people took umbrage if they were not seated in their exact order of precedence.

Mr. Hwfa Williams, her husband, who is seldom mentioned by social historians, had initiated the Sandown Park race meetings and I went to it when the Grand Military meeting was revived after the years of war.

He had also re-popularised roller-skating, and made it 'the

rage' it had been earlier in the 1880's and in 1910. This was something I had learnt to do when I was a flapper, as my father was stationed for a short time at Seaford on the south coast. There was a rotunda on the front and we would roller-skate round it for hours on end.

At the end of the twenties ice-skating (which superseded the *thé dansant*) came in, which was far more graceful and appealed to far more people. Nevertheless I remember going to roller-skating halls where it was considered very dashing to mix with the proletariat and roll round and round the floor, being almost deafened by the noise.

Another craze was the motor-scooter. The first was hailed with great excitement. There were to be scooter-ways on either side of the roads and the manufacturers prophesied 'a new era in locomotion'! But it was to prove expensive and unreliable. After Sir Philip Sassoon, the handsome, enigmatic, multi-millionaire Member of Parliament, took a bad toss by confusing the stop-lever with the accelerator, it went out of favour.

Sir Philip Sassoon had started the war as secretary to General Rawlinson, then had himself transferred as secretary to the Commander-in-Chief. He was supposed to have wired a florist:

'Stop flowers to Lady Rawlinson, but send them to Lady Haig.'

Later when Lloyd George became Prime Minister he wired:

'Send flowers to Mrs. Lloyd George.'

On Easter Sunday a woman friend wired Sir Philip:

'Christ is risen, apply for secretaryship!'

The pogo-stick was news, and we were all photographed hopping about like kangaroos. Mah-jongg, which came from the U.S.A. in 1923, was less strenuous and very social. Women had lessons in this Chinese game, and sat all the afternoon calling out 'Chow', 'Kong', 'Poong', and talked of the 'East Wind' and 'Red and Green Dragons'.

One 'unforgettable' friend of the early twenties was Meggie Albanesi—the actress. She was young and beautiful in a dark, silent manner which haunted one. She was also an overwhelming success, but she lived on her nerves. She always thought she could have done better. She was always dissatisfied with her performance, even while the producer, the manager, the actors and the public were in ecstasies over her.

I met Meggie in 1921, when she was in *The Cinderella Man*. This was a delightfully romantic story of a young man (played by Owen Nares) who had experienced three unhappy love affairs. A psychiatrist—the first time we had ever heard of one!—in a series of flashbacks showed him how the girls he thought he loved had changed with time. Of course, he realised his true love is the little Cinderella girl who had been waiting for him just at hand!

'You were so good!' I told Meggie.

'No, my voice wasn't right!' she would reply.

In *East of Suez* in 1922 she gave a marvellous performance. Somerset Maugham brought us all the mystery, drama and menace of the East. The critics ran out of adjectives to describe Meggie, but she sat crying in her dressing room.

'Meggie, you were wonderful!' I said over and over again.

'I should have done better,' she wept, 'and I will.'

She was the first perfectionist I had met, and I didn't understand. Now I think she personified all we wanted for ourselves and couldn't put into words—we longed to express all those hidden, half-formed aspirations we felt but couldn't explain. Meggie tried to portray what she sensed behind the façade of self.

She died in 1924 having achieved one theatrical triumph after another. She was rehearsing for a great play and the whole profession mourned her.

A few days before her death she went to see *Outward Bound* by Vane Sutton Vane. It was a strange, rather creepy play, in which a variety of people found themselves in the smoking room of a liner. They do not know why they are aboard. One by one they reveal their characters. Finally, in a conversation with the barman, Scrubby, who is a modern Charon—the ferryman of the Styx—a young drunkard says:

'We are—now answer me truthfully—we are all *dead*, aren't we?'
A pause—then Scrubby answered very quietly:
'Yes, sir, we are all dead. They don't find out as soon as you have as a rule.'

'A strange influence that has upset me very much,' Meggie told her mother.

What is so interesting is that, when *The Cinderella Man* was produced, psycho-analysis was considered a lot of rubbish. A woman committed suicide when under psycho-analytic treatment, and the Westminster coroner said:

'I am not a scientific person, but it sounds to me like jargon.'

The Press in general agreed: even the progressive, up-to-the-minute *Daily Mail* said:

'. . . by letting the bottled-up emotions have free vent—subconscious inhibitions often bring about a general weakening of mind and body.'

The Church was delighted to find something new to condemn. A preacher pronounced psycho-analysis to be 'dogmatic and confused with sex', and accused it of giving 'unbridled licence to free sex-expression'.

On the other hand the Freudians were busy warning everyone how dangerous self-control could be to mental health.

'If I do, I'm a bestial, unbridled animal,' one man said. 'If I don't, I'm likely to be a lunatic!'

At a party I was introduced to a rather drab-looking middle-aged woman with untidy hair.

'I'm sure Barbara could help you,' my hostess said to her, 'she writes.'

'I'm sorry,' I said, 'I didn't catch your name.'

'Marie Stopes!'

I hardly dared to tell people I had met her.

It was through Dr. Marie Stopes that sex had become the most controversial subject of the day. Sexual liberty had become easier through the new contraceptives, although only a handful of women knew anything about them. In 1922 Dr. Marie Stopes—a doctor of science and a leading expert on coal—had hired the Queen's Hall for a meeting to advocate the use of birth-control. She wore a large picture-hat.

The fury aroused by Dr. Marie Stopes seems incredible today. People denounced her as a corrupter of morals, a friend of prostitution. The Bishop of Woolwich protested that the use of contraceptives was 'for the satisfaction of physical desire only'.

Dr. Stopes replied by saying that after she had opened her clinic in the East End she had received in three months twenty thousand requests for procuring abortions from overworked and sick mothers, many of whom had been told by doctors that they would die if they had another child.

The Catholics gathered their forces against Dr. Stopes, and she was forced to bring a libel action, in which she stated that she believed herself to be 'a channel of divine inspiration'.

This made the K.C. for the prosecution shout:

'Dr. Marie Stopes will have you believe that God sent down this beastly, filthy message.'

But although Dr. Stopes was denounced, abused and charged with incredible crimes, in 1923 the Cambridge Union carried a motion in favour of birth-control, and by the thirties the battle was won.

But before this there were many tragedies. A friend of mine fell in love. She was gay, impulsive, reckless—the model for one of Michael Arlen's gallant heroines. Her lover was brilliant, distinguished and fascinating; he was also much older than she and had a wife and family.

One day she came to me—deliberately offhand.

'I'm going to Paris.'

'Paris! Why?'

'I'm having a baby.'

'Oh no! But Paris?'

'Things can be arranged in Paris. What else can I do?'

What could she do? Her father was well known and involved politically with the man she loved. To 'face the consequences' would have destroyed not only her reputation but that of others more important.

She went to Paris and she died of 'peritonitis'.

A favourite joke of the period was about a clergyman who discovered a mother with three illegitimate children.

'Dear! Dear! Most regrettable!' he exclaimed in horror. 'What are the poor little things' names?'

'Innocence, Ignorance and Damned Bad Luck,' was the reply. It wasn't really funny!

Another of Geoffrey's older friends was the Dowager Lady Michelham, who had been the model for Constance Collier in Somerset Maugham's most criticised play *Our Betters*.

She had a peculiarly deep voice and an odd accent, and though Constance Collier mimicked her cruelly I don't think she minded. She was a personality in an era of personalities, with her long strings of enormous egg-size pearls, her puckish sense of humour, and her huge parties of guests eating off gold plate. She was the first hostess to introduce after-dinner cabaret performances in a private house. Before that time there had been music—of what we would call the 'highbrow' sort—but Cupid Michelham had exhibition dances—Dorothy Dickson and Carl Hyson for one turn.

On a television programme 'Abroad with Behan', which I flew up to Newcastle to do in 1969, Dominic Behan in his delightful Irish brogue asked:

'Why are you so taken up with etiquette?'

'I'm not,' I answered. 'I wrote a book on etiquette to help people. Women dread doing things wrong, whether it's opening a bazaar or arranging a meeting of the W.I. They hate to feel embarrassed.'

I then told him my most embarrassing moment. It was at the first big dinner party I was asked to by Cupid Michelham in 1920. About thirty people sat down at a huge table covered in orchids and set with gold plates. I had never seen gold plates before.

The first course was a slice of canteloupe melon. I picked up a gold spoon. At the first touch the melon leapt off the plate and disappeared under the table. I sat crimson with embarrassment while it was retrieved by a disdainful footman with powdered hair, and another slice placed in front of me.

Cupid and I went to Oxford University to visit her second son, Jack. I remember he had a naked electric light bulb and told his mother he couldn't afford a shade. As he was one of the wealthiest young men in England, this was rather surprising. But I've found so many rich people have strange meannesses.

For instance Sir Ernest Cassel made his grand-daughter Edwina pay for her laundry out of the small dress allowance he gave her. When Lady Bland-Sutton died they found a large box marked: 'Pieces of string too small to be used'. Once at No. 10 Downing Street I saw an ex-Vicereine of India slip some of Mrs. Attlee's meringues into her handbag!

One very rich woman who never tried to pretend she was poor was Lady Astor, who in 1919 was the first woman to take her seat in the House of Commons.

In one speech she wound up by saying:

'Now, my dears, I'm going back to one of my beautiful palaces to sit down in my tiara and do nothing, and when I roll out in my car I will splash you all with mud and look the other way.'

Her audience roared with laughter.

I knew and admired Lady Astor. Who didn't? A Virginian by birth, Protestant and later a Christian Scientist, she was very outspoken, and 'Astorisms' became a regular source of amusement. One was never quite certain if she was ingenuous or knew the full value of her remarks.

'I like the common man,' she said once, 'because I am common myself, but I follow the uncommon man.'

On a platform she was fanatical against alcohol but when I lunched at the Astors' house in St. James's Square with Bill Astor he offered me a drink. I looked surprised, and he said:

'Mother doesn't approve, but she wants to be hospitable, so our guests have what they want.'

It was, however, the most repeated joke of the period when Lady Astor on a platform exclaimed:

'I would rather commit adultery than drink a glass of beer!'

And a man's voice from the back of the hall demanded:

'Who wouldn't?'

It was an extraordinary coincidence that at the time the name of her secretary was Miss Brew!

Lady Astor started the first evening receptions attended only by women. Without drink, without men, they were, not surprisingly, very dull, and there was no rush for invitations.

At first her fellow Members of Parliament did not take Lady Astor very seriously—a woman in the House of Commons must be a freak—but they grew to respect her, love her for her warm heart, and be infuriated by her unceasing interruptions.

Another friend who, like Geoffrey, had his own aeroplane, was also in the Navy. Lieutenant Glen Kidston was a Bentley Boy, for he was a racing driver of Bentleys, but in 1925 he attained in a 1,990 c.c. Bugatti a speed record at Brooklands with an average of 96¾ miles an hour.

Glen was extremely attractive, amusing, dashing, and a wonderful dancer. It's difficult to portray how much that counted in those days. We danced, we motored, we flew. Glen had the fastest speedboat in the South of France. He took the best film of big game I have ever seen.

Early in 1931 he told me he had bought an aeroplane which had belonged to Alfred Lowenstein.

'Why on earth have you done that?' I asked.

'I did it on an impulse,' he replied, 'it's a good aeroplane.'

The Belgian multi-millionaire was one of the supermen of the new world-power of International Finance. These men, in the post-war years, superseded kings, governments and military conquerers. Lowenstein was in himself an 'economic interpretation of history'.

All the year round suites were reserved for him at Claridges in London and the Ritz in Paris; he maintained a fleet of aeroplanes to transport himself and his entourage to his 'palaces' in Biarritz and Brussels. The Prince of Wales was frequently his guest at Melton Mowbray.

Hydro-electric power and the development of artificial silk made Lowenstein one of the three richest men in the world. Then, during a battle with the banks over the International Holdings Company, Lowenstein was killed. When his aeroplane was high over the Channel he opened the entrance door and stepped out. It was suggested that he thought it was the lavatory, but a French doctor who examined his body when it was recovered from the sea found 'toxic matter' in the organs. There was after his death naturally a huge slump in his holdings.

'I don't like the idea of your buying Lowenstein's aeroplane,' I said to Glen, 'it makes me feel creepy. Sell it, buy another— why saddle yourself with someone else's bad luck?'

Glen laughed.

'I tell you, it's a good machine, I'm not superstitious.'

'But I am,' I persisted. 'Don't fly it—I beg you.'

I suppose it was a premonition, but how many people really listen to premonitions? How many will change their plans? And how often are we wrong?

Early in 1931 Glen set off from Croydon for South Africa. I waved as Glen smiled at me from the pilot's seat. He taxied down the runway.

'I'm wrong, of course I'm wrong,' I told myself, but I felt miserable and depressed. I knew there was something dark and sinister about that aeroplane, I felt I would have sensed it even if I hadn't known its history.

A month later Glen crashed into the side of a hill in Africa. The reports said the aeroplane was overloaded. His sister sent me three of my photographs which he had carried with him. Another useless, perhaps avoidable, death? But Glen had also contributed towards motor and speedboat racing and flying—people learnt by his mistakes.

Lady Plunket was another person I loved who was to die in an aeroplane crash, but not until late in the thirties.

Dorothé Plunket was lovely, tiny, the most exquisite dancer of the period. She should have been a professional, for her mother was Fanny Ward, the American actress, who was the first person we ever heard of who had her face lifted.

Dorothé had put up her hair when she was only thirteen so that she could wash dishes in a canteen for troops in the war. Jack Barnato, one of the South African diamond millionaires, proposed to her when she was fourteen, and waited three years to marry her.

When he died she took up flying. She had done forty hours solo, preparatory to taking her pilot's exam, when the aeroplane in which she was going to make her test crashed, killing everyone on board.

Dorothé had wanted to be a nurse, but instead she took to driving her car very fast round Brooklands. More than anything she loved to dance. She married Teddy—the good-looking, delightful, six-foot-tall Baron Plunket—and had three adorable sons, one of whom was a page at my wedding.

Dorothé radiated happiness, kindness and sympathy. She was the first person who showed me that a woman should not only try to amuse and entertain other people, but understand, help and encourage them. The second woman who influenced me so tremendously in my contacts with people was Edwina Mountbatten.

Dorothé always made me feel I was the one person she wanted to see, the one person she wanted to listen to, and she had the same effect on everyone she met. The shyest, dullest, most boring man or woman blossomed when she drew them out and smiled at them. No one ever felt lonely or ignored when Dorothé was there.

She was in looks a living personification of a fairy. She always seemed too fragile and too lovely to be true; exquisitely dressed, she floated on tiny feet. She was never unkind, she never repeated gossip, she always produced an extenuating excuse for anyone who was criticised.

148

'I'm sure there must be a good reason,' Dorothé would say when people denounced something controversial which a young person had done.

'Let's give them a chance,' was one of her favourite maxims.

Yet without gossiping, without being catty, she was so amusing, so entrancing to be with. Everyone loved her, men, women and children, and when she died half London was in tears.

Dorothé was very superstitious. She wouldn't put her left arm into a sleeve first, or her left foot into a shoe.

'If you ever put on a garment inside out,' she warned me, 'you must jump over it three times before you put it on again.'

I'm ashamed to say I always follow this advice; for I can't forget how seriously Dorothé took these things.

Dorothé was a close friend of the gentle, shy Duchess of York (later to be Queen Elizabeth), and the Marquess and Marchioness of Londonderry treated her like one of the family. But she had friends in every walk of life. No one could resist her charm, and when she gave exhibition dances and charity balls in private houses, the audience were clapping her personally as much as they applauded her undoubted talents.

Dorothé and her husband were burnt to death in America when the aeroplane in which they were travelling caught fire. This was, I felt, a bitter waste; for Dorothé had contributed nothing to flying, only to life and our lives in particular.

CHAPTER SIX

Don't put your daughter on the stage,
Mrs. Worthington;
Don't put your daughter on the stage.
The profession is overcrowded and
The struggle's pretty tough,
And admitting the fact,
She's burning to act,
That isn't quite enough.

NOËL COWARD

By 1921 everyone had gone 'movie mad' and *The Glorious
Adventure*, which was the first British film in colour, had a
society cast which reads like a page from *Debrett*. Lady Diana
Cooper, thrush-blue eyes and pale gold hair, played the lead. This
was her first venture. She was to make another film in 1923
and star as both Madonna and Nun in *The Miracle* in New
York.

She rushed home to canvass for her husband Duff Cooper at
Oldham. She hated the canvassing. Who doesn't?

'I marvelled when they did not bang the door on our silly,
smirking, out-to-please faces,' she said.

Duff Cooper got in with a majority of thirteen thousand over
Labour. My brother was to like him so much when he got into
Parliament, and I always admired his sensitivity, his honesty and
above all his courage. He was the only person who resigned on
principle when Neville Chamberlain came home after Munich
with the farcical promise of 'peace in our time'.

Diana Cooper played in *The Miracle* at the Salzburg Festival
in 1925, then returned to America to go on tour. Then she
turned down more contracts because she could not bear to be
away from the man she loved and to marry whom she had

fought against parental disapproval. Despite all jaundiced predictions they were blissfully happy.

'If I had more guts,' she wrote to Duff from Chicago, 'I'd stay for the extra two thousand pounds, but I can't wash out a holiday with you. There are not enough of them in the summer of life. I feel sad days will never cease. I'm tired. . . .'

What Noël Coward was to call 'the heady quality of applause' was not all the fun it was cracked up to be.

Lady Asquith, always sensational, said of her son:

'If Anthony goes into the film business it will be over my dead body.'

But fortunately nobody listened! And Anthony was to produce many excellent British films in an effort to compete with America.

Film actresses, like the stage sort, were still under the cloud of Edwardian disapproval. Professional actresses were not accepted unless, of course, they were very pretty and fascinating Gaiety girls! Then like Gertie Millar, who became the Countess of Dudley, and Rosie Boote, the Marchioness of Headfort, they were elevated by marriage to the top table!

Lord Robert Innes-Ker, whose mother was the Dowager Duchess of Roxburghe, startled everyone in 1920 by marrying José Collins, of *The Maid of the Mountains* fame, by special licence.

One of the American newspapers put the general attitude towards this romance very clearly:

'Bobbie Innes-Ker is always a gay and reckless character, and his intimacy with actresses and music-hall favourites has existed for years, but it was hoped he wouldn't marry into the footlights out of consideration for his distinguished relations. Queen Mary probably would not care to receive Miss José Collins, even when disguised as Lady Robert Innes-Ker, when, on the other hand, the future King would certainly be very pleased to meet her.'

José was, however, despite all the predictions, to be a great success with her brother-in-law and with all her husband's relations.

When I was offered a leading part with Nelson Keys, whom C. B. Cochran considered the best revue artiste of his age, in a show George Grossmith was interested in, my mother nearly had a fit. The idea of my becoming an actress was unthinkable. And when, in the forties, my daughter Raine, while still at school, was offered a film part, I was equally positive she should not take it.

'I think it's a wonderful opportunity,' Mrs. Michael Bowes-Lyon, sister-in-law of the Queen, said to me then. 'Raine acts well and looks beautiful, why do you object?'

'I should hate that sort of life for her,' I replied feebly. The old-fashioned convictions die hard.

I think one of the reasons I was so positive was that, unlike my mother, I had seen the theatre at close quarters. I knew a young man called George Curzon, who had retired from the Royal Navy with the rank of lieutenant-commander. He was the son of the famous Ellis Jeffreys—a unique actress who was much admired by King George and Queen Mary—and through his father he was related to all the lovely exciting Curzons.

George was acting in a play at the Apollo called *The First Year*. Ernest Truex, an American, played the lead. It was a hot summer and I used to sit in his dressing room during the matinée eating strawberries which we had bought in Berwick Market, and talk to the other performers when they were not on stage. I got intensely bored with their obsessive preoccupation with themselves.

They were interested in nothing but their own performance: whether the lights were right or wrong; if another actor had moved too far up stage so their lines were lost; or if someone was late on cue. George once ticked me off:

'You didn't tell Ernest what a wonderful performance he gave this afternoon.'

'Was it any different to yesterday?'

'No, but he wants to think so, and actors must be encouraged and praised.'

What it taught me was that everyone wants to be praised, everyone wants encouragement. I felt these older men and experienced actors would think it impertinent on my part if I discussed their performances. But, of course, I was wrong.

I was to learn that interest and encouragement are things nobody resents and everyone wants. In fact, no one can have enough of them. As Lord Wavertree used to say:

'Never mind about laying on flattery with a butter-knife! People, especially men, can take it by the bucketful!'

I knew then that the professional stage was not for me. But

that did not prevent my longing to appear in the limelight with all my friends. Lois Sturt, Lady Allington's daughter, was the only one of my really close friends who was lucky enough to get into the movies. She had a part in *The Glorious Adventure* as Nell Gwynne. She couldn't have been better cast. She was in real life pure 'Restoration'. She had dark flashing eyes, was impetuous, fearless and completely unpredictable. There was nothing she wouldn't do. She loved dressing up and was to be in all the pageants I produced.

She always had rather unusual men in love with her and finally she married Viscount Tredegar, who was a character straight out of fiction. He had lived in the Vatican as Privy Chamberlain of the Sword and Cape to the Pope; he stood for Parliament as a Conservative candidate for Limehouse and made himself an expert on unemployment and housing because he owned most of Bow and Bromley; he was the world's leading authority on Dr. John Donne; he was a gourmet; a music-lover; a poet; the owner of a menagerie and had remarkable gifts as a bird-tamer.

Evan Tredegar, who looked like a Prince of the Renaissance, wore huge rings and dressed in picturesque flowing capes and coloured waistcoats. His castle in Wales, Tredegar Park, was full of treasures. The one he liked best of them all was his macaw who pecked everyone. In the house in South Street, where he and Lois lived, there was a cage of live monkeys halfway up the stairs.

Evan Tredegar's mother as a hobby made exquisite copies of birds' nests. There was a rumour that she had also made a large model with mud, so that she could sit in it herself.

The first time I trod 'the boards' was in an enormous theatrical show at Covent Garden. Called *Chiquita*, it was written by Wilfred Eyre, a young man I often dined with, and I was extremely impressed by his production. He wisely had professionals in the leading parts but it was also 'the first presentation of a super-chorus of society amateurs including Lady Diana King, Lady Eleanor Smith, the Hon. Ivy Somerset, Miss Barbara Cartland, etc.'

My second stage appearance was doing a three-legged dance at an 'All Dancers' charity matinée at Daly's. My partner was the lovely little Marchioness of Queensberry, who at sixteen had played the lead in *Mr. Manhattan*, married into the peerage, and left the stage for good.

Then we both did a dance with the 'Ruthven twins'—the strikingly attractive and dashing twin daughters of Lord Ruthven —who were the joy of every gossip-writer. They were tall and dark with rather big feet, bodies which looked angular, and they were tremendously *chic*. They were both to take part in the many pageants I devised and even at one time to go on the stage as 'The Ralli Twins'. They had long necks and they made fashionable first a gold neckband and then the first pearl 'chokers'.

Excited by Wilfred's success I agreed enthusiastically when it was suggested I should write a revue for a charity in which the Duchess of Rutland—Diana Cooper's mother—was interested. Unfortunately they couldn't find a theatre, and *The Mayfair Revue* had to be produced very sketchily at the Hotel Cecil which had just been demobbed, having been the Air Ministry during the war.

The *Bystander* said rather scathingly:

'*The Mayfair Revue* drew a goodly number of people, including Dame Clara Butt, who seemed delighted with the efforts of young ladies on the stage to appear exactly like chorus girls.'

One thing which was much better than the performance was the dresses. I had been asked if I would help a young undergraduate just down from Cambridge who wished to be a dress designer. He was good-looking, enthusiastic, eager and so charming that everyone wanted to help him. He certainly produced the most attractive clothes and he was delighted to make gowns for the cast very cheaply. His name was Norman Hartnell.

'Norman, can you design dresses for Lord Bethel's daughters? They are doing a song and dance.'

'Of course, will they pay?'

'Yes, a reasonable amount, and they are certain to send you their friends.'

'Splendid, I'll draw something for them to see. Do you think eight pounds for each dress will be too much?'

The dresses were lovely and we weren't the only people who

thought so. They were stolen from the hotel after the dress rehearsal, and Dorothy and Grace had to rush to Shaftesbury Avenue at the last moment to get themselves something to wear.

Norman was to design for me many wonderful dresses, including my presentation dress for Buckingham Palace. I even gave him an idea. I asked him to make me the first long wedding dress worn since the war, and the first tulle one anyone had seen. Unfortunately, I designed it myself! Norman went on to design the lovely, ethereal tulle wedding dresses for Daphne Weymouth and Lady Lettice Lygon which made his name.

He also made me a grey flannel coat and skirt. We all wore them when the men started to wear—almost as a uniform—grey flannel Oxford bags. I was wearing it on Derby Station where a young man was seeing me off to London. Suddenly he said:

'Oh, Barbara, you look so lovely, will you marry me?'

The magic of Hartnell was transmitted even to grey flannel!

There were other amateur, but undoubtedly theatrical, efforts. In 1922 the Sitwells burst upon an astonished world with *Façade*. I remember the laughter and the rudeness which were evoked by their idea of speaking their poetry unseen through an enormous mask designed by John Piper, which occupied the centre of the stage.

A trumpet-shaped instrument made of fibre was used, which was later taken up by the Admiralty and used by sea captains for short orders from the bridge during a storm.

Edith Sitwell, who looked like a Gothic statue, was acclaimed by her friends, mostly painters, musicians and poets, at the first performance in Carlyle Square, but when fifteen months later *Façade* was shown at the Aeolian Hall the audience hissed and was so hostile that Edith was warned not to leave the theatre until most of the people had dispersed!

The newspapers had a heyday:

'*The Drivel they had to Hear.*'

'*Noël Coward Walks Out.*'

'*Meaningless, Rhythmless, Childish Words.*'

It seems fantastic that such high passions should be aroused. Osbert relates:

'For several weeks subsequently we were obliged to go about London feeling as if we had committed a murder—in fact we had created a first-class scandal in literature and music.'

Yet in 1926—so strange is public opinion—the *Sunday Times* reports:

'*Façade* was the jolliest entertainment of the season.'

That pioneers in anything have a rough passage was something I was to discover all through my life. Only the dull, the unimaginative, the fat cows contentedly chewing 'the cud', are immune from the slings and arrows of those hostile to any new idea, any spark of originality!

Not content with a revue, I wrote a play called *Blood Money*. It was produced at the Q Theatre and created a lot of excitement because it had been banned.

When the Lord Chamberlain was dispensed with in 1968 I went on B.B.C. to argue the case with John Mortimer the Q.C. and playwright, who began by being aggressive, in the modern manner, and saying:

'I've never read any of Miss Cartland's books—thank God!'

He then went on to say that I didn't know what I was talking about, having never written a play or had one banned.

'Actually, my first play was banned,' I replied, and had the satisfaction of seeing him really put out.

'I hadn't been told this!' he said angrily.

What he meant was that he hadn't been properly briefed, but as the defendant I had certainly scored a point.

My play was banned because I had used the title of a living Indian prince. But when I asked the Lord Chamberlain to choose another name, he obliged, while pointing out it wasn't his usual practice!

Blood Money opened at Kew. The best notice said: 'For a first effort it proved more than promising.'

The worst reported: 'It is an immature specimen of the sex-ridden drama.'

What I felt was wrong was that Edmund Willard, a brilliant actor, was miscast. I had written a part for the conventional type of rather brainless English gentleman.

It is interesting to see how, just as the top actresses all looked like Vere de Vere duchesses, so top actors looked like dukes. The most outstanding was Owen Nares, the matinée idol of the war years.

'He looks such a gentleman,' my mother always said in surprise.

She and her friends would have been even more surprised if they had known, as all the theatrical profession did, that Owen Nares had a habit of sitting completely nude in his dressing room with his feet in a washbasin. If people walked in he just gave them his charming, heart-throbbing smile which filled the theatres in every play in which he appeared.

Three great actor-managers, all most distinguished to look at, had died during the war. Sir Herbert Tree, Sir George Alexander and Sir Charles Wyndham. Another knight, Sir Charles Hawtrey, had as a successor in his comedy roles Ronald Squire, who had a wickedly attractive chuckle and a very polished manner. He also had an amusing way of talking which made everything he said sound witty. Once I was discussing if there was life on the moon—a subject we were interested in even in those days—and Ronald said to me:

'My dear young lady, when you were busy being born they produced the first supernatural play called *A Message from Mars*. I thought then, and I think now, this planet is quite good enough for me!'

The most dynamic of the post-war theatrical producers was Gilbert Miller, a good-looking American, with huge shoulders on a short body, who took over the St. James Theatre in 1920. He loved England, because his father, an actor-manager, had been born here and he crossed the Atlantic during the war to produce *Daddy Long-Legs*.

Gilbert had an amazing memory and always remembered everyone's troubles or complaints, and enquired about them. No one could help being flattered by his interest.

After one failure he only produced straight plays. One of his greatest successes was *The Last of Mrs. Cheyney*, with Gerald du Maurier—by then a Sir—which ran for 514 performances.

Gerald du Maurier, ugly, fascinating, compelling, was the pioneer of naturalness on the stage.

'Don't force it!' he would say when he was rehearsing with another actor. 'Do what you generally do any day of your life when you come into a room. Bite your nails, yawn, or lie down on the sofa!'

Gerald disliked ardent love-making.

'Must you kiss her as though you were having steak and onions?' he would ask.

Gilbert Miller discovered Leslie Howard, a handsome and sensitive actor, who became symbolic of all good breeding and glamour. He introduced Leslie to America, where he appeared in a light comedy called *Just Suppose*. The audience laughed at Leslie as the boisterous equerry to the Prince of Wales, and wept when H.R.H. put his duty to his country before love and said goodbye to his American sweetheart. As Leslie's daughter Doodie was to say later:

'No one in 1920 could foresee how the real Prince would rewrite the script!'

Also in America Leslie played Napier Harpenden in *The Green Hat*. It was the smash hit of the twenties both as a book and a play. It made Michael Arlen a fortune and Leslie a star.

American women watching adoringly 'the perfect English gentleman', had no idea it was most unpublic school, as they thrilled to sentences like:

'You are my dark angel and my tower of delight in the twilight of the world.'

From being the most popular young actor in America, Leslie returned to England in 1928 as actor and producer. With Gilbert Miller he presented *Her Cardboard Lover*, starring Tallulah Bankhead, who filled the theatre with screaming, hysterical women. His second play, *Berkeley Square*, made him the leading matinée idol both sides of the Atlantic.

It is in *The Scarlet Pimpernel* that I shall always remember him.

'You were exactly as I had imagined Sir Percy Blakeney,' I told him once.

The shy look which was one of his most charming characteristics made it almost seem as if he was blushing.

'Thank you,' he smiled. 'I only wish I had Sir Percy's ingenuity at getting out of uncomfortable situations.'

I guessed he was referring to his private life. His daughter Doodie wrote after his death:

'He never had enough energy to run after a woman; it was rather that he sometimes lacked the energy to run away.'

Leslie made a lot of money but he developed 'rich-man's disease'—a dislike of spending it. His idea of sixpence under a plate by way of a tip was not well received in smart restaurants. He was killed in 1943, when the commercial plane in which he was travelling from Lisbon to England was shot down by the Germans.

The stage in the twenties was filled with the most entrancing people and they made an effort to be smart, well made up and glamorous at all times. How boring it is today to see stars arriving at the theatre by bus, wearing an old mackintosh, a head-scarf over their heads and ill-cleaned boots beneath their mini-skirts.

Gertie Lawrence would arrive at the stage door in a big Hispano Suiza car, with orchids on her shoulder and invariably an escort of smart young men with top-hats and white gardenias. But even the poorest little trouper would make an effort.

'It is very exciting to be stared at in the streets,' a young actress said to me. 'It gives me a thrill—those are the people who pay to see me.'

It was not only a question of how actors were dressed when they were outside the theatre, it was something much deeper. Before the war the actors and actresses knew that the real job of the theatre is illusion, and they created it.

MacQueen Pope, the greatest authority on the stage, says:

'They and all the players kept themselves aloof. They did not mix.'

Actors and actresses lived in a little world of their own. They were people of mystery. They knew quite well that they were not considered respectable by the men and women of the ordinary world. They were not thought of as 'ladies and gentlemen', and they didn't want to be.

At the very beginning of the twenties the great actors accepted few invitations. Then it became fashionable to mix one's guests and it was considered smart to have leading actors and actresses at one's dining-table. But it was still difficult to get the real artistes to come. People like Cyril Maude, Fred Terry, Julia Neilson, and even Sir Gerald du Maurier, felt that society interfered with their work and their studied aloofness. Work should come first.

There was, of course, in those days no radio or television, nor recordings, to provide additional income, things which inevitably were later to lessen the value of the stars by over-familiarity.

'In the past they had to act well,' MacQueen Pope says, 'or get out.'

It was the 'starlets', as they were to be called, who broke down

159

the barriers. Sylvia Hawkes, reputedly the daughter of a London ostler, took London by storm. She was a mannequin at Revilles in Hanover Square when I first saw her. Then she appeared in the chorus at the Winter Garden in *Tonight's the Night*. Following this she was in the first cabaret show ever seen in London, *The Midnight Follies*.

We met again staying at the Duke of Sutherland's house near Guildford. Later the Duke and Duchess took her abroad in their yacht. She was slim, fair, wide-eyed and very, very lovely.

Lord Birkenhead once said to me:

'It's extraordinary, she has every traditional attribute of breeding—a beautiful neck, beautiful hands and beautiful feet.'

One evening in 1926 I went into the Berkeley for dinner. The gossip-columns of the evening papers were full of the Earl of Shaftesbury's denial of Lord Ashley's engagement.

'*My son is not engaged to Miss Hawkes, nor is there any question of his marrying her.*'

Tony Ashley was a dance partner of mine. I found him sitting with Sylvia in the Berkeley looking very happy.

'Come to our wedding tomorrow!' he said.

'You're being married?'

'Eleven o'clock at St. Paul's, Knightsbridge, by special licence!'

I went to St. Paul's to find a large and curious crowd but few friends.

'The bride's mother was present,' the Press reported, 'the bridegroom's relations did not attend.'

The crowd cheered the bride, the Press stood on the pews to take photographs. Sylvia wore a white satin dress which had been made for her in twenty-four hours. Lord Northesk, who had married Jessica Brown, the attractive, high-kicking American dancer, signed the register.

Sylvia was to have five husbands in all, one of them being Douglas Fairbanks senior. But in the twenties she crashed through the last snotty taboos which the Edwardians had created between stage and society.

The stage, whether we knew the performers or not, was very much a part of our life. We went to every new show, we discussed it, criticised it, and were absorbed by it just as today people are absorbed by the television. But actors and actresses

The author in 1923.

My parents in Scotland *(above left)*. I bought my hat in London's Brompton Road for 3s.6d. and the cherries for 1s.6d. *(above right)*. In 1925 *(below)* with my brothers, Ronald 18 *(left)* and Tony 13.

Flying through the twenties: the glider *Barbara Cartland* was later to carry the first aeroplane-towed glider mail, from Manston in Kent to Reading.

Bright young people of the twenties: Lady Louis Mountbatten *(top left)* was co-heiress with her sister, Mary Ashley *(bottom left)*, to the vast wealth of their grandfather, Sir Ernest Cassel. The Countess of Dalkeith *(top right)* was the loveliest bride of 1921 when she became the Duchess of Buccleugh. Paula Gellibrand *(bottom right)* caused a sensation when she lunched at the Ritz in a hat trimmed with wisteria.

MRS. WILLIAM

Lady Plunket *(top left)* danced her way through the twenties; half a million people watched Lady Diana Cooper play in *The Miracle (bottom left)* and both Anne Messel *(top right)* and Loelia Ponsonby *(bottom right)* were known for their beauty.

In 1927, wearing the cloche hat and fur of the decade *(opposite top left)* and a sequinned and diamanté dress, given to me by a young student called Norman Hartnell, for my first presentation at court in 1925. In 1923 I was in Deauville *(opposite below)* with *(left to right)* the Marchioness of Queensberry, Philip Dunn and Noël Coward. In 1928, I was again presented at court *(above)*.

The spirit of the twenties: the Hon. David Herbert, Lady Plunket and Mr Walter Crisham in one of the many dances they gave for charity.

were very real to us. We copied them, we tried to look like them.

By the middle of the twenties all the young leading ladies had all been tempted into the night-clubs. I can remember Gertrude Lawrence making an entrance into the Embassy Club looking like a mermaid in a Hartnell gown embroidered all over in Nile-blue sequins. Round her shoulders there was a cape of pleated tulle. She glittered, she sparkled, everyone's eyes turned towards her.

I almost expected people to clap, and I think it was with difficulty we restrained ourselves. Then with a smile that embraced the whole room, she moved to her table, one of the most important tables in the room, next to the one which was called 'the royal box', because it was kept for the Prince of Wales.

I always think of Gertie the first night of *Private Lives* standing on the hotel balcony in her white fringed Molyneux dress singing in her funny off-key voice:

> 'Some day I'll find you,
> Moonlight behind you,
> True to the dream I am dreaming.
> As I draw near you
> You'll smile a little smile . . .'

She was me, she was every woman in the theatre. We were singing in our hearts, believing it, living it . . . 'Some day I'll find you again.'

Gertie, whom I loved, didn't mind making herself up to look ugly in a character part, but most of the leading ladies wanted to look glamorous. Evelyn Laye could have looked nothing else when the curtain rose to show her as Helen in the most beautiful imaginative stage bed I had ever seen, designed by Oliver Messel.

Oliver, a product of the early twenties, became, before he was thirty, the leading stage designer in England. Max Reinhardt thought him a genius and said so. Oliver invented—by using colour and materials never before envisaged—a new genre in stage effects.

He designed a restaurant for me which I was helping to make profitable for some friends. From a dull square room without windows, it became a place of imagination and loveliness. Oliver was always original, always producing the unexpected but invariably something beautiful.

He had a round forehead, satanic eyebrows, pointed ears, flashing white teeth, curly hair, and looked like a fawn. He was a clever mimic, but was never cruel. He had a passion for dressing up, and should have lived in the Regency days.

Oliver's success in the theatre dates from the day C. B. Cochran saw his Exhibition of Masks. His success has never gone to his head, he is still 'a little boy'—shy, modest, charming and loved by everyone who works with him.

Oliver's sister Anne, now the Countess of Rosse, made one think of nymphs dancing in the shadow of green trees, of the mist above a still lake, of moonlight on the sea. She had that intangible liquid beauty which is in movement.

How difficult it is to write of the twenties without mentioning the blonde beauty of Margaret Bannerman in *Our Betters*. She was the ideal British Venus. This was a play in which Somerset Maugham with cynicism and satire showed what life was like in what was still called 'the upper classes'.

He was accused of using 'his wealth of wit and fancy' to adorn 'decadence and hedonism'.

As a man he always seemed to me to be tortured inwardly. We all knew about his paralysing shyness which caused his stammer, but no one can explain why, when he was surrounded by great wealth, comfort and priceless antique treasures, there should be that ingrained streak of sadism running through his work.

I felt the answer lay in his cold dark eyes and sensitive sardonic mouth. He suffered and he wanted others to suffer too. It was as if he had never forgiven life.

Edith Day was the popular phenomenon of the period. She was a prima donna, ballerina and magnificent actress all rolled into one. She sang 'Alice Blue Gown', which has become a classic, with such artistry that she stopped the show.

Edith sang magnificently but there was more to come. When she danced, light as the proverbial feather, she did a back kick actually touching the back of her head with the sole of her foot! The audience went mad, we stood up and cheered and cheered!

No one seems to get excited today. Marlene Dietrich is the only actress recently who has seemed to vitalise an audience. I heard a lot of masculine 'Bravos' the last time she appeared in London, but no one rose from his seat.

Edith played the lead in a very romantic musical spectacular in 1927 called *The Desert Song*. It was set in Morocco, with Riff warriots galloping over the sands and the handsome Harry Welchman as 'The Red Shadow' carrying Edith (as Margot) out into the moonlit desert.

On St. George's Day, after a large wedding at St. Margaret's, Westminster, with twelve small bridesmaids dressed like rosebuds, my husband and I went to Claridges Hotel. We were leaving for the Continent next morning—an arduous journey by train from Victoria, boat across the Channel, then two and a half hours in 'The Golden Arrow' before we reached Paris. We had dinner and then I said suddenly: 'Do let us go to *The Desert Song*.'

There was only a box on the second tier left. We sat there hand in hand and I was carried away by the throbbing music, the beauty, the romance!

I didn't know where Margot's love story ended and mine began.

Of course, I can never forget the elfin grace of Jessie Matthews. Her big eyes and almost childish appearance made us feel she was finding the world as surprising and difficult as we did. When she sang 'My Heart Stood Still' she became a star, but she still tugged at our hearts as the little girl who hadn't really grown up. We identified ourselves with Jessie because we were instinctively resisting the passing years. As Noël said in *The Vortex*:

'It's funny how Mother's generation always longed to be old when they were young, and we strain every nerve to keep young.'

Like Peter Pan we wanted to be young 'for ever and ever'. Why? Was it because we were afraid of what we would find? Afraid of the world treating us as it had treated those shell-shocked young men, those legless, armless heroes with disfigured, burnt, distorted faces, often with sightless eyes?

There was one man who, before the war, had been tall, good-looking, athletic and was also the owner of vast estates and possessor of one of the greatest titles in England. He contracted polio in the trenches. It would take him ten minutes on crutches to get from his car to a seat in a restaurant. But with enormous courage and determination he managed it.

We would lunch together and I knew without it ever being put into words that he wanted love and a woman to prove to

163

him that he was still a man. I couldn't help him, but a leading lady of the theatre with a beautiful face and a very beautiful body did. She made him very happy and I shall always salute her.

One really lovely girl from Vienna introduced a new note into C. B. Cochran's revue *This Year of Grace*. Instead of dancing quickly and vividly as we had expected, Tilly Losch moved slowly and gracefully like a figure from a stained-glass window to the 'Air on a G String' by Bach. Noël Coward, who had written the revue, was doubtful of this number's success. He begged 'Cockie', as everyone called him, even on the night of production, to take it out. For once in his life he was wrong. 'Gothic', the name of Tilly's dance, was one of the most popular turns in the revue.

Tilly and I travelled to Canada together during the war. There were submarines stalking us, the ship was overrun with children, there weren't enough lifeboats or lifebelts, it was very rough. Tilly lay in bed looking lovely, composed, mysterious, and ate caviar.

'It's so uncomfortable when a ship dances,' she said.

Tilly had green slanting eyes which gave her an entrancing sphinx-like enigmaticness. She hated black cats, but was herself cat-like in the way she disliked to feel she was being dominated or owned. She did not like people to sit too close to her, she loathed other people to listen to her conversation if she was concentrating on one person. She hated trams, motor-cars, taxis and aeroplanes! If she had to travel she liked big ships.

She adored the theatre, which was her love—her passion. She liked swing, Greta Garbo, films and eating. She had to diet, and would discuss it very seriously.

'The bread-and-butter diet—it is good?'

'The banana diet—every day bananas, bananas? Oh no!'

'The hay diet—protein one day, starch the next. I should forget!'

'Oh dear, I do so like my food!'

She craved for Neapolitan ices—one could buy them just outside the theatre; Indian Krapfen a special chocolate and whipped cream biscuit; stewed beef and horse-radish sauce.

' 'Fey are my ruin, I cannot resist 'fem!'

She could not pronounce 'th'.

Of course, like everyone in the theatre Tilly was superstitious. If she saw a chimney-sweep she had to hold a button of her dress until she saw a white horse—I always blow a kiss to the sweep. Tilly crossed her fingers if she met a cross-eyed man, and would always enter the theatre with her right foot forward.

I wrote a song which said:

> 'Don't trust luck—he's only a fantasy,
> Luck's a will-o'-the-wisp.
> Don't trust luck or life's a travesty,
> Built on an idle wish.'

But I didn't believe it!

Tilly married the Earl of Carnarvon—the popular 'Porchie', who had an unerring eye for a fast horse, a high pheasant and a pretty woman. The marriage failed and Tilly went to live in America. Here she not only danced but painted. At the first exhibition of her art, she said:

'I feel terrible, as if caught dancing across the stage naked.'

She had nightmares in which all her paintings turned into monsters and then came tumbling over her like a pack of cards.

A year or so ago I went to an exhibition of Oliver Messel's drawings and portraits in London. When I arrived he was talking, as I thought, to a little schoolgirl with a navy-blue beret on her red hair. It was Tilly!

'You have sold your soul to the devil!' I said accusingly. 'How could you look the same as you did forty years ago, in *This Year of Grace*?'

What a show that was! All London was singing:

> 'A Room with a View and you,
> And no one to worry us,
> And no one to hurry us through this
> dream we've found . . .
> We'll be as happy and contented as
> Birds upon a tree,
> High above the mountains and sea . . .'

Masie Gay had a very amusing song called 'Up, Girls, and at 'Em', about the women who were always trying to swim the Channel—the one thing in the twenties I never wanted to attempt.

165

Gertrude Ederle was the first woman to succeed in 1926. Her time, fourteen hours, thirty-nine minutes, was two hours faster than any man had swum it before.

Binnie Hale, always to be connected with *Tea For Two*, was a dear friend. She married a man called Rayne and had a daughter exactly the age of my Raine. We used to have tea parties when the children were small. I adored seeing her in *Sunny*, which ran at the Hippodrome for 363 nights. It was not surprising, as the music was by Jerome Kern.

With Binnie in this show was Jack Buchanan, who always in his top-hat and tails looked 'West End'. He was accepted both sides of the Atlantic as the 'Prince of Fashion'. He introduced the double-breasted suit and dinner-jacket, which caught on because the Prince of Wales adopted them.

Jack and I gave away the prizes at a 'Servants Ball' held at Harrods. I don't believe you could fill a ballroom with this elusive race today.

In 1921 Jack was in a revue called *A to Z* in which he sang 'And Her Mother Came Too'.

> 'My car will meet her,
> And her mother comes too.
> It's a two-seater,
> Still her mother comes too.
> At Ciro's when I am free,
> At dinner, supper or tea,
> She loves to shimmy with me,
> And her mother does too!'

It was a song which was rumoured to have been inspired by Elsie Janis's mother, who in real life was the exact prototype of a stage 'Mum'. Elsie Janis was a very successful American star who came to London to play the lead at the Palace—and her mother came too.

Elsie was the most brilliant mimic I've seen—so penetratingly accurate that Gaby Deslys left the theatre when Elsie took her off! Her props were very simple: a couple of hairpins with which she would pin back her hair. She didn't have to dress up—she *became* the person.

Elsie loved Basil Hallam, the original 'Gilbert the Filbert—

166

the Knut with the K'. He was the idol of the town, but was sent white feathers during the war so he joined the Balloon Regiment. He was killed when his parachute failed to open.

Elsie had a lovely voice. She and Basil sang:

'I'm here and you're here, so what do we care?'

The trouble was her mother was there as well!

Mrs. Bierbower was forceful, indomitable and overpowering. The words 'no' or 'impossible' did not exist as far as she was concerned. Nothing stopped her once she had made up her mind! People loathed her, feared her, avoided her. Elsie adored her.

There was a closeness between Elsie and her mother that people felt was almost frightening. Wherever Elsie might be, Mother knew what was happening to her, what she had done and what she had said. Mrs. Bierbower would praise or blame her about it immediately Elsie came into the room. No one told her—she knew!

But Elsie had a magic which drew celebrities of all walks of life to the suite which she and her mother filled with dogs, a coloured cook and a chauffeur who always drove on the right-hand side of the road as he did in America.

Many of the men I knew asked Elsie to dinner or supper with them, but invariably 'her mother came too'.

'I'll bet you a fiver I'll get her to come out alone!' some man would say.

'I'll take you but you'll lose your money,' was the invariable answer. He always did.

Elsie said her epitaph should be: 'Here lies Elsie Janis—still sleeping alone.'

Mrs. Bierbower had one weak spot—like so many Americans she loved a lord. When Lord Lonsdale, the great sporting personality with his yellow buttonhole, yellow Rolls and yellow-liveried servants, dined with her, she was so impressed that she said to her butler:

'John—fetch a seventy-five-cent Corona for the noble lord.'

A to Z gave Gertie Lawrence her first leading part. She conquered London and the show ran for 433 performances. Part of the music was by the best-looking actor on the stage—Ivor Novello, known at the very beginning of the twenties only for his wartime marching song—'Keep the Home Fires Burning'.

Everyone who worked with Ivor loved him. He and Noël Coward were the kindest authors, actors, producers and managers there have ever been. They would write in a part for an ageing out-of-work actress; they would 'carry' a number of decrepit old actors in every show. How much they gave away in loans and presents to the hard-luckers is incalculable.

I did not meet Noël until 1923 when we bickered at Deauville because we both hated the party we were in. I was furious when he called me 'Queen Gloom', but we made up. This was just before *The Vortex* took London by storm. I had now grown more sophisticated, but even so Noël astonished us with the idea that dope-taking wasn't confined to cloakrooms of low night-clubs like the '43'. Decent people, even someone's mother, might take it!

I remember sitting stunned as the curtain fell, and then noticing as Noël took his curtain-calls that his wrist was covered in blood. Apparently when he swept the bottles and pots of cosmetics off his mother's dressing-table in a grand gesture he had cut a vein.

'I bound it up with my handkerchief,' he said later, 'but it bled effectively throughout my author's speech!'

How little I realised as we trailed round Deauville with the rich and the famous, all attempting to create new and complicated patterns of adultery, that Noël was to be 'The Master' of the modern theatre.

'I felt that I was seeing a side of life,' he wrote later, 'which should by rights be glamorous to eyes unfamiliar with it; all the correct adjuncts were there: champagne, beautifully gowned women, high-powered gambling, obsequious *maîtres d'hôtel*, moonlit terraces—a perfectly arranged production with all the parts well cast according to type. I think, perhaps, that there must have been something wrong with the dialogue. The author must have had a common mind because soon I became bored and wanted to go home.'

I went home! I think now, looking back, we were, Noël and I, both too young!

In those days Deauville consisted of two luxury hotels, the Casino, the *plage fleure*, the Bar de Soleil, Ciros, a few luxury shops, the post office, the police station and many large, expensive villas. And how smart it was!

There was the Aga Khan—plump, dark-complexioned and black-spectacled, who won the Derby five times, and was 'God on Earth to millions of his followers'. He stayed with Teresa Magliano, the mother of Aly Khan, for three weeks every year at the Villa Corizia, and married her in 1923 at a secret Moslem ceremony in Bombay. Aly was twelve years old.

I saw the tall, astigmatic King of Sweden, who spluttered and dribbled so much when he spoke that Elsa Maxwell used to warn her guests to wear raincoats if he accepted an invitation to one of her parties.

King Gustav was an indefatigable tennis player and had a reverence for top players. Once when Suzanne Lenglen and Henri Cochet were late for lunch he insisted on waiting for them, saying:

'There are many kings and emperors, but there is only one Lenglen and one Cochet. I can wait. They are the aristocrats and I am the commoner today.'

I felt in the Casino that watching these gay, colourful, bejewelled throng round the green baize tables was the ghost of the fabulous Gaby Deslys. With her fair fluffy hair, tip-tilted nose and big wistful eyes, she personified to me and to many of my generation everything that was romantic and glamorous.

While I was growing up I had searched the magazines for pictures of Gabys wearing fantastic jewels, low-cut gowns and enormous hats of costly ospreys and birds of paradise—the forerunners of those worn by Mistinguett in the Folies Bergères.

Gaby was a success in the Parisian 'cocottes' of the nineties, and the originator of the theatrical trend towards glamour which reached its fulfilment twenty years later in the person of Marlene Dietrich.

Gaby was quite open about her life. When questioned about priceless jewels given her by infatuated lovers, she said:

'Money is woman's only bulwark against the world. I give nothing back!'

She always wore long ropes of pearls hanging nearly to her knees. These were the cause of riots in Portugal among the peasants after Gaby announced that they had been given her by the very young King Manoel. He was then forced to abdicate.

Years later Gaby admitted the pearls had really been a gift from a rich Argentinian and she had involved the King merely for publicity. But when Gaby went to Lisbon she was nearly lynched and escaped only under police protection.

I saw King Manoel with his habitual long cigarette holder gambling at Deauville. He had only reigned for two years then came to live in England. He was philosophical about his exile.

'I have outlived any resentment at being deposed,' he said. 'I enjoy the life of an English gentleman and would be reluctant to exchange my present surroundings for the turmoil of state-craft.'

King Manoel enjoyed England as had Gaby Deslys. She had a house in Kensington Gate, where the rent was paid by Gordon Selfridge. She was the first woman I ever heard of to have roses tattooed on her breasts. Although I never saw her, when she died I felt that the world was less colourful without her. Perhaps subconsciously my passion for beautiful hats emanated from her.

Another king at Deauville was King Alfonso of Spain, tall, dark, handsome, gay and indescribably fascinating—like a king in a musical comedy. He once told me he was offered a pound a word for anything he cared to write for a newspaper.

'I refused,' he said. 'Even if I am deposed, I have to behave like a king.'

He used to drive himself at Deauville in an Hispano Suiza at eighty miles an hour and was always on show on the polo ground where he rode and played magnificently. His team nearly always won because he had brilliant players in it, like Lord Rocksavage.

One of his favourite stories, which he told me himself, was when he visited the vineyards of the Marquis de Lur Saluces.

'Is it true,' he asked, 'that to make your Château d'Yquem the peasants no longer trample the grapes with their feet?'

'Yes, sir,' the Marquis replied, 'it is true.'

'Alas,' King Alfonso sighed, 'I thought your wine had recently lost some of its flavour!'

The decade 1919–29 was known as the 'La Belle Epoque'. It was a period of wild extravagance, especially at Deauville. In 1922 the Great Syndicate had come into being, and Nicolas Zographos had announced 'Tout Va', meaning that the Syndicate would cover any bet, however large.

Previously, the bank was put up to auction to the highest offer, the most persistent of those competing for this being Gordon Selfridge; André Citroën, whose biggest publicity stunt for his motor-cars was to light up the Eiffel Tower with electric serpents and thirty-six cascades of lights, and James Hennessy, the Brandy King, a white-moustached, spry, little man who won the Grand National with Lutteur III in 1909, and £20,000 from Zographos in 1922.

Zographos, whom I met, looked rather like a Greek Charlie Chaplin, had charming manners, and a phenomenal memory for cards. He had a strange habit of polishing his Rolls-Royce every day, drank only orange juice and when he died left £5,000,000. No gambler before or after him has left such a vast fortune acquired entirely from baccarat.

Of course, I was also introduced to François André, the former undertaker's assistant who was the uncrowned King of Deauville and who run it shrewdly, brilliantly and profitably. He always carried an umbrella.

'Nothing is good that isn't expensive,' André would frequently say. 'I don't want anyone to sneeze without it costing at least a hundred sous.'

Deauville made nothing out of me. Noël gave me a few francs and I won at the Casino. I collected the money, hoarded it like a squirrel and didn't play any more!

I think the play which impressed me most in 1920 was *The Garden of Allah* at Drury Lane. It was the first spectacular melodrama I had ever seen. It was the story of a Trappist monk who broke his vows, came back to the world, fell in love with a divorced woman, married her, then felt God was stronger than earthly love and returned to his monastery.

Godfrey Tearle, tall, commanding and extremely good-looking, was magnificent as the monk, while the settings had everything—Arabs, Moors, dancing-girls, donkeys, horses, dogs, sheep and real camels. There was even a baby camel which gambolled about and became a great favourite.

The *pièce de résistance* of the show was a sandstorm—the wind howled and the whole desert seemed to sweep over the encampment, there were pillars of sand like Dancing Dervishes, the roar of the storm, and then, as quickly as it had risen, it subsided and dawn came serene, clear and peaceful.

It was a triumph of stage effect, but I was there on the first night and when the sandstorm began I found myself covered with a yellow film which tasted like biscuit. When the scene ended, the applause and cheers nearly took the roof off and there were nineteen curtain-calls. But the young man I was with exclaimed:

'Good Lord! You're Chinese!'

'So are you!'

'By Jove, so is everybody!'

The first twelve rows of the stalls were covered in the pease-meal which had been used as sand! It had surged over the foot-lights as the gauze curtain which was supposed to protect the audience had by mistake not been let down. We laughed, but it took ages to wash my face and brush all the yellow out of my hair before I could go on to a night-club.

Godfrey Tearle told Ethel Mannin—a clever author and a friend of my brother Ronald—that he missed a lot of fun in life because of his handsome-hero-clean-English-manhood appearance.

'Everyone thinks I'm so nice,' he sighed.

He was indeed nice and he had a directness and simplicity which made women not only swoon over him but want to cosset him as well. He took his acting very seriously, and with reason; for he was the outstanding actor of the twenties.

His father was an actor-manager and as a child Godfrey accompanied his father, mother and their company wherever they went. He loved theatre, thought theatre and talked theatre. He was nine when he had his first part in *Richard III*. When finally he became a leading man (the word 'star' hadn't yet come into fashion), his looks, his height, his charm, and his great silver-toned voice, packed every theatre in which he appeared.

I was at a theatre party when a stage-struck friend of mine said gushingly to him:

'Oh, Mr. Tearle, you were simply marvellous tonight! Who can teach me to act like you?'

'Acting cannot be taught,' he answered gravely. 'It can only be learnt and the best way to learn it is on a stage facing an audience. It also has to be felt. One must *be* the part.'

Later he grew lazy. He 'acted' instead of 'being' his parts. He was still magnificent, he still played with genius, but the fire within him was a little dimmed. Yet when he died one of the more brilliant lights of the theatre went out.

The Garden of Allah was written by Robert Hichens. I loved his exciting and colourful but rather long-winded books. I can never think of him without remembering an extraordinary curse in which he was involved.

An English Peer was visiting North Africa with some friends. Robert Hichens showed them the sights, one of them being an ancient mosque. As usual the doorkeeper asked them respectfully to remove their shoes, but the English Peer strode past him. Inside the mosque, where the faithful were at prayer, a priest with a long beard and the high black hat of Islam stopped the Englishman and spoke to him in Arabic.

'I can't understand a word you say,' the English Peer ejaculated, and pushed him aside.

'He wants you to remove your shoes,' someone explained.

'A lot of nonsense! I'll do nothing of the sort,' the English Peer retorted. He looked round the mosque and left.

The party returned to a restaurant and sat outside drinking. While they did so the English Peer looked across the street.

'Why, there's the old josser who spoke to me in the mosque!' he exclaimed. 'He obviously doesn't like me! If looks could kill . . .'

'Be careful he hasn't a knife,' someone laughed.

Robert Hichens held up his hand.

'Don't,' he begged, 'don't laugh! It's not funny, the priest is putting a curse on you. It's a terrible one—I know of it.'

'Good Lord! I don't believe that superstitious nonsense!'

The English Peer returned home. The first thing that happened was that his eldest son, a little boy of seven, was walking along the pavement with his nannie when he ran into the road and was killed instantly by a lorry. The next he heard was that his wife, whom he loved, had been killed in an aeroplane crash. The third, that a very dear friend had died in Paris.

The English Peer could not help connecting these overwhelming tragedies with the curse. He wrote to Robert Hichens, who by now was at his villa in the South of France, asking his help.

Robert Hichens crossed the Mediterranean and sought out the priest with the long beard. He begged him to take off the curse, offering, on the English Peer's instructions, any money he required to do so.

The priest shook his head.

'The curse must wear itself out!' was his reply.

Mary Rose, produced in 1920, moved me tremendously. It was my 'search for the miraculous'. Everyone who saw this Sir J. M. Barrie's masterpiece found it a play of magical beauty which they could never forget.

'You have given us glimpses into the mysteries of life, and death, and time that have sent us away strangely taken, almost beside ourselves.'

That was written by the hard-boiled critic of *The Times*.

It was the story of a young woman, happily married, who hears voices calling her to a forbidden island. Finally she listens to the voices and visits the island, as she thinks for the day. She is away, in fact, for thirty years and returns to find everyone she knew dead or old, while she is still radiantly young.

It seemed so real, so possible that Fay Compton, exquisitely beautiful, could disappear and come back unchanged and unaltered, since time for her had stood still.

I told Fay Compton this and she answered:

'I feel like that, too. Sometimes, when I come on the stage in the third act, I feel I really have been away.'

It was that which made it so real.

I tried to write a play for Fay Compton rather on the same lines as *Mary Rose*. Fay was very sweet and encouraging, but alas I was no J. M. Barrie and I couldn't get my third act right.

Mary Rose was to be linked in my mind later with *An Experiment with Time*. This was written by J. W. Dunne, who had designed the first British military aeroplane in 1906. He now tried to invent a method of demonstrating that time was only relative through recording one's dreams. He proved quite simply that when we are asleep we are released from the imprisonment of the Third Dimension and see in our dreams images from the past, the present and the future.

Ronald and I experimented as Dunne directed, and one night I dreamt of Anne Boleyn, Mary Cunningham-Reid and a film camera. The next morning I had a letter from Mary, I opened the newspaper to see Merle Oberon had agreed to play Anne Boleyn in a film, and when I went outside I saw a film unit taking a shot in the street.

Another play which had an esoteric meaning for me was *Hassan* by James Elroy Flecker, produced with music by Delius in 1923. It was a blend of beauty, poetry, music, colour, drama and tragedy. It was the story of a man with poetry in his soul—a confectioner in Arabia who fell in love and sought his ideal only to find he had lost all he had . . . and then he started all over again.

Watching we all felt we were pilgrims—reciting Flecker's wonderful words:

'We are the Pilgrims, master; we shall go
Always a little further: it may be
Beyond that last blue mountain barred with snow,
Across that angry or that glimmering sea.'

Henry Ainley played Hassan. He had a golden voice which made one vibrate to the sound. I came out of the theatre feeling I had passed through a deep emotional experience. Flecker had died in 1915. Why are there no plays to make one feel like that today?

Right down the ages in every country the theatre has always educated the public. It is the theatre that has opened to its audience the doors of beauty, of drama, of knowledge of themselves. That is why the theatre is so important. Perhaps I am old-fashioned, but I shall never feel that the cinema can have the same impact. I can be moved by a great film, but it never establishes the same contact with me as a performance with the human touch of living and breathing actors.

I had seen very few plays before I came to London in 1919. One—called *Mr. Wu*—I had seen by mistake, when my governess took me to what she believed was a musical comedy. I can remember her embarrassment and also my bewilderment! I couldn't understand what *Mr. Wu*—Matheson Lang as the big Chinaman—wanted to do to a white woman!

But the theatre has had a glamour and glitter in England since the days that Will Shakespeare wrote plays which became perhaps our greatest heritage. I believe that the theatre has a tremendous influence on its patrons; the plays they see remain in the mind, they make people think, they should inspire and help.

Hassan remained in my mind. It was not only its beauty that I remembered, but it first gave me the urge to go out and explore the world. I love the East, it is now a part of me; and I think the idea of what it could mean to those who love it was born that night when I sat watching one of the most beautiful plays that have ever been put on the stage. There are some lines that have always remained with me:

'When the wind beneath the moon
    is drifting like a soul aswoon,
And harping planets talk love's
    tune with milky wings outspread, Yasmin.

Shower down thy love, O burning bright!
    For one night or the other night,
Will come the Gardener in white, and
    gathered flowers are dead, Yasmin.'

It is difficult for people today to realise the excitement and elegance of the theatre in the early twenties. All the women wore their best evening dresses, all the men in the stalls wore tails and a white tie.

On arrival at the theatre, I generally found I knew so many people that it was almost like a big party. I waved to my friends, and sometimes if somebody important came in, especially an actor, the people in the pit at the back of the stalls would burst into applause. The celebrity would bow, everyone would stare, and it was all very exciting and raised the tempo.

My escort would buy two programmes, but not chocolates— it was not the smart thing to eat in the stalls, although occasionally ladies indulged themselves at matinées. These were very well attended, for most women had nothing to do in the afternoons.

Of course, one was not offered ice-creams. It was not until 1922 that J. Lyons introduced the ice-cream brick to England and installed a plant capable of producing 400 gallons an hour.

But in the afternoon there was tea, served on a tray with milk, sugar, biscuits and a slice of fruit cake, and in the evenings the bar was well patronised in the interval by the men, many of them ordering champagne. There was nothing so vulgar to be had as beer. Ladies did not leave their seats.

The lights would go down and we would settle ourselves with a little sigh of anticipation. The stalls were a kaleidoscope of colour, glittering jewels and expensive furs. The boxes would be full. Sometimes an elderly woman would wear a tiara to match her diamond necklace or bracelets on her wrists worn over her long, white kid gloves.

176

The younger generation had given up gloves. It was considered very daring that a man should not wear them, and could put his hand on your bare back if you were fast enough to wear a backless dress!

The conductor would stand up in the limelight to receive a round of applause. Then he would tap the music-rest with his baton and the music would start. There was no 'potted' music in those days, even for straight plays, but a full orchestra, consisting of men who had played in the same theatre for years and years, and considered themselves part of the show. They also, of course, wore evening dress.

It is hard to put into words the thrill I experienced as the curtain rose. Nowadays children see plays on television almost before they can sit up. They are used to actors, they are used to 'make-believe'. I had to make my own. When I saw 'make-believe' in front of my eyes, the illusion and the wonder of the theatre were breathtaking.

In 1920 there was a great deal of talk about the dancing craze being a threat to the theatre. The theatre adjusted itself, as it has done down the centuries, and before long jazz bands were a top-line attraction. People flocked to see them in the theatre, and to hear them play the tunes they had already got to know and like on gramophone records.

But the most serious menace to the theatre came in 1922, when the British Broadcasting Corporation came into being.

'It won't last,' the theatrical managers said. 'You'll see, it will only be a flash in the pan. People will soon get tired of sitting at home crouching over their sets, and listening to something they can't see.'

But for some people who didn't want to go out, who couldn't afford the theatre, or were not living in a city, the radio seemed a miracle. Tens of thousands began to listen in and find it an all-absorbing hobby. What is more, the British Broadcasting Corporation began to make its own dramatic stars. At first they were not performers so much as announcers—the voice was very important. Elocution teachers found themselves flooded with new clients.

This new force made the footlights flicker, and more and more of the theatrical profession began to go on the air. One of the first was George Robey, the beloved comedian who was the last person to make men laugh before they went out to Flanders, and who set the whole world whistling his duet with Violet Lorraine —'If you were the only girl in the world'.

Radio moved swiftly. The Marconi Company put a crystal set de-luxe on the market, and 'listening' stopped being a craze and became a necessity. Listening to broadcastings became part of everyone's life. The theatre did not at first realise it, but this was the most serious menace it had ever faced, far worse than the cinema, of which it had been afraid earlier. This was progress, this was something which was going to close many theatres in the future, if not quite yet.

A play which also affected me, but in a different way from *Hassan*, was *The Constant Nymph* with Edna Best as the girl who dies after she runs away with Noël Coward, as the young husband unhappily married.

'Edna was instinct,' Herbert Farjeon said, 'with the dogged, passionate faith of youthful love.'

It was a very moving show marvellously acted and produced by the hardest taskmaster in the theatre, Basil Dean. He made it the most discussed play for the two years it ran to a packed theatre.

But while Noël was uncannily well cast as a musical genius, he hated the part, and after a month John Gielgud, who had understudied him in *The Vortex*, took over.

Lord Birkenhead asked me to go with him to a dinner which was being given for the author of *The Constant Nymph*, Miss Margaret Kennedy.

'You write, too,' he said, 'you had better come along with me and see I do it right.'

Proudly I accompanied the greatest orator of the day to the dinner. He told me that he had had a long and tiring session in the House of Lords, and he drained a large glass of brandy before we set off. From a seat in the centre of the hall I watched Lord Birkenhead at the top table and thought nervously that he seemed sleepy and uncommunicative. Finally he rose to speak. He made a clear, concise, brilliant and very flattering oration. Unfortunately he made it about H. G. Wells and never even mentioned Margaret Kennedy!

I cried all through *The Constant Nymph*, just as I cried through most of *Cavalcade*, the most unforgettable spectacular I have ever

178

seen. Sir Patrick Hastings, the toughest barrister of the period to be up against, cried too, although he was furious with us for referring to it afterwards.

I suppose the most exciting actress of the twenties was Tallulah Bankhead. I met her almost as soon as she arrived in London to star in *The Dancers*. She was red-headed, with a smouldering, pouting face. But much more than that, she had a vibrant personality and a strangely arresting voice like hot honey and milk.

She startled all London in 1923. She was 'news' and everyone talked about her. Her entrance into a restaurant was sensational. Old gentlemen told me with shaking voices there had been nothing like it since Lily Langtry.

'Dah-ling,' she said to me. 'I hear you write plays—write me a really goddamn wicked one.'

This was not in keeping with her father's idea of Tallulah. I sat next to Senator Bankhead—a white-haired country gentleman of the old school—at a dinner party at the Savoy.

'How pretty your daughter is,' I remarked.

'Tallulah is just a sweet pretty gurrl,' he replied. 'She has high spirits, but there's no harm in that.'

Other people were more critical. Hannen Swaffer wrote:

'London would be very dull without Tallulah, especially now Mrs. Meyrick has gone to gaol. We should not have anything to talk about.'

Tallulah described herself as 'Pure as the driven slush', but Cecil Beaton had other ideas, and said:

'She is Medusa, very exotic, with a glorious skull, high pumice-stone cheekbones, and a broad brow.'

Tallulah was not only talked about; she was the rage. People abused her, protested against her; but she was electric, compelling, magnetic. When she arrived at a party everyone woke up and it became a noisy success.

She was always unpredictable. She and Sir Patrick Hastings, who had written a play in which she played the lead, were walking to the theatre after lunching at 'The Ivy', when a small street-urchin sidled up to them and said:

'Stand on me head for sixpence.'

'I stand on mine for threepence,' Tallulah retorted.

She did! It was lucky that there wasn't much traffic about at the time.

Tallulah was the first person I knew to have fans who screamed as they do today for the pop stars. What was so extraordinary was that they were mostly women. She produced a female mob hysteria which had not been seen before in England.

It was to be repeated and exceeded when film stars started coming to London. Mary Pickford, Ronald Colman, Greta Garbo and Harold Lloyd became household names, but, of course, the heart-throb of the period was Rudolf Valentino.

Rudolf Valentino is still spoken of as the greatest screen lover of the generation, but not everyone swooned at his appearance. Eddie Marsh, patron and helper of many authors and playwrights of the people, wrote to Ivor Novello:

'I lunched with Lady Birkenhead today and met—whom do you think?—Rudolf Valentino. He really is a bit of a shock—just a dago waiter with brown skin and octoroon hair. Upon my word, I thought him the ugliest man at the table—the others being the Duke of Sutherland and myself. I didn't talk to him—he seemed quite pleasant and unassuming, but without a particle of charm.'

No one has ever received such adulation from women. He was everything they longed for and dreamt about in a lover. When he appeared in *The Sheik*, by E. M. Hull, he made thrills run through the female audience like electric sparks. I had already read the book over and over again, and of course I quivered to:

'Her body was aching with the grip of his powerful arms, her mouth was bruised by his savage kisses. She clenched her hands in anguish. "Oh God," she sobbed, with scalding tears that scorched her cheeks. "Curse him! Curse him!" And with the words on her lips he came, silent, noiseless, to her side. With his hands on her shoulders he forced her to her bed. His eyes were fierce, his stern mouth parted in a cruel smile, his deep, slow voice half angry, half impatiently amused.

' "Must I be a valet as well as lover?" he asked.'

It may sound strange, but I think of Alice Delysia, the French star of so many Cochran shows in the twenties, almost every night. She said to me once in her fascinating broken English:

'Never forget, Barbara, when you go to sleep to keep your

hands open, your fingers out. If you clench your hands, then they will age much quicker.'

So I remember Delysia and stretch out my fingers. I can see her at the London Pavilion wearing nothing but diamonds. That was the impression her emboidered sheath gave and very dashing it was in those modest days when a naked tummy would have brought in the Watch Committee.

Delysia was a superb cook, she would walk in the rain, darn Norman Hartnell's socks and look seductive, entrancing and very 'naughty' in the first solid sequin dress he ever designed. Only a Frenchwoman could have been so versatile.

When I had supper with Delysia once at the Savoy, her favourite dishes had all been ordered—eel soup, pig's trotters and black pudding. I didn't seem very hungry that evening!

Delysia was Charles Cochran's favourite leading lady and that was a compliment beyond price from the world's Greatest Showman.

After I had produced at the Albert Hall in 1930 a really big pageant—'Britain and Her Industries'—I felt as if I had received a million-pound prize when Cockie said to me:

'You've given us a magnificent show, Miss Cartland. I want it to be the finale for the midnight matinée at the London Pavilion.'

My dress, representing the White Star Line, was a colossal canvas hoop holding a replica of a lighted ship and three other girls! The stage of the London Pavilion is tiny!

I wriggled through the wings in bits and pieces followed by the rest of my pageant all in enormous dresses specially designed so as not to be dwarfed in the Albert Hall! The Prince of Wales literally had to step over us and squeeze himself to the front to make an appeal for the Charity.

It was not money which interested C. B. Cochran, but the ideal of providing the best possible entertainment for the public. He gave us the scintillating spectacular musicals of the twenties which kept us dancing and singing. There was *London, Paris and New York*, with Nelson Keys as the star; *The League of Notions*, with the 'Dollies and their Collies'; *The Fun of the Fayre*, with lovely Evelyn Laye; *Mayfair and Montmartre*, which was withdrawn after Delysia lost her voice and other losses were £20,000; *On with the Dance*, the hit being Noël Coward's 'Poor Little Rich Girl'; *One Damned Thing After Another*, with Jessie Matthews,

Sonny Hale and Edythe Baker with her vast white piano; *This Year of Grace*, which will always be remembered for Noël's:

> 'Dance, dance, dance, little lady!
> Youth is fleeting—to the rhythm beating
> In your mind.
> Dance, dance, dance, little lady,
> So obsessed with second best,
> No rest you'll ever find.'

Cockie brought us Dusé, Sarah Bernhardt, Georges Carpentier, Florence Mills, the Russian Ballet, Beatrice Lillie, the Lunts, Spinelli, the Wembley Rodeo and *The Miracle*.

He was bland, smiling, with an easy, almost lazy manner. He never swore, never backed horses and lost his temper only twice in his life. The last verse of A. P. Herbert's tribute on his fiftieth year in the theatre went:

> 'To men like you we pay no living wage,
> And all their work is swept away like snow.
> Yet you have left your footprints on the stage;
> The world is richer for the "Cochran Show".'

CHAPTER SEVEN

Bright young people
Making the most of our youth,
They speak in the Press
Of our social success,
But quite the reverse is the truth.
Psychology experts we often perplex,
And doctors have warned us we'll
end up as wrecks.
They take a degree if they find out our sex!
What could be duller than that?

NOËL COWARD

THE newspapers had used up almost every adjective in describing the modern young woman.

'She is a vapid pleasure-loving nymph,' a novelist called Winifred Graham said. 'There is no comparison between these travesties of womanhood, painted and dyed and awaiting their cocktails, and their mothers.'

We were reported as being 'vulgar, absurd, improper, fast, over-sexed, abominable, shaming, humiliating'.

Someone more kind did refer to us as 'such enchanting, sexless, bosomless, hipless, thighless creatures'.

'As flat as a herring-bone!' Yvonne Arnaud said firmly. But she was always round and cuddly, so it may have been jealousy!

The *Daily Express*, in an attack on the modern girl's brother, referred to him as 'weary, anaemic, feminine, bloodless'; 'dolled up like a girl'; 'and exquisite without masculinity'. They would never fight—their fathers had died for a degenerate offspring.

But apart from making us more defiant, we didn't worry very much about what was being said about us. We were all too busy, dancing and enjoying ourselves. Life was fun and life was amusing, and if we did read the newspapers—which wasn't often—we weren't really perturbed at what we saw written about us, because we had heard it all too often at home and from our relations.

Then the young really gave the newspapers something to write about, when the Bright Young People came into being. It started in a very modest way, as such movements always do. Lady Eleanor Smith, who was the clever attractive daughter of Lord Birkenhead, and the Yungman sisters, who were the daughters of a very well-known London hostess, Mrs. Richard Guinness, devised a series of hoaxes which they played on their friends, and which they found exquisitely amusing.

Eleanor masqueraded as a Russian princess, and deceived a rather pompous young man with long stories of her adventures. She spoke broken English, she fluttered her mascaraed eyelashes at him, and her tales became more and more dramatic.

Finally the young man became suspicious. He rang Eleanor up.

'I think you're making a fool of me,' he said accusingly.

'I can't think what you mean,' Eleanor replied.

'I don't believe in that Princess friend of yours,' he declared. 'I think she's a hoax, in fact I have a suspicion it's you?'

Eleanor laughed.

'How can you say such things,' she replied. 'But I'll tell you what we'll do. The Princess is going to a dance tonight, I expect you're going too. Look out for her, I'll be along later, and then you can see if I am she or she is me.'

The young man, rather bewildered, did as he was told and went to the dance. When the Princess arrived he saw the Yungman sisters curtsying, and several young men he knew bowing over her hand. He was immediately ashamed of his suspicions of Eleanor, and going up to the Princess he also bowed low and raised her hand to his lips. There was a shriek of laughter, and Eleanor took off her wig!

The story was repeated all over London. Everybody thought it very amusing, except, of course, the young man in question.

The next exploit was more adventurous. The first abstract paintings were beginning to be noticed in London. Edward Molyneux, the dress designer, was busy buying them both in London and in France. He made a huge collection, few of them costing over twenty pounds, which he sold later for over a million. It is a pity we also didn't have the sense to stop laughing at abstract paintings and start collecting them. But we thought them quite ridiculous.

'Just dabs and blobs!' we cried. 'Who would look at things like that!'

Brian Howard had a brilliant idea. He painted a number of pictures in imitation of the more advanced abstract school. He had them framed with rope and gave them pretentious titles, like 'The Adoration of the Magi'—a picture of many cubes, lines and splodges—'Leda and the Swan', which looked as if he had upset the paint pot, while 'The Portrait of my Brother' was very lurid.

When he had produced quite a number of these, invitations were sent out to 'the first Exhibition of Pictures by Bruno Hat, in Mr. and Mrs. Bryan Guinness's house'. There was an accompanying biography, saying that Mr. Bruno Hat had come to England with his father in 1919 from Lübeck. It was explained that a month previously a number of examples of his work had been shown in Paris, and the opinion there was so favourable that immediate arrangements had been made for a large exhibition in the early winter.

Everyone who received an invitation trooped to the Guinnesses'. No one had the least suspicion that it was anything but a genuine exhibition of modern art.

A girl with the catalogues and prices sat at a table. Mr. Bruno Hat himself sat in a wheelchair. He wore dark glasses, a drooping moustache, and the sort of dark clothes which a penniless German artist might easily wear if he had to put on his Sunday best for such an important occasion.

Everyone else looked very smart, and we walked round staring at the pictures and trying to pretend we understood what they were about.

'This is really a new approach to art,' someone said to me. 'You've got to empty your mind of all the former conceptions which are now out of date, and let this seep gently into your consciousness.'

I tried to pretend I understood what I was being told, when a large, rather bossy woman walked up to Mr. Bruno Hat and spoke to him in German. He made some strange sounds, and one of the

Guinness girls hurried forward to explain that Mr. Hat could speak only a strange dialect of his native language.

It was not until the next day that the hoax was exploded, and then, naturally, everyone pretended they had guessed it all the time. But I was there, and I am positive that no one had the slightest idea that our legs were being pulled. It was very cleverly done and all very harmless.

Another joke was for Eleanor, Teresa—who was always called Baby—and Zita to dress up as press reporters and visit film stars as representatives of non-existent newspapers. They were never exposed, and the film stars had no idea they were wasting their time.

Then Zita, Eleanor and Loelia Ponsonby, and a number of other girls, invented a new sort of paper-chase, which we had all played as children. The two chosen as hares had five minutes' start and they rushed all over London using buses and the Underground and leaving clues behind them in as many places of public interest as possible.

It was such fun that the men wanted to join in and that meant the chases had to be held in the evening. The men suggested bringing their cars and that was how the treasure hunts began.

Nineteen-twenty-four was Wembley year, and someone had the bright idea of a treasure hunt over that gigantic stadium. It rained, so I didn't go. But the general idea caught on, and soon motor-cars were rushing all over London filled with young people hunting for hidden treasure.

At one hunt I remember there were fifty cars and we all assembled on the Horse Guards Parade and then went racing down the roads, juggling and jostling for position. So it was very lucky it was 2 a.m. and that there was practically no traffic.

Cries of 'Tally Ho!', 'Gone Away!' and shrieks of laughter woke more respectable householders. Most of the cars were open, so the girls' hair got blown about. As the men drove they often stood up to wave and shout at their friends. By the time we had crawled about on a pavement near Seven Dials for a clue, our dresses were pretty dirty and some even managed to get them torn. It was a blessing there were no photographers! The last clue was at Norfolk House, St. James's, where there was breakfast and a dance band. It was all madly gay and we danced until breakfast-time.

Loelia Ponsonby, whose father was Head of the Royal House-hold, was on the treasure hunt which sent the competitors to Buckingham Palace.

'We bore down on the sleeping palace with screeching tyres,' she relates,[1] 'jumped out of our cars and rushed up and down the railings, looking for the clue in the sentry boxes and shouting and screaming while every moment more cars kept arriving.

'Next day,' she continues, 'my father came home with a story of the extraordinary things that had happened at Buckingham Palace the night before, how swarms of lunatics had tried to break in, the Captain of the Guard had turned out every available man and telephoned for reinforcements, when suddenly the whole crowd had disappeared as mysteriously as they had arrived. My father laid on the agony, tremendously amused to be in the secret, and I was able to fill in the gaps and tell him that the reason for our sudden departure was that we had found, at the foot of the memorial to Queen Victoria, the next clue: a bunch of white roses with a card, "All good Cavaliers will know where this should be laid", which had sent us helter-skelter down the Mall to Whitehall.'

Loelia had a magnolia complexion and a raven's wing shingle. She was intelligent, introspective and sensitive. The last man she should have married was the spoilt, autocratic Duke of West-minster, with his inhibitions and hatred of conventional people. But Loelia said:

'I fell more and more in love with this—to me—godlike figure.'

The marriage electrified Mayfair.

'That nice girl! He's old enough to be her father and has been married twice already!

'He wanted to marry Coco Chanel.'

'He was infatuated with Gertie Millar.'

'He believes a pure young girl is his only chance of having a son.'

Colourful and exciting, everything about the Duke was big, including his vices and virtues. He was called 'Bend Or' by all his friends after his grandfather's Derby winner in 1879. He bought an aeroplane in 1909 and hunted boars at Mimizan in France. In 1912 he was fined for driving a motor-car at nineteen miles an hour!

[1] *Grace and Favour*, by Loelia Duchess of Westminster.

At the outbreak of the war he went out to France with a Hotchkiss machine-gun mounted in his Rolls-Royce, and fought the Germans almost single-handed. In 1915 he raised and armed his own armoured-car squadron which he took to Egypt to fight against the Senussi in the desert. During this successful engagement he rescued sixty starving British merchantmen and won the D.S.O.

'He would have received the V.C.,' a general once told me, 'if there had been a senior officer present to report on his gallantry.'

The Duke held the record at Monte Carlo for winning the maximum on black twenty-three times consecutively. He owned two famous yachts, *The Cutty Sark* and *The Flying Cloud*; introduced afforestation in Cheshire, the Lake District and Scotland; hired special trains, one with a baggage wagon for his pack of foxhounds; and pulled down Grosvenor House in Park Lane to make way for the Grosvenor House Hotel!

Of course he was a 'godlike figure'!

Clues for the treasure hunts got more and more complicated. Lord Beaverbrook even printed fake copies of the *Evening Standard* with a clue hidden in the imaginary news. At the Hovis Bread factory on the Embankment the seekers were given a loaf of brown bread with the clue baked in the middle. By now the *Daily Mail* was also on the trail:

'CHASING CLUES—NEW SOCIETY GAME
Midnight Chase in London
50 Motor Cars
THE BRIGHT YOUNG PEOPLE'

Everyone paid ten shillings into a pool which furnished the prize for the successful pair. This meant that sometimes the sum to be won was nearly £100, and there was not only a lot of tense competition but a lot of cheating.

I was sitting in the Berkeley Restaurant with a young man one evening, and one of the Bright Young People came in with her escort and sat down at our table.

'I'm exhausted,' she gasped. 'We're on a scavenger party and we've been given the most impossible things to collect: a policeman's helmet—and if we take that we're sure to be arrested! A red hair from an actress—the only one I can think of is Fay Compton, and I'm much too frightened to ask her. And a pipe that has been smoked by Stanley Baldwin! We knocked on the' door of No. 10 and the policeman was very rude, so we just gave up.'

'Scavenger parties' became the vogue, but it meant we made more of a nuisance of ourselves rather than just being noisy. On one 'scavenger' I started off well. I was driven by a young man who was good at problem questions. I was hopeless at them as I'm hopeless today on TV quiz games.

The first object we collected was the cap of the commissionaire at the Ritz; the next a name-plate from one of the embassies; then we searched a mews for a horse's bridle. We searched and searched but we couldn't find one. So we started to talk, and found that we were so much more interesting than the scavenger hunt. I never did know who won!

The Bright Young People never formed one exclusive group. Brian Howard, who had a strong influence on his set, was described by Daphne Weymouth 'as a sinister impresario: with epigrams cracking from his lips and dark eyebrows raised he looked mockingly down his nose at his protégés dancing like puppets as he pulled the strings'.

Brian's coterie at Oxford was known as 'The Hearts'. His friends included Evelyn Waugh who was to be famous as a satirist, John Sutro, Henry Weymouth,[1] who married Daphne, Harry Stavordale,[2] who in order to go to the cinema at Eton which was out of bounds used to dress up as an old woman, and Michael Rosse,[3] who was to become the stepfather of the Earl of Snowdon. Brian designed their racing colours and set the fashion in shirts, long before Mr. Fish thought of tucks and frills.

It was Brian who inaugurated the idea, about the time of the clue-chases, of 'Follow my Leader' through Selfridges. Daphne, tall and sparklingly beautiful, goddess-like Lettice Lygon, David Plunkett Green, over six foot, who wore a red satin-lined evening cape and was mad about jazz, and his sister Olivia, who had a dead-white expressionless face made up like a mask, and many of their friends would rush in and out of the departments, up

[1] Viscount Weymouth.
[2] Lord Stavordale.
[3] Earl of Rosse.

and down in the lifts, even climbing over the counters. Selfridges took it sportingly, while the papers gave it headlines.

On the way home from dances the same crowd used to congregate outside Powis House and in chorus shout: 'Good night, Lady Po-Po-Powis.' It was her name that evoked the serenade, and there is no record of Lady Powis having been awoken by the noise.

Sir Anthony Lindsay-Hogg and some of his friends let off fireworks unexpectedly in the garden of a house in the country belonging to one of the older generation. There was a tremendous row about this and they were made to apologise. It was a long time before they lived down the stigma of 'frightening old people when they had just gone to sleep'.

Sir Anthony looked like a very tall kindly sheep. He was exquisitely and meticulously dressed and had a soft seductive voice. He was always in debt as he was waiting for 'Granny' to die. To spite him she lived to be ninety-four.

It was also a B.Y.P.—Gavin Henderson—who actually set the Thames on fire at Henley. Even their elderly critics felt this was something of an achievement.

The B.Y.P.s' efforts all started in rather a childish way but with a touch of individuality. They were really just children's games. It was only when outsiders began to destroy the youthful fun by introducing drink, dope and vice that the whole thing deteriorated into something unpleasant and beastly.

At first they were just Bohemian parties, the best that London had ever seen. There was a Russian party, for which an entire studio had been redecorated for a single night to represent a Russian cabaret. This was given by the Countess Anthony Bosdari, whose husband had been one of the most attractive 'gentlemen-about-town' for many years.

There followed a party given in Burlington Gardens by David Tennant and his wife Hermione—the actress. It was called the Mozart Party because all the guests wore eighteenth-century costume, and the playing of the 'Jupiter' Symphony by a small orchestra was followed by dancing. This was all highly respectable, and no one could say a word against it.

Fancy dress was not exclusive to the very young. After the war everyone wanted to get away from the gloom of wartime clothes and wartime austerity. The Duke and Duchess of

Sutherland were the first who gave fancy-dress dances. They held these in their tennis court at Hampden House in Mayfair, which they covered with special flooring and converted into a tented ballroom lined with tapestries.

It was the Prince of Wales's idea that the guests should try to disguise their identity completely. This meant that most people brought two or three changes of costume, and as they were all very distinguished, the longer they could remain unidentified the better.

The Prince of Wales arrived at one of these balls dressed as Bonny Prince Charlie, but later changed into the garb of a Chinese coolie, and kept people guessing for a long time as to who he was.

On another occasion the highlight of the evening was a procession of boats. Mrs. Richard Norton was among the crews. The Prince of Wales, Prince Henry and Prince George arrived as Eton boys but changed during the evening. Lord Blandford (later to be the Duke of Marlborough) came as a female Channel-swimmer.

Mrs. Dudley Ward started one ball as a little girl and ended as a donkey; a party from White's Club came as monks; another lot were dressed as cocks and hens equipped with eggs which were 'laid' on the ballroom floor.

It was at this party that two waiters with unusually large noses started to ply the company with champagne with such unsteady hands that people looked surprised.

'Surely the Sutherlands could get better servants than that,' they whispered to each other.

The waiters grew more and more unsteady and suddenly fell to the ground with a great noise of clinking cutlery.

'The damned fellow is dead drunk!' someone exclaimed.

There was a hoot of laughter as the waiters turned out to be Prince Obolensky and Lord Bessborough, who not only had fooled their friends, but had acted so realistically that they had to prove that they really were sober.

Of course, with people chopping and changing their clothes, even arriving disguised, these parties produced the great problem of the twenties—the uninvited guest. There was really nothing to prevent complete strangers from hiring a fancy dress and slipping into any party.

The Duke of Sutherland told me that this must have happened

many times, and he often related the story of one of his friends who at a party he was giving suspected that one of the guests had come uninvited. He walked up to him and said in a low voice:

'I say, old man, do you happen to know the host here?'

The stranger looked round and answered decidedly:

'No, thank God, do you?'

It seems extraordinary how everyone wanted to dress up, the young, the old, the distinguished, the beautiful, statesmen, diplomats, aristocrats.

Lady Diana Cooper gives a vivid picture of a fancy-dress ball at Lord and Lady Ribblesdale's:

'There was a fancy ball at Ava Ribblesdale's last night, and all the women looked fifty per cent worse than usual—S. as Little Lord Fauntleroy quite awful, P. as a street Arab just dirty. Venetia and I had been to Michael Herbert's where was Willie Clarkson with brilliantined beard and frock-coat, his whole apparatus and a lot of French porters' clothes. Rosemary Ednam[1] looked well as the "Artful Dodger". The rest of us were porters. We thought we were pretty funny all dashing into the room shouting "Porteur, porteur!" Gerald Berners[2] was good as a hunting man with a marvellously funny mask by Oliver Messel. He had announced his intention of going as Nurse Cavell but was dissuaded. Winston[3] as Nero was good. F.E.[4] went as a Cardinal. The dressing-up was of course the best part but spoilt by your not being there, as everything is.'

No one was too grand to dress up at another Sutherland party given in 1928. Prince George arrived as a chef, the Prince of Wales in a robe of the Ku Klux Klan. Lady Louis Mountbatten and Mrs. Richard Norton were white ostriches. Duff Cooper was one of three blind mice, Lord Berners in white mask and veil as a 'monkey bride'.

Lord Berners was a great eccentric. He had a small harmonium installed in his car as he often, when out driving, felt inclined to compose 'motifs' inspired by the countryside. The lining at the back of his car was stencilled with butterflies. To see him playing

[1] Viscountess Ednam.
[2] Lord Berners.
[3] Winston Churchill.
[4] Earl of Birkenhead.

the harmonium, a monocle in his eye, haloed by butterflies, made passers-by gape. But later Lord Berners terrified people when he took to riding through the villages in an open car wearing a frightening mask. He had a number of these, each more horrific than the last.

The Sutherlands' and Ribblesdales' fancy-dress balls certainly bore no relation to some of the other parties which took place. As Evelyn Waugh said in *Vile Bodies*, there were:

> 'Masked parties, savage parties, Victorian parties, Greek parties, Wild West parties, Russian parties, Circus parties, parties where one had to dress as someone else and almost naked parties in St. John's Wood, parties in flats and studios and houses and ships and hotels and night-clubs, in windmills and swimming baths.'

One party which shocked everyone was when Brian Howard and Elizabeth Ponsonby, a cousin of the quiet, shy Loelia, and one or two others, hired the St. George's Baths at the height of the heat-wave. It seemed to them a good idea if their guests might swim during the intervals of dancing and supping. But unfortunately they engaged a Negro band.

The *Sunday Chronicle* said:

> 'Great astonishment and not a little indignation is being expressed in London over the revelation that in the early hours of yesterday morning a large number of Society women were dancing in bathing-dresses to the music of a negro band at a "swim and dance" gathering organised by some of Mayfair's Bright Young People.'

My mother was horrified.

'Fancy dancing in bathing-dresses!' she exclaimed. 'I've never heard of anything so improper!—and watched by black men! I'm very glad you weren't there!'

The invitations for the Baby Party read:

> 'We are having Romps from ten o'clock to bedtime. Do write and say you'll come, and we'll love to have Nanny too. Pram-park provided. Dress: anything from birth to school age.'

The *Daily Express* gave the party a lot of publicity the next morning:

'The so-called young people arrived in perambulators. They rode rocking-horses in the gardens, chased each other on donkeys and scooters, and bowled hoops. Screams resounded in the brilliantly lighted square (Rutland Gate, Knightsbridge). The guests were dressed as babies in long clothes, Girl Guides, Boy Scouts, nurses. They had comforters in their mouths and carried toy boats, dolls, pails and spades. An attempt was made to take the donkeys into the house. They were led up the steps, a butler pushing them from behind. Late in the evening the crowd was scattered by the violent ringing of a fire-bell. It was only some of the Bright Young People arriving in a taxi-cab. Cocktails were served in nursery mugs, and the "bar" was a babies' pen.'

There was violent criticism this time not only in the home from irate parents but from writers to the newspapers.

'This disgusting exhibition . . .'

'Immature, vulgar posturings from a class of people who should know better.'

'This is the type of behaviour which leads to Communism!'

There was more to follow. A 'Pyjama and Bottle Party' provided the newspapers with a bonanza. The *Daily News* reported gleefully:

'The hundreds of guests came in pyjamas, the first arrival was a pretty flaxen-haired girl of about nineteen, wearing pyjamas with stripes of salmon pink. Her contribution was a bottle of 1840 champagne which was immediately consumed.

'Mr. & Mrs. X (the host and hostess) were attired in sleeping-suits of orange. Many of the men's pyjamas were trimmed with lace. The bottles of refreshments which the guests were expected to bring provided an amusing diversion. There was gin, hair-restorer, health salts, distilled water, beer, ink, petrol, Ethyl, smelling-salts, Thames water, Jordan water, cabbage water, and water from a pool alive with tadpoles! The party was supposed to drink these "refreshments". . . . All the while, in another room, the orchestra was playing dreamy music.'

One could say, of course, that Bright Young People on the whole were 'caught' in full limelight of publicity. The fact was they couldn't avoid it. What was unfortunate was that, as always happens, a very different type of people began to give parties, and to claim that they, too, belonged to the Bright Young People.

194

And so the idea, which at the beginning had been gay and amusing, simple and light-hearted, degenerated into something rather sordid and unpleasant.

Sexy wasn't a word we threw about much in the twenties, but that is what the parties became, orgies which shocked and disgusted not only the newspapers and the older generation, but also ourselves.

I wrote in one of my articles:

'Mayfair is suspected of being a haunt of vice and degeneracy. The neighbourhood is no longer connected in surburban minds with Duchesses, tiaras and gold plate, but with licentious orgies, pyjama parties and dope.'

Who shall blame anyone for not understanding that these were not the Bright Young People, but the social climbers, the outsiders, the hangers-on who were coining in on the act. They wanted to earn a title for their degeneracy, but there was no gaiety about it.

All through the twenties the real young had been trying to be original, to think up something new. In 1921 Oxford University had a 'Hide and Seek Club', which used to meet at Boars Hill or in the gardens of professors' houses. Cambridge, not to be outdone, had a 'University Pavement Club' which was a protest against the rut of modern life.

The members met on King's Parade and sat on the pavement for an hour playing marbles, nap, tiddlywinks or noughts and crosses. Passers-by were invited to join in, 'in order to secure that unanimity which is essential to pavement life'!

There was also the Oxford Railway Club formed for the pleasure of drinking on trains at night. Both universities had climbing clubs, and every year at Oxford someone made the classic climb up the Martyrs' Memorial to place a chamber-pot on the top.

This was all in the spirit of the Bright Young People. One of these who had started the cult, but who was far too clever to remain in it for long, was Lady Eleanor Smith. She was dark, like her father the famous F. E. Smith, the first Lord Birkenhead, with wild hair swept back from her oval forehead. She had black eyes which could flash with anger or excitement and there was an air of purpose and urgency about her, as if she had to hurry to get everything she could out of life. Eleanor told us she was of gypsy descent.

'My great-grandmother's name was Bathsheba,' she said. 'She was dark, handsome and temperamental, with brilliant eyes, an olive complexion and jet-black ringlets.'

Eleanor made it sound so convincing that we believed every word of it, and accepted that her great interest in gypsies and circus people was due to the fact that she was a blood sister of theirs, and therefore drawn to them instinctively.

It was not until many years later that her brother, Freddie Birkenhead, was to expose the truth. He explained that their grandmother, a nonconformist schoolmistress, had a dark complexion.

'This,' Freddie writes, 'was my sister's sole and slender excuse for claiming a gypsy descent. Her hallucination about Bathsheba led to some serious misunderstandings. Not only did I foolishly accept her account and quote it in a previous book, but I also misled Sir Winston Churchill into introducing this travesty of fact in his brilliant work *Great Contemporaries*. Later it reached Nazi Germany, and we learnt at the end of the war that our family had been booked for total extermination on account of its impure gypsy blood.'

Eleanor for a bet spent the night with Zita in the Chamber of Horrors at Madame Tussaud's, wrote 'Women's Gossip' for an evening newspaper, and became a film critic.

She hated both jobs and threw them up at a moment's notice to wander with the Great Carmo Circus. She was completely under the spell of the Big Top, and even on one occasion took the place of a bare-back rider who was ill.

She wrote several delightful novels. *Red Wagon* was the first, which was a great success, then *Ballerina*—inspired by Anna Pavlova before she died—was adapted for the stage, with Frances Doble—Sacheverell Sitwell's sister-in-law—and Anton Dolin as the stars.

It was put on at the Scala Theatre, and during the dress rehearsal a strange thing happened. The stage revolved to show a woodland glade, and a snow-white figure in a fluffy *tutu*, its head bound with swans' feathers, moved on to the stage.

Eleanor watching from the stalls thought that Frances seemed much smaller, then as the figure glided into the spotlight she saw it was Anna Pavlova!

Anton Dolin saw it, too. He gripped Eleanor's hand and went deadly pale.

'This is uncanny,' he muttered, 'it's awful . . . what have we done? Oh God—Why did we ever bring up the past?'

Dolin had put on his understudy Borek, and now the white form stood effortlessly upon one *pointe*, pirouetted three times—something Frances couldn't do—and drifted like swansdown into Borek's arms as the curtain fell.

Three other people who had also watched were white and dazed.

'We can't all have seen—what we saw,' one of them mumbled.

Afraid, Dolin and Eleanor ran to the pass door, Frances stood there on the stage.

'I'm sorry . . .' she said to Dolin, 'let's take it again.'

'Take it again? Why?'

'I couldn't dance. I must be awfully tired. My mind suddenly seemed to go blank. Will someone get me a glass of water?'

Later Dolin affirmed:

'We can't deny it. For a moment that particular spirit from the past took possession of Frances's mind and body.'

On the last night Frances Doble untied her pink ballet shoes and declared:

'I shall never walk upon the stage again as long as I live.'

She never did.

Eleanor adored her father, but the Birkenheads always teased each other. One day Lord Birkenhead came home with the news that he had been offered a lot of money to write a series of articles called 'Milestones in My Life'. His family asked which incidents he proposed to use. He told them.

'You might have put in your marriage!' Lady Birkenhead said reproachfully.

'And the birth of your first child!' Eleanor added.

'I said milestones, my dears,' Lord Birkenhead replied, 'not millstones.'

One of Eleanor's claims to fame was that in 1923 she was charged by the Men and Women's Christian Temperance Union with having 'publicly smoked a cigarette on the quad of Magdalene College'. In the same year it was reported in the *New*

Statesman that a young lady in a small restaurant had a cigarette knocked out of her mouth by an elderly and scandalised waiter.

In 1919 there were all sorts of different restrictions as to where you could and could not smoke. In old-fashioned restaurants they frowned on women smoking, and in many cases asked them not to do so. In the West End it was taken more or less for granted, even while the waiters would raise their eyebrows at each other. But it was still improper for women to smoke on top of a bus, and if the conductor didn't ask her to put it out the other passengers would do so.

Virginian cigarettes were first called 'stinkers', then 'gaspers', and were considered a little vulgar. Edwardian gentlemen had smoked Egyptian cigarettes, and it was only during the war that Tommies had got used to the cheaper type, especially Woodbines. I remember the first record we ever had played on our very squeaky gramophone before the war was called 'Little Willy's Wild Woodbines'. It was a moral story about how little Willy smoked his father's cigarettes, and then was violently sick.

Cigarettes in 1925 were ten for 6*d.* and twenty for 11*d.* Scotch beef was 1*s.* 10*d.* a pound, Scotch whisky was 145*s.* a dozen. A whisky and soda at most night-clubs was 1*s.* 6*d.* Bicycles could be bought for 30*s.* and any type of perambulator was available on weekly instalments of 1*s.* 9*d.* Wallis's best Staffordshire Willow Pattern china service—eighty-three pieces—cost £3.

Eleanor took part in one of the most elegant parties of the period. The Circus Party, which took place in July 1928, was given by Norman Hartnell. He rented Strathmore House, No. 17 Bruton Street, where Princess Elizabeth was born. The invitation card read: 'Come as a Circus Character', and as only two hundred and fifty guests were invited the invitations were as coveted as vouchers for the Royal Enclosure at Ascot.

There were performing wolves which skipped merrily round an arena, acrobats, a somewhat lethargic bear and other stunts.

Eleanor led her white pony, with a scarlet saddle and jingling with golden bells, up the stairs. But the Marchioness of Carisbrooke, wearing a riding-habit of violet cloth and a top-hat, left her horse outside.

Ferraro, the beloved head waiter of the Berkeley, who spoilt all the young of the twenties, did the food and the buffet-table was decorated with pale green animals in ice. The ballroom, which was a complete circus ring, was hung with scarlet and magenta curtains.

The supper room was in gold tissue and the breakfast room for kippers and cocoa at dawn was hung with a huge checker design of silver and emerald metal.

The Earl of Northesk and Nelson Keys came as two barkers. The Earl of Hardwicke and Sir Anthony Lindsay-Hogg came as cowboys. The Ruthven twins, really in the spirit of the party, came as gorillas. Lily Elsie looked lovely as a sailor-boy in a blue velvet suit with Ivor Novello dressed the same.

Norman greeted his guests tail-coated as the Ring Master, but at midnight he reappeared smothered in sequins as a clown. The only tragedy of the evening was that Gwen Mond (later Lady Melchett) got hit on the head in the coconut-shy.

Gwen, the wife of Henry Mond, whose father in 1927 had created the giant organisation known as Imperial Chemical Industries, was the first person to wear a nylon dress and a nylon nightgown. She told me how the zip received its name.

Made in the factory, it was shown to her husband on the jumper of one of the office staff. He pulled it up saying:

'So this is how it works, z . . . z . . . zip!'

Someone exclaimed:

'What an expressive name for it!'

And zip it became.

The Bright Young People had a vocabulary of their own; we talked about parties being simply 'too sick-making' or 'too tired-making', or that somebody or other was 'too boring'. If we thought a young man was rather pretentious, or tried to worm his way into society, he was 'smooth', but real cads were 'too grizzly for words'. Everything else was 'too perfectly amazing!'

According to one commentator, it was the age 'of tired, monotonous drawl, of tired, monotonous metaphors, such novelty as there is coming mainly from America'.

I don't believe a word of this. I talked in a gay, excited way because I felt gay and excited. I never knew anybody who drawled, and I think this is just another instance of trying to find something rude to write about the age and the people who lived in it.

Hilaire Belloc even said:

'The world is to end next summer. I don't believe it, it's too good to be true.'

No one could write of parties in the twenties without including Mrs. Corrigan's. A telephone operator in Cleveland, she had made a blind date with a steel millionaire and married him the following morning.

When he died six months later his wife inherited all his steel holdings. These she sold for $80,000,000 in cash. Laura Corrigan came to England and was presented at Court by the American Ambassadress in 1922.

On arriving in London she rented the house of Mrs. George Keppel (the last love of Edward VII) in Grosvenor Square, and asked for the owner's guest-list to be included in the lease. Mrs. Keppel agreed but raised the rent.

Mrs. Corrigan started her sensational parties by asking anyone who would come, but in a few years only royalty, smart society and press reporters could get in.

She introduced cabaret acts we had never seen before, acrobats, tap-dancers, and in the tombola were gold and diamond cigarette-cases, cuff-links and vanity-cases. In 1926 Mrs. Corrigan, inspired by the Bright Young People, made her guests provide the entertainment.

We couldn't have improved on the programme which was headed: 'All Star Theatre, 16 Grosvenor Street, July 12th.'

Guests were in fancy dress for the dinner party, which was just like any other except that all the men were given silver pencils and the women silver mirrors.

Afterwards the fun began. 'The Plantation Group' included Lady Louis Mountbatten—B. Natural (always am)—her cousin, the Countess of Brecknock, and Lord Ashley—B. Sharp (in business). There was a dancer—Beauty Nimple Legs. 'This little darling,' said the programme, 'is the favourite of the Terpsichore', and was, of course, Lady Plunket.

Mrs. Corrigan used to make innumerable 'malapropisms' which were sneered at and repeated with glee, especially by those who enjoyed her hospitality. Her first was to describe her house in Grosvenor Square as 'my little ventre-à-terre'. Another was when she said of a cathedral that it had 'magnificent flying buttocks'.

When Elsie de Wolfe, the decorator, who was also Lady Mendl,

200

showed Mrs. Corrigan her villa at Versailles, she pointed out the indirect lighting, which was new in those days.

'I just love this confused lighting,' Laura Corrigan gushed.

Mrs. Corrigan always wore a wig, owing to some accident in her early life. It was said she had a smart one which represented 'just come from the hairdresser', a dishevelled one 'just off to the hairdresser', and a windswept one.

One of Lady Cunard's more piquant remarks was when Laura Corrigan asked her what she was going to wear at the Opera that evening.

'Just a tiara and my own hair,' Emerald replied.

As the years passed Mrs. Corrigan got grander and grander. To get the people she wanted to her parties, she sent the invitations out with co-hostesses who were too important for anyone to ignore. The card always bore the magic word 'decorations'.

Always a showman, she engaged experts to teach her and her friends the 'Big Apple' when it came in and the 'Lambeth Walk'. Presents, like their recipients, got more and more impressive. Prince Frederick of Prussia and dukes were presented with a pair of gold mounted sock-suspenders! Lower titles received initialled braces with solid gold tabs, women were given gold and tortoise-shell combs in pink leather Cartier cases.

It was some years before Mrs. Corrigan's guests realised that the prize-winners were never commoners. Loelia Westminster (the 3rd Duchess) wrote:

'She worked through the Duchesses in strict order of precedence and shortly before the war she reached me. When I was handed the gold cigarette case, there were cat-calls and boos from my friends which Mrs. Corrigan took as a sign of my appalling unpopularity. It was beyond me to explain that what they objected to was the raffle being rigged.'

But Laura Corrigan had guts. When the Germans overran France in 1940 she was living there, but refused to escape to America and remained in Paris. She sold her fabulous jewels one by one. The fat repulsive arms of Hermann Goering were covered from wrist to elbow under his uniform with bracelets he bought from the ex-telephone operator from Cleveland. She spent the proceeds in feeding French prisoners of war held by the Nazis.

Another type of party was introduced, called 'A Murder Party'. I don't know who invented this ingenious idea, but Lady Ribblesdale asked the American-born Queen of original parties, Elsa Maxwell, to arrange 'a murder' in her new house in St. James.

Elsa Maxwell had just disrupted Paris with her version of the 'scavenger hunt', which was to provide the most unusual object. The manager of the Casino de Paris put in a riot call for the police when two 'hunters' rushed on to the stage, grabbed one of Mistinguett's slippers and then took the rest of her shoes from her dressing room, so that she was forced to finish her act in bare feet.

A black swan in the Bois put up such a fight when one of her feathers was purloined that two men were taken to hospital. Elsa's landlady had hysterics when a donkey which had been borrowed from a pedlar started to kick out the walls of her apartment.

It was a more serious matter when Lady Mendl, whose husband was a member of the British Embassy, was accused of creating an international incident by trying to procure one of the pompons a French sailor wears in his cap. A stiff note of protest was sent to His Majesty's Government in London!

The prize was won by the Grand Duchess Marie of Russia, who produced a *pot de chambre* with two big blue curious eyes painted inside.

The whole point of the Murder Game was that people had to be fooled into thinking a crime really had been committed. Elsa Maxwell chose Zita Yungman, the originator of the B.Y.P., as the 'victim' and the small dapper Duke of Marlborough was to be the murderer, although unlike Zita he was not in 'the know'.

Two weeks before the event Elsa Maxwell started planting clues, and on the night she inserted special Turkish cigarettes into the Duke's gold cigarette case.

Zita was found after Lady Ribblesdale had sent her butler upstairs to ask why she was late for dinner. The butler reported the door was locked. After it was broken down the guests were speechless at what they saw.

Zita was lying on the bed with a huge blood-stain (tomato ketchup) on her breast. There was a revolver on the floor, a

Turkish cigarette-end on the bed. Two actors impersonating the police arrived and demanded to inspect everyone's cigarettes. They found the Duke had the same brand as the one by the bedside. They also produced threatening letters signed 'M'.

'Your Grace, why did you murder Miss Yungman?' the detectives said seriously.

The Duke looked absolutely stunned! The room was plunged into darkness. Dishes crashed to the floor, there were screams and detectives were heard shouting 'Stop that man!'. When the lights went on again Zita was seen sitting at the table laughing.

The Duke took it all in good part, but he was not so amused when the *Daily Express* announced on the front page:

'DUKE OF MARLBOROUGH MURDERS BEAUTIFUL GIRL IN LADY RIBBLESDALE'S HOUSE'

In very much smaller type a subheading read:

'Elsa Maxwell Stages a Party.'

There were parties day and night, but the 'smart' people still wanted to disguise themselves. It was as if they all wanted to escape from reality into a gay, irresponsible world of pretence.

Even Christmas carols were an excuse to don masks and become incognito. Oggie Lynn, the very social singing-teacher of the time, arranged a carol party. They planned to appear at theatres during the interval, at restaurants and hotels. To their friends they sent postcards saying: 'The Mayfair Carollers will sing in your street at . . . hour on . . .'

Four days before Christmas, wearing dominoes, black masks and tricorne hats, their music in red velvet covers, their collecting-boxes looking like snowballs, they drove round London. The choir included Lady Maud Warrender, Lady Maidstone, A. P. Herbert, Lady Diana Cooper and the 2nd Duchess of Westminster.

Lady Howard de Walden, who had a lovely voice, organised the collections. At the first theatre, not recognising the Duchess she told her to collect in the gallery.

'I don't think you know me,' Violet Westminster said coldly, 'I am the Duchess of Westminster.'

For a moment Lady Howard de Walden was taken aback. Then she said lightly:

'Well, that's all right, you will have a still greater success.'

Which she did! The choir collected £500, mostly in half-crowns and pennies, and it was a tour de luxe. Lady Curzon of Kedleston provided a magnificent supper and wine. At Claridges a lot of money was collected, only J. M. Barrie refusing to contribute because he was annoyed at their intrusion!

This seems to be the only unwhimsical action recorded against the creator of Peter Pan. He even had a delightfully fanciful way of paying his alimony. His ex-wife had married the novelist, Gilbert Cannan, twenty years her junior. They subsisted largely on the money Barrie gave them. This he handed over each year at a *tête-à-tête* dinner held on his suggestion on the divorced pair's wedding anniversary.

A Bright Young Person who did the unpredictable was the Countess of Seafield, who, being small and sandy-haired, looked exactly like Queen Victoria when she was young. She had a great sense of humour, a charmingly unassuming nature, a stutter, and was the richest peeress in her own right in Scotland. She fell in love with Derek Studley-Herbert, a very good-looking, gay young man whose claim to fame was that he had been President of 'Pop' at Eton and Captain of the Oppidans. He had very little money. After some stormy interviews with Nina's trustees, one of whom was the Mackintosh of Mackintosh, who inevitably thought them too young, they became officially engaged.

Then suddenly one day they felt they couldn't face an enormous and pompous wedding. So they were married secretly by special licence. Everyone was furious, especially Nina's tenants and relations in Scotland, who felt they had been 'done out' of the proper wedding festivities and all the trappings.

American hostesses of the twenties must include American-born Lady Cunard, who adored Sir Thomas Beecham and spent all her money helping him to restore Covent Garden. She had made her first appearance in England under the chaperonage of the eccentric Lady Cardigan.

The first thing you saw when you visited the Cardigans' house was the head of Ronald, the charger the 7th Earl had ridden at Balaclava, as it had been stuffed and hung in the hall. King Edward had one of Ronald's hoofs mounted as an inkwell.

Lady Cardigan would take everyone to see her bridal chamber, which contained a bed surrounded by looking-glasses, draped with white net, roses and satin. Her feet were supposed to be the smallest in the world, and to draw attention to them she used to order the butler to change her boots in the drawing room.

Lady Cardigan would go to the meets of the Melton Hunt in a brougham, with her saddle on top, wearing a leopard-skin coat over her habit and a tiny billycock perched on her yellow curls. She would ask everyone if they had seen her horse, but the whole performance was a farce as there wasn't a horse and she hadn't been on one for years.

It was Lady Cardigan who arranged her protégée's marriage to Sir Bache Cunard during the South African War. Lady Cunard in the twenties was like a small parakeet, or, as Mrs. Ronald Greville described her, 'a yellow canary of prey'. She had a nose like a beak and a receding chin. Her chin was the misery of her life. She had it massaged and given electric treatments but nothing succeeded in bringing it forward!

A ruthless, indefatigable 'lion' (social species) hunter, it was said that Lady Cunard could 'flick her guests into animation like a practised ring-master.' She certainly eventually entertained everyone of consequence except Queen Mary, who disliked her, ending triumphantly with the Prince of Wales and Mrs. Simpson. She dreamt of being 'Mistress of the Robes' to Queen Wallis but it was a short-lived fantasy.

Lady Cunard was called Maud until 1926 when she changed her name to Emerald. She had a magnificent emerald necklace which she habitually wore in the evenings. When asked why she had taken the name of Emerald she said:

'Since I am nicknamed "The Emerald Queen", I have adopted it as my Christian name.'

Every contemporary history speaks of her parties, her effervescent personality and her conversational sallies. Lytton Strachey's description of Lady Cunard is interesting:

'My smart life proceeds a-pace,' he says in 1919. 'I find it mainly simply comic, and distinctively exhausting. No pasturage for the Soul, I fear! Lady Cunard is rather a sport, with her frankly lower-class bounce; she makes the rest of 'em look like the withered leaves of Autumn. But she herself, I fancy, is really pathetic too. So lost— so utterly lost!'

Nancy, Lady Cunard's daughter, whom she had neglected as a child, hated her and was a social rebel. Nancy, with whom Michael Arlen was madly in love, was the model for his story *The Green Hat*.

When Lady Cunard introduced Michael to her guests at a luncheon party she pulled him across the room and cried: 'This is Michael Arlen—the only Armenian who has not been massacred!'

Nancy wore African bracelets of ivory from wrist to shoulder, encircled her blue eyes with kohl, and wore her short gold hair curved over her cheek-bones like scimitars.

At one party to which she had been dragged by her mother, she suddenly in the middle of the dance-floor screamed:

'I hate this! I hate it! I hate it!'

It didn't seem to me distinctive enough to arouse such passion, but she could be very violent!

Nancy came out in 1911, she married at eighteen and had a divorce. She was not a contemporary but she was pointed out as 'a terrible warning' to many of my friends who knew Lady Cunard.

'You don't want to be like the Cunard girl!'

'Being Bohemian never helped anyone!'

'If you think you can go out with your face painted like Nancy Cunard, you're mistaken!'

Needless to say this made her doubly interesting. We longed to know what she was doing, whether she was in England or France, with her mother or in her flat over the Eiffel Tower Restaurant in Percy Street. We knew she wrote poetry, that she was interested in Negro art, and there were incredible rumours:

'I tell you they were together in Venice.'

'He's a brilliant pianist.'

'He's handsome and not as black as some! He has Red Indian blood in him as well!'

It was some time before Lady Cunard learnt of the connection between her daughter and the Henry Crowden of Eddie's 'South Alabamians', a Negro quartet.

Then Margot Asquith, taking the stage as usual, arrived for lunch and produced her bomb.

'Well, Maud, what's Nancy up to now? Is it dope, drink or niggers?'

206

Lady Cunard had many enemies. The people she had snubbed and ignored and refused to invite to her house now had their revenge.

Nancy came to London with Henry, but few of her old friends saw her. The majority were deeply shocked:

'I can't think how she can!'

'It's only because she hates her mother!'

There was a story that Sir Thomas Beecham had declared: 'She should be tarred and feathered!' Whether this was true or not, Nancy felt she was being persecuted. She became wilder and more rebellious than ever. Even Henry found her impossible. Lady Cunard continued to entertain. She had another knock-out blow, this time delivered by Sir Thomas Beecham.

She had persuaded herself in the thirties that he was impotent and no longer unfaithful to her. But one day when she was having tea in his hotel suite, a young soprano burst in and demanded hysterically that he make an immediate choice between 'me and that Lady Cunard'.

Without a moment's hesitation, like playing 'oranges and lemons', Sir Thomas replied.

'I choose Lady Cunard.'

But in 1939, while in America, she learnt by chance from a luncheon guest that Sir Thomas was obtaining a divorce to marry someone else.

She died in 1948 and her ashes were scattered in Grosvenor Square. It was then found that her emeralds were false.

Sir Thomas Beecham was witty, charming and sardonic. He was extremely fastidious about his appearance and everyone chuckled when his braces broke during a concert in New York and he had to conduct with one hand and hold up his trousers with the other.

His scathing remarks to the audience and the orchestra always made news. To the Albert Hall chorus during Messiah, he said:

'I know the weakness of human nature, but when you sing "All we like sheep have gone astray", kindly do not look so pleased about it.'

Another American hostess—London was full of them—was Lady Colefax, who was a deadly rival of Lady Cunard and very unlike her except that they both were on the 'lion' hunt. Lady Colefax was a little hedge-sparrow compared with the flamboyance of Lady Cunard's bird of paradise, in fact, she looked anybody's respectable aunt from the country.

But she had a fierce determination to have a salon and the oldest joke at the time was that the 'only sound in the King's Road was Lady Colefax climbing'.

The Sitwells played one of their pranks on her. One evening when she was giving a large and important party they installed a loudspeaker in their car. As the door of Argyll House opened to receive each distinguished guest they loudly and wittily mispronounced each name.

The Sitwells, who always had more imagination than anyone else, once borrowed Lady Crewe's house in Chelsea in order to award prizes for the 'worst literary efforts of the year'.

Osbert and Edith received the guests dressed in the deepest funeral black with solemn faces looking, as Beverley Nichols said, 'like literary undertakers'.

The prizes for the 'Worst Book of the Year', the 'Worst Poem of the Year' and other 'Worsts' were things like a glazed fish in a glass case, and a mangy stuffed cat playing with some moulting mice under a glass dome!

The Bright Young People was really an extremely good name for us. We were bright, we were gay, we were original and we did enjoy ourselves. If a few people got mobbed up and made fools of in the process, well it didn't really hurt them. We made a lot of other people laugh. Quite frankly, I think that the Bright Young People brought a great deal of brightness to a world which was still sadly in need of it.

CHAPTER EIGHT

Mary make-believe
Dreamed the whole day through,
Foolish fancies
Love romances,
How could they come true?

NOËL COWARD

ONE of the things which is most difficult to put into words is the effect which being brought up in a manless household had on us. Adolescence, as we know now, is the most important formative period in a child's life, but during those years we had practically no contact with men.

My father had become a legend, and that meant I could scarcely think of him as a person. I had seen so little of him and, though he was very fond of his children, we always took second place to my mother, whom he adored. I was brought up on the story of how, when I was born, there were complications, and the doctor asked my father conventionally:

'Which do you want saved, the mother or the child?'

'Damn the child,' my father had replied, 'save my wife!'

When he came home on leave during the war our joy and excitement were automatic. He was a soldier returning from the war—someone brave who was fighting for us—a hero!

'How you've grown!' was the obvious remark he made to us.

Then he would whisk my mother away—to London, to Eastbourne, anywhere where they could be alone. They didn't want to be bothered with us during their precious hours together, and we seldom saw him again even to say goodbye.

I was so lucky to have an exceptionally wonderful mother who was understanding, sympathetic and young in her outlook. She gave me love, ambition and a standard to live up to which I have never ceased trying to attain. She was both an inspiration and a spur.

But because she had loved my father wholeheartedly she gave me a very glamorised view of men, which, combined with the romantic novels I devoured, produced a picture of the male sex in my mind which had no link with reality.

Many of my friends were at odds with their mothers, and were therefore completely lost in their contacts with the older generation. Sandwiched between Edwardian restrictions and their own wild desire for freedom, they found themselves isolated in a no-man's-land of ignorance.

If their fathers had been killed, as mine had been—and this was almost universal—it meant that the succeeding years were more devoid of men than they had been during their fathers' lifetime. It would have been considered wrong and fast for a widow to entertain.

We therefore had no contacts with and no knowledge of older men, and the young ones with whom we danced and laughed gave us really very little insight into the character or feelings of this unknown sex. In fact, older men, and for that matter older women, were looked on as strange beings very far apart from us, who possessed, we felt, no ordinary human feelings such as we were experiencing.

It was not surprising that we believed this, first because of our ignorance of men of any age, and secondly because many of my contemporaries who had fathers alive had very strange and eccentric ones.

The Sitwells, for instance, Osbert, Sacheverell and Edith, had an incredible father in the person of Sir George. He was in the years to come to fill book after book of Osbert's autobiographies, and to project his personality so strongly and so pervasively over the years that it was difficult to remember any other character being mentioned.

Sir George Sitwell was always building, always altering, always telling people how to do things, always convinced that he knew better than anyone else. He is a delight to read about, but he must have been hell to live with.

During the war Sir George read a letter in *The Times* concerning 'the possible benefits in reviving the medieval habits of payment in kind'.

He thought this an excellent idea, and in 1915 wrote a letter to Sacheverell's house-master at Eton saying that, having been particularly hard hit by the war, he could not afford to pay the usual fees at the beginning of the next term, but instead would deliver their value in pigs and potatoes!

Sacheverell, who experienced a very uncomfortable time at Eton after this letter, wrote desperately to Osbert, who was at the front. The letter reached him at the same time as a letter from Sir George saying that in view of the economies he had to make he had cut off his allowance.

But Osbert, already grown up, was equal to the challenge. He wrote to his father saying:

'I come home on leave in about a fortnight, and as I have no allowance now, I've been able to arrange, I'm glad to say, that the guard on the leave-train should accept potatoes instead of my fare.'

Sir George was furious, not because he thought Osbert was being impertinent, but because he felt his son was giving away potatoes that belonged to him.

In a notebook entitled 'The Wisdom of Life' Sir George had written: 'Never open a letter from a correspondent known to be troublesome until after luncheon.'

Osbert does not relate at what hour his letter was read, but there was a satisfactory conclusion: Osbert's allowance was restored and the school fees were paid by cheque.

The Curzon girls, Cynthia and Alexandra, were also contemporaries, and they had George Nathaniel, the 1st Marquis Curzon of Kedleston, as their father. Lord Curzon, whom Max Beerbohm described as 'Britannia's butler', was a man of great gifts of intellect. He had been Viceroy of India, and held many important posts in the Cabinet. Unfortunately he suffered fools most ungladly, and he presented to his equals and inferiors, especially to his inferiors, a façade of extreme aristocratic class-consciousness and pomposity, which left people either speechless with rage or convulsed with laughter.

We were not to know, until all the biographies were written, how deeply Lord Curzon had suffered as a child from a mother who ignored him and from a sadistic governess. All his life he was to yearn for love, and in his dealings with women he could be pathetically sentimental. But the man in the street resented his autocratic manner and the way he obviously looked down on the 'lower classes'.

'Curzonisms' were repeated and re-repeated. A friend referred to his marble pillars, only to have Lord Curzon say haughtily:

'My pilasters are alabaster.'

In 1919 Lloyd George, Churchill, Birkenhead and Chamberlain were to nickname him 'Lord Alabaster'.

A verse written about him in 1883 when he was at Oxford was to cause him much distress in his future life. It ran:

> 'My name is George Nathaniel Curzon,
> I am a most superior person,
> My cheek is pink, my hair is sleek,
> I dine at Blenheim once a week.'

In 1920 when Lord Curzon was engaged in a mortal fight for his political future he wrote to his wife:

'Never has more harm been done to one single individual than that accursed doggerel has done to me.'

Lord Curzon was a tremendous snob, he simply didn't believe Consuelo Balsan, ex-Duchess of Marlborough, when she told him she had never regretted not being a duchess any more.

When Cynthia Curzon asked her father if she could marry the young M.P. for Harrow called Oswald Mosley it is said that when George Nathaniel reached for *Debrett* she handed him a telephone book.

It is amusing in the light of future events to read Lord Curzon's description of his future son-in-law:

'Very young, tall, slim, dark, rather a big nose, little black moustache, rather a Jewish appearance.'

Richard Norton's father, Lord Grantley, was so absent-minded that when he went up to change for dinner he would often take off his clothes and go to bed. He had a passion for buying houses. He inherited five, but was always buying others and moving, often without even telling his family. His relations would arrive to stay for Christmas to find they had come to the wrong place, and they had no idea where to find him.

One day Lord Grantley was travelling by train when he saw a very attractive house standing on a small hillside. He instantly desired to own it. He got out at the next station, went to the largest house agent's in the town, and told them to buy the house for him.

'We have no house of that description on our books,' the agent informed him.

'Find out the name, the owner, and what he wants for it, and be quick!' Lord Grantley instructed him.

The whole office went into action. Lord Grantley sat down and waited. Presently the agent came up to him triumphantly.

'The house is called Elton Manor,' he said. 'The owner is an old gentleman called Lord Grantley.'

When Lord Grantley was eighty-seven he was cited as a co-respondent in a divorce action. He was furious when the judge adjourned proceedings while he considered whether the allegation could be admitted at such an advanced age.

'You'd think,' Lord Grantley growled to his son, 'the fellah was implying that I'm past it.'

But the grounds were allowed and a decree nisi granted, to Lord Grantley's delight and satisfaction!

My understanding of older men wasn't enhanced by my maternal grandfather, who had died just before the war of a heart attack brought on by one of his tyrannical rages: one of his pig-sties was set on fire, and he didn't consider that the local Fire Brigade had arrived speedily enough!

He was, in fact, typical of the period: extremely handsome, blue-blooded, delightful to meet; charming in the company of outsiders, while he made his children's life a misery with his rages and the restrictions he imposed. When they were small he boxed their ears until my mother had abscesses in hers.

When they were older he invariably said it was too hot for the horses to take them to the tennis tournament or a cricket match, and they would have to bicycle. If they arrived home late they started the meal at the course where they came in, nothing was allowed to be kept for them.

As children they never ate peaches or any other fruit from the garden unless they stole it. When they were older, if anything annoyed him he would cut off their allowance.

I remember that when he and my grandmother drove over to see us at our house in Pershore their visit inevitably ended with my mother rushing upstairs to cry on her bed. It was not something which endeared the older generation to us, and it certainly gave me no understanding of the great and vital men that I was to meet in 1924.

By this time I had found myself a job, writing snippets for the gossip-column of the *Daily Express*. Quite by chance I had met a young man at a cocktail party who had asked me to send in some contributions, promising to pay me the immense sum of five shillings for every paragraph that was published.

I thought this seemed an easy way of earning money without exerting myself, and I contributed a large number of social paragraphs to the *Daily Express*, when one morning the telephone rang, and I was told that Lord Beaverbrook would like to meet me.

A car was sent for me and I was taken down to Hurlingham, where, in a small house called The Vineyards, I met the man whom Lady Diana Cooper was to describe as 'this strange, attractive gnome with the odour of genius about him'.

I knew nothing of Max Beaverbrook's background. I had heard, of course, as I was working on the *Express*, that he was a meteor in the newspaper world. He had bought the *Express* only at the end of the war, and Lord Northcliffe had told him it would be a failure. In fact for the first two years it had seemed as though Northcliffe might be right—the *Daily Express* lost £20,000 the first year that Beaverbrook owned it, and £50,000 the next year. But the tide turned and circulation leapt ahead.

So much has been written about the leading men of the period, but I wish now, as one always wishes, that I had been older and more observant when I met them. As it was, when I used to sit at lunch and dinner at The Vineyards with Lord Beaverbrook, Lord Birkenhead, Winston Churchill and Sir James Dunn, I thought of them as Four Old Wise Men, while perhaps I should have seen them as Four Great Adventurers—men who by their sheer vitality and drive had boosted and invigorated the world in which they lived.

Leo Amery, a great politician—who helped my brother—talking of F.E. and Winston, said to me:

'They were always political adventurers—brilliant, eloquent, patriotic and public-spirited in a way this new generation does not understand the word. For them there were always new horizons, new mountains to climb, new rivers to cross!'

I watched Prince Charles on the television a short time ago

trying so hard to answer the question about what he thought of his parents, and he said rather hesitatingly:

'I have only just begun to think of them as people.'

I knew exactly what he meant because to me in those days older men were not people. I couldn't believe that they suffered, that they were ever unhappy, depressed or despondent as I and my contemporaries often were. I couldn't believe that they felt deeply about anything except finance and success, which we had not yet tasted. They were creatures apart, made of granite or gold, but not of fears and tears, of shyness and half-formed aspirations which we felt would never come true.

It was not until quite recently, when I read Lady Diana Cooper's memoirs, that I realised how wrong I was. In those days she was one of the mighty—already grown up. She was not so very much older in actual years, perhaps eleven or twelve, but time is very relative when one is young. The fact that a person is even two or three years older creates an immense barrier, and Diana Cooper, with her wonderful beauty, her ducal parents, the background of Belvoir Castle, her acquaintance with everyone who was important, was as remote from me as the moon from the earth. And yet to my astonishment she writes:

'I felt my every movement was being analysed, criticised and condemned. I felt fat, unspiritual, unsuitable and stupid.'

Could Lady Diana really have felt like this? The woman whom over half a million people had paid to watch playing the Madonna, and who had managed to seem so completely suitable for the part? On another page she says?

'All these contorting nervous fears and fatigue breed terror of other kinds, never properly under restraint.'

'But how could Lady Diana not be utterly and completely controlled?' I asked myself. Then I began to look back and realise how stupid I had been, how all that I had seen and heard had in my ignorance passed over my head, and so much of what I had been told had no impact because never for a moment had I believed that the person who was speaking was of the same material as myself.

This gulf exists today between the old and the young, although in nothing like the same degree as existed in the early twenties between those who had been brought up without fathers and those who we thought were old simply because they had added more years to their lives than we had yet attained.

Max Beaverbrook was forty-four when I met him, and I know now that he was passing through a particularly difficult and unhappy period of his life.

Bonar Law—'the unknown Prime Minister'—whom he loved, had died, and Max once said to me almost savagely, as though the words were torn from his lips:

'Do you know what it's like to watch someone you know dying slowly day by day, to know that you cannot help them, that you can do nothing for them? Have you any idea what it is like to sit there, wanting to give them a part of yourself, a part of your life, some of the years you still have to live, and knowing that you are helpless?'

Another time he said to me of Bonar Law:

'He would have been the greatest Prime Minister we've ever had, but—he died in my arms.'

I didn't know then what an enormous part Max had played in politics, or indeed how Bonar Law had once tried to take his own life when he had retired to the South of France. It was before he knew he had cancer of the throat, but he sent for Max, or rather he told him what he had tried to do, and Max had abandoned everything to go to the help of his friend, and still was powerless to help him.

'I watched a man die.'

He was to say it over and over again because it had happened just a few months before I came into his life. His thoughts still dwelt on it, he was still deeply and emotionally involved.

One of the points the critics had against Max was that he 'destroyed young men'. I don't think that was true. Max could be ruthless—he had learnt to be so in the hard school in which he had grown up—but after Bonar Law was no longer there I am sure that he was searching all the time for someone to love and admire, as he had loved and admired this man twenty years older than himself.

He was like Metternich, the great Austrian statesman, who all his life searched for the ecstasy he had felt in his first love affair, and who subsequently had innumerable loves, every one of them lacking in the springing joy and beauty which had come to be the standard by which he judged all women.

Max, I am convinced, measured all men by what he himself had felt for Bonar Law, and when sometimes he believed in them for a short while, and they failed him, he hated them because they had revived within him the hope that he would once again love and trust a man who could to him become another hero.

I came into Max's life also at the time when he was experimenting with so many things—trying out the new, distrustful of the old. He employed a craftsman who was making him a special new sort of furniture. With his money he could have bought the most fabulous treasures in Britain, but instead he encouraged some obscure workman to chisel away and create for him something no one else possessed.

He had also suddenly come to a decision that he should know more about music. There were Russian orchestras brought by fast cars from Southampton where they had docked, to sing for Max the very moment they set foot on English soil. There were elderly men playing oboes, harps, violins and cellos in the garden. This was not because there was any artistic merit in going back to nature, but because The Vineyards was so small that the only way one could get away from the musicians was to put them outside.

I was never particularly musical, and I suffered acutely during this musical phase of Max's, just as Daphne Weymouth was to suffer when he decided that everyone should eat roast chicken and fresh green vegetables and potatoes and nothing else. Daphne once went on a cruise with him, and she described how greatly she minded when they arrived in Paris and ate at restaurants renowned among gourmets for their cuisine.

'It was torture for me,' she said, 'catching pungent whiffs of garlic, seeing the people at all the other tables eating snails, canard à la presse, truffes sous la cendre, and delicious crustaceans. Often I was close to tears.'

I think this must have been the time when Max inspired Jimmy Dunn with his passion for natural food. I remember great mounds of grated carrot being brought in for every meal, and also a story which has always made me laugh.

They had heard that a very famous health expert was visiting England from Canada. He was brought to see Max and Jimmy Dunn as soon as he arrived, and they told him proudly of their

217

diet, explaining how their fresh vegetables were grated, and how they consumed great quantities of them.

The health expert listened respectfully, and then he said:

'If God had meant you to eat like a cow, he would have given you four stomachs.'

I seem to remember the food at The Vineyards and at Cherkley (Max's country house) being very indifferent. While later in life Max took tremendous trouble over food and wine, in my day both Winston Churchill and Lord Birkenhead were continually complaining!

'Where did you get this claret, Max?'

'The grocer's, I think.'

'It tastes like it!'

It was as if Max, while playing with the idea of things about him being beautiful, was not interested in himself. I didn't realise then how deeply the fact that he had been teased as a boy about his looks had eaten into his soul.

He was the youngest of five children, and his father was a Presbyterian minister who had emigrated from Scotland to Canada in 1864. He was a strong preacher on the eternal damnation of sinners, and he disciplined his children to save them from the fires of hell. Max's mother used to beat him when he was a rebel—and this was very often.

What I ought to have understood at the time and didn't was that Max was deprived of love in his childhood, when it was most necessary to him. He had no golden memories of romance, or of his mother's belief and trust in him. I think what he remembered most was wanting to escape, and being ashamed of being so poor (although later he used to boast of it), and a dislike of his own appearance.

He must have given up any thought of changing himself. He bought his clothes at Harrods, or rather his valet bought them for him. They were rather badly fitting, nondescript navy-blue suits, and his shoes, purchased in the same way, had thick soles.

Men who have had an unhappy childhood are either determined that their children shall never suffer or else they want them also to find the world as rough and difficult as they did.

Max and I motored down to see little Max and his younger brother Peter, who were at a preparatory school, and we took them out to lunch. They were charming, good-looking little boys.

'What public school are you sending them to?' I asked.

'They will go to Westminster,' Max replied.

'A day school!' I exclaimed. 'Why don't you send them to Eton or Harrow?'

'They're not going to start life on my back,' he retorted, 'and they're not going to be given any advantages because they are Lord Beaverbrook's sons. They will start at the bottom, they will start as "no one".'

'But can't you see that's impossible?' I cried. 'How can they possibly be no one when they are Lord Beaverbrook's sons? It would be so much better for them to go to a school where many boys are the sons of important men. They are far more likely to be singled out in a school where they are big fish in a small pond.'

We argued fiercely, but I couldn't convince him. He wanted his sons to start at the bottom. It was ridiculous, and yet he would vie with his friends in claiming how much he had suffered in his childhood.

'I earned my own living when I left school at sixteen—selling newspapers.'

'My first full-time job was washing bottles for a chemist at a dollar a week!'

'I was continually hungry!'

'I slept on the floor in the insurance office where I worked. I hadn't more than $1.50 a week, and I borrowed that to keep myself from starving.'

Max would relate his sufferings, perhaps exaggerating some of them; and yet there is no doubt that he had indeed struggled against privation and poverty.

One thing, I think, that Max had never forgotten was that when he had become rich and famous, and had just been elected a Member of Parliament, a friend said to his mother:

'You must be proud of your son.'

Mrs. Aitken replied coolly:

'Which son? I have several.'

Once a big dance was being held in Newcastle, New Brunswick. Max, always ambitious and studying law, wanted to be present. He was told by a friend that as a law student he could get an invitation. He hired a tail-coat, white shirt and tie, and waited. Nothing happened, and he told me how he contacted his friend and complained that he had not yet received a card.

'I'm sorry,' the friend had replied, 'you can't go, after all. They have learnt that in the past you sold newspapers in the streets—we can't have newsboys in this Assembly.'

'How mean!' I exclaimed on hearing this story. 'You must have minded terribly. What did you do?'

'I went home,' Max replied. 'I put on that dress-suit and I sat in front of a mirror. I looked at my reflection, and I said to myself, "The day will come when they will be glad to ask me to their goddamned Assembly".'

Apart from his early days in Canada, Max must have endured in England many personal rebuffs and snubs more wounding than anything he had encountered in his boyhood. He was ugly, short and brash—a defiant cover for his shyness—and because he was a Canadian he was all the more ready to resent the aristocratic indifference of those whom he met in the House of Commons and in society.

Yet despite all this he was an ardent Imperialist and a completely convinced Conservative. People who have written of Max have so often stressed his obsession with money, his desire for power, his almost cynical interest in the social scene; but the thing I remember about him most is his close and unbroken loyalty to the three friends whose company meant more to him than that of anyone else.

One of these was the brilliant F. E. Smith—the 1st Lord Birkenhead. He, too, would boast of his poverty and of the hard life he had endured as a child.

'I made my own way in life unaided. Hungry and threadbare, I had nothing to help me but my own brain.'

This in fact was as much a fictitious picture as his daughter Eleanor's story that they were descended from gypsies.

F. E Smith's early life had not been one of grinding poverty, but was happy and reasonably prosperous. I suppose it made his rise to power seem all the more poignant when he pretended that he came from the gutter.

One story that was true, which Lord Birkenhead would tell over and over again, was the time at Oxford when he decided to call a meeting of his creditors.

'I remember when I was in very straitened circumstances at Oxford,' he would begin.

'We've heard that story before,' Winston Churchill would growl.

'Barbara hasn't heard it,' F.E. would reply, determined to continue, whatever the opposition.

He admitted to having been wildly extravagant, he was heavily in debt, and in June 1895 he realised that having enjoyed himself at the expense of his studies, his prospects were not particularly good, and he didn't think he had distinguished himself in his Finals.

At this moment he would say dramatically:

'I realised that only my skilful tongue stood between me and disaster.'

He invited all his creditors to his room, he settled them comfortably in chairs, and then frankly he told them the position.

'I have made many passionate appeals in my life,' he said, 'but never one which came more sincerely from the depths of my heart, or one which affected me more personally.'

To the shopkeepers, tailors, boot-makers and other tradesmen he spoke with the eloquence and fire which was to make him the most outstanding advocate of any generation. He told them of his dazzling prospects, and he told them too how stupid they would be to ruin him when he was destined for a Fellowship and a long residence in Oxford.

'I then left them,' F.E. said, 'to discuss it amongst themselves. I have never waited the verdict of a jury with more apprehension.'

When he went back he thought he had lost his case, but finally his tailor proposed that an extension of credit should be given him.

'I have never forgotten that man,' F.E. said. 'I can see his face now; to me at that moment he looked like the Angel Gabriel.'

'And did you go on buying your suits from him?' I asked.

'I still order two a year,' F.E. answered.

I learnt early in my acquaintance with the Four Adventurers that they needed an audience. I suppose in a way I was a perfect audience because I was prepared to listen wide-eyed, and maybe open-mouthed, to everything they told me. I was also so young and so ignorant that they could repeat old stories, old anecdotes, and know that to me they were as new and fresh as on the day when they first happened.

Max had once said to me that a man wants to spread his tail like a peacock, he wants to be admired, he wants to be able to show off. I think that in a way these great men enjoyed showing off to a young girl. They certainly talked to me, and perhaps at that particular time they needed someone to talk to.

Lord Birkenhead had been Lord Chancellor until a Socialist Government had come into power and he had lost office. He was when I met him only in the Shadow Cabinet. I had a feeling at the time that he was depressed, that he felt he had already passed the zenith of his power, and there could be no greater position for him than that which he had already enjoyed.

Once, when we were staying at Cherkley, Lord Beaverbrook's house in the country, he received a horoscope which had been 'done' for him by Lord Wavertree. He read it to me: it said he would have 'one more great rise and then a great fall'.

'I can't imagine what that great rise will be,' he said scornfully, 'unless, of course, a grateful people make me King.'

'Why shouldn't you be Prime Minister?' I asked, not realising it was something which no one else would have dared to say to him.

'I have held the highest post in the land,' he said, 'having been Lord Chancellor.'

He said it in a voice which held some reserve behind it, some bitterness and perhaps resentment.

I didn't know until very much later that two years earlier, when the Coalition Government had been in power, the Unionist junior Ministers had asked to be allowed to submit their anxieties over the Irish question to the whole body of Unionist Ministers of the Cabinet.

At this meeting Lord Birkenhead had, for some completely unknown reason, adopted an arrogant attitude that was offensive. He lectured the junior Ministers for their silliness and want of loyalty, he antagonised them and made them more indignant with every browbeating sentence.

At the time Lord Birkenhead could have had no idea how his attitude damaged his reputation and standing; if ever he had had a chance of leading the party, he had destroyed it then.

Max told me that Bonar Law used to quote an Arab proverb appropriate to F.E.:

'Easier to keep a live coal in the mouth than a witty saying.'

I was also told that F.E. had once lost a great sum of money by being witty. A wealthy Lancashire ship-owner, Sir Robert Houston, promised to make him one of his heirs. Sir Robert was very proud of his red beard, which, as he got older, kept its original colour. He was also a right-wing Tory die-hard.

One evening at a dinner party someone mentioned Sir Robert, and F.E. remarked:

'Of course, he's the original dye-hard!'

It was an expensive joke. Sir Robert cut him out of his will.

F.E. was often to repeat to me what he had said so memorably in his rectoral address at Glasgow University, that 'The world continues to offer glittering prizes to those who have stout hearts and sharp swords'. But his sharp tongue made him many enemies, while his charm and his kindness won him many loyal and adoring friends.

'He has a genius for friendship,' they said of him. 'If he gives you his hand, he gives you his heart.'

What I found so attractive was that he had a gift for talking to and with the young. He never patronised me, he never condescended, he never seemed to speak down to me. He talked to me as an equal and I, like so many others of my generation, loved him for the compliment.

In October 1924, in the General Election which followed the exposure of the Zinoviev letter, we sang:

'Since Ramsay Mac
Has got the sack,
It ain't gonna rain no mo'.'

The Conservatives swept the country and F.E. was appointed Secretary of State for India under the leadership of Stanley Baldwin, who had become Prime Minister, to Lord Curzon's tearful dismay and disappointment.

Lord and Lady Birkenhead gave a great reception at the India Office the following summer. F.E. asked me at the last moment if I would like to go.

'How can I?' I enquired.

'I will get one of the secretaries to send you a card,' he said. 'Bring a young man with you. It will be a sight to remember.'

How right he was! I have never forgotten the glitter and pageantry of the guests gathered in the huge open hall of the India Office. The Indian princes with their turbans and jewels, and the saris of their women, created a kaleidoscope of colour, and it was the first time I had seen diamonds worn in an Indian woman's nose. There were Arabs in their flowing robes with mysteriously veiled wives, and the English, as usual, looked more magnificent, more decorated and more bejewelled than anyone else.

One of my friends was Bibs Charteris, an angelic character who married the Earl of Plymouth. When he was Under Secretary of State Lord Plymouth often gave official parties for overseas visitors. One of these was attended by a Sultan from the Malay States.

'I'm so glad you could come,' Bibs said to him with her usual enthusiasm. 'Will you have a White Lady?'

The Sultan looked staggered, then smiled delightedly: he had not expected English hospitality to be so generous!

At Lord Birkenhead's party the Duchess of Sutherland wore a tiara which was almost a helmet of huge diamonds, and the Duke, in knee-breeches, had the blue ribbon of the Knight of the Thistle across his breast.

My pleasure was slightly dimmed by the fact that the young man I had taken grumbled incessantly that he only had two small medals, while everyone else was festooned with them. Also, in the excitement of the moment, I had forgotten that I should have worn gloves. Everyone else wore them, and I was blushingly conscious of my bare hands.

My embarrassment was increased when Lord Wavertree told me:

'Before the war it was always said that one could tell a lady by her gloves!'

Lord Wavertree—the brother of my great-uncle—was a dedicated astrologer, and followed the stars long before the newspapers ran them as a daily guide. He had the horoscopes cast of all his horses for mating and racing purposes. The stars, however, must have misled him when he sold Prince Palatine, the winner of the St. Leger and of two Gold Cups, for two thousand guineas.

However, Uncle Willie, as I called him, leased Minoru to Edward VII as a three-year-old. Minoru won six races, including the Two Thousand Guineas and the Derby. This was the only occasion on which the Derby has been won by a reigning monarch. The King was mobbed at Epsom by a demonstration of loyalty and affection, the police were overpowered, and everyone present on the course sang 'God Save the King'.

Uncle Willie was in character an odd mixture. He was extremely shrewd where money was concerned, having negotiated the sale of Walkers Breweries for £6,000,000. He would always pay the first-class fare of his guests if he thought they were poor, and when they left gave them money to tip his servants.

At Horsley he had a large collection of pornographic books and pictures which he kept in a locked room, and the most fabulous Japanese gardens in Great Britain, for which he employed thirty gardeners.

The Duke of Sutherland was another notability I met with Lord Beaverbrook. He would come to those small, intimate lunches at The Vineyards, and though he was younger than the other men, he also seemed to me a being from some celestial height. He was very good-looking, tall, fair, with blue eyes, the possessor of the greatest acreage of land in Great Britain, and had recently sold his coal-mines, bringing him in a great sum of money to add to his already enormous wealth.

In Scotland the Duke of Sutherland's home was Dunrobin Castle, an enchanted fairy-like place on the sea with its turrets and towers silhouetted against the hills. I was to love it dearly, just as I was to love Sutton Place, the house the Duke bought from Lord Northcliffe, and which, with its beautiful Elizabethan brick, its huge ancestral hall and its peacocks strutting proudly on the terrace, was the most romantic place I have ever seen.

I had, of course, heard about the Sutherlands' magnificent fancy-dress parties, their yacht—*The Sans Peur*—in which they journeyed to Africa, and the kings and queens they entertained.

I knew the Duke was the best big-game shot in the world, and that he had been Under Secretary for Air in the last Conservative Government—an achievement at thirty-five. He was also extremely proud of his position as President of the Air League of the British Empire.

He owned so much, he had so much to do, he was ambitious and full of enthusiasm. I thought he must be the happiest man it was possible to meet.

'Don't you think a man is entitled to take a little happiness when he can find it?' the Duke asked me soon after we met.

I looked at him in astonishment. Then as I grew to know him

better I found that, although he was too much a gentleman ever to say so, his marriage was not a happy one. The Duchess was beautiful, fêted, painted by all the great artists, acclaimed by her friends and the hundreds of hangers-on who trailed behind her, and who are part of every ducal entourage. But they had no children.

Often at Sutton the Duke would appear to be the odd man out, an onlooker not a participator in the gay crowd of distinguished people who, from the King and Queen of Spain to Douglas Fairbanks Senior, filled his house. I felt often that some of the things which were said to him were wounding and hurtful.

Later Duchess Millicent was to tell me secretly how much she worried about her son's happiness, but there was nothing she could do and like all the mothers in the world she could only pray that somehow things would 'come right'.

The Duke began to seem a little vague. People said he was slightly deaf because he didn't always hear what was said to him, but it was not until many years later that it was discovered that every night of his life he took a sleeping pill. Sometimes one, sometimes two; it was his escape from the world. It was a barrier between him and things that could hurt—these little pills which one day would take his life away from him before he should have died.

The most exciting person at Max's parties was, of course, Winston Churchill. It was impossible when he was present not to find oneself watching and listening to him. It wasn't so much what he said, because F. E. Smith was vocally far more brilliant; it was a kind of aura about him, that irresistible Churchill magnetism which was to show itself from the moment he was born to the moment he died.

He had in 1924 been through a very bad time. He was without a Parliamentary seat, he had become the target of political brickbats for having deserted in turn both Conservatives and Liberals, and when he stood for Westminster he had been beaten by a narrow margin of forty-three votes in a poll of 22,000. When he lost in Manchester the Stock Exchange had telegraphed him jeeringly:

'What is the use of a W.C. without a seat?'

As always when Winston was up against it he was very voluble in defence of himself. I heard him explaining what had happened, arguing that he had been right in the course he had taken, and speaking as if it was only a question of days or hours before an impatient electorate carried him shoulder high to victory.

He was not defeated, he was undefeatable; and yet there must have been some hurt in knowing that his brilliance was unappreciated, that his political acumen hadn't more support in the country. But, as usual, he was looking ahead, prophesying, and rightly, that the Socialist Government would not last, and that the Liberals would inevitably withdraw their support from the MacDonald administration.

Already he had been chosen as prospective candidate for a rural constituency of West Essex, or the Epping division. He told us about it, extolling its virtues as a place wholly desirable, the sort of people he would want to represent, and which must, without reserve, want him as their representative.

One thing I learnt about Winston Churchill was that he had an amazing capacity for concentrating on what he was doing to the exclusion of all else. He would set up his easel in the garden at Cherkley and paint the bushes and shrubs on the terrace, depicting them in what seemed to me strange colours. When he did this he didn't seem to be thinking of anything else, he didn't even seem to hear what was going on around him. I realised that this perhaps was one of the powers all these great men had.

I knew that F. E. Smith, when he was working at the Bar, would often not open his brief until he was on his way to the Law Courts. Then, as he travelled in a taxi, he would read it, and by the time he reached his destination he would be word perfect.

'He has a photographic memory,' I remember saying to my friends when I spoke of him.

I saw how Winston could concentrate on his painting, on a book he was reading, or on the notes he was making, and be completely unconscious of everything else around him.

Max used his powers of concentration on the person with whom he happened to be. He would draw someone out, not by coaxing methods but by direct questions. It seemed as though he wanted to tear them apart to find out what made them tick, to search inside them to understand what they were thinking and feeling.

Very few people could withstand this method, which as Max

grew older became a fine art. Most people expanded to him, they blossomed, they gave him what he wanted to know, and then, alas, far too often there was nothing left to give, and he threw them away.

'You write well,' he said to me when we first met at The Vineyards.

'Thank you.'

'But you could write better.'

Then came the flow of questions.

'Who are you?'

'Where do you come from?'

'Why do you write?'

'What do you think?'

Max taught me to write. He told me that to get style he had read the books of one particular author he admired, and nothing else, until he could imitate him without being conscious of doing so.

I would write my paragraphs and take them to the Hyde Park Hotel, where Max had his office surrounded by telephones. He would read what I had written and pull it to pieces.

'Why do you say that?'

'I don't know.'

'Can't you see it's superfluous?'

'Yes, I can see that now.'

The offending words were crossed out, my untidy effort was finally initialled and sent to the *Express*.

Max's third great friend, besides F.E. and Winston, was Sir James Dunn. Jimmy was a Canadian, like himself, a man of great wealth even then. When he died he left £25,000,000. He was a financier and had been knighted during the war. He was a barrister of law in Canada, but didn't practise. He was rough and bluff, dominant and domineering. He was the least polished of the Adventurers, and the least reserved or controlled. He would rage at the servants, be excessively rude in restaurants; and yet, when he wished, he exercised a charm which matched his blue eyes and the blue shirts which he habitually wore.

Jimmy Dunn fell in love with me and asked me to marry him. My mother was appalled; he was not only far too old in her opinion, but he was already married, in the process of having a divorce, and had a grown-up family.

I had no intention of marrying anyone who I felt was old enough to be my grandfather, but I was fascinated by the life Jimmy lived, which was more spectacular and more glittering than that of his friends.

He had rented an enormous house at Roehampton called Templeton, which belonged to the Hon. Frederick Guest, the Chief Whip of the Lloyd George Liberals, an energetic, middle-aged man who combined politics and air-racing.

His counterpart on the Conservative side was Sir George Younger. Freddie Guest believed a Whip shouldn't interfere in politics; Sir George was continually meddling. One day F.E. asked him crushingly:

'Since when has the cabin-boy mounted the bridge?'

Templeton had a huge garden in which floodlit parties took place. It was the first time I had seen floodlit gardens, and certainly the first time I had ever met the amazing collection of people whom Jimmy called his friends. There were statesmen, politicians and actresses, Bright Young People, film stars and millionaires. There were Russian orchestras and singers, ballerinas and bands.

It was all incredibly luxurious—a yacht in which to visit Deauville (hired from F.E.), a fleet of Hispano Suizas to carry one from place to place, special tables in restaurants and night-clubs, whole floors of hotels booked at the places he wished to visit. It was grand living by a man who was virile, forceful and vivid, like a character from a Wild West film.

At my unenjoyable weekend at Deauville, Jimmy's guests were typical—Duff Cooper and the lovely Lady Diana en route for New York and *The Miracle*; an unknown young man named Noël Coward; my friend the Marchioness of Queensberry, who ran away with Jimmy when the weekend was over; the best-known polo player in Europe; Phyllis Satterthwaite, who coached King Gustave V of Sweden at tennis; Ruby—Jimmy's ex-mistress—who was a delightful woman, and her very pretty adopted daughter, who was the result of an illicit liaison between a hospital nurse and a doctor; and a number of other now faceless creatures with tingling laughs.

Ruby had kept Jimmy's interest for many years because she discovered that being a strong, overpowering man, he liked weak, helpless women. Whenever he appeared to be getting bored with her she had a surgical operation. He was completely and whole-heartedly devoted while she was ill.

But Jimmy had a social complex. I remember when we were having lunch on the yacht as we left Southampton, Duff Cooper asking me, as I came from Worcestershire, about Lee and Perrin's Worcestershire sauce.

'It's an interesting story,' I replied, and picking up the bottle I began to read the label, which said: 'Made from the original secret recipe preserved for many generations in a nobleman's family. . . .'

'A nobleman's family indeed!' Jimmy stormed, suddenly going off into one of his rages. 'You're always talking about noblemen! Who are they, and who cares about them these days? They are finished, out of date, an anachronism! The world today is for those who have brains and know how to use them!'

There was never any point in trying to argue with Jimmy, he could shout one down. Only one woman was ever to tame and control him, and that was his third wife—Christoforides. He was happier with her than anyone else. Being with Jimmy was always like riding a rough sea—there were squalls and tempests, sudden bursts of sunshine, never a dead calm.

At Templeton I saw Lord Birkenhead and Lord Rochdale play a singles tennis match for a stake of £100. F.E. unfortunately had been entertaining the Law Society of America for nearly a week. He drank an enormous amount, but his practice of taking daily exercise, which would have killed a weaker man, made him seemingly untouched by the late hours he kept, or the brandy and cigars which were his habitual diet. But on this occasion his exercise had been curtailed, and Lord Rochdale won very easily.

Once during a weekend in the country F.E. played thirty-six holes of golf in the morning, rising early to do so. After luncheon we rode for two hours on Scottish ponies which Geordie Suther-land had brought down from Dunrobin, and which were inevitably given too many oats and too little exercise. I remember falling off because I hit my head on a bough riding through the woods. The moment we got back to the house F.E. demanded tennis. He played three sets, and then as everyone sank exhausted into chairs on the terrace, he announced amid groans:

'Now I would like another round of golf before dinner.'

It was exercise which kept him so fit and made him seem

untouched by the excesses of his diet. When one sees his pictures, and reads his brilliant but often hurtful speeches, it is difficult to reconcile them with the picture of F.E. diving happily off his yacht with a lighted cigar in his mouth, and performing his favourite trick of coming up from the depths of the ocean with it still alight.

How many stories there were about him! The one I liked best, which happened just after the war—which I made him tell me himself—was when he was lunching at the Ritz. A general who had spent the war at the War Office stopped at his table to speak to him.

'You have a lot of medals, General,' F.E. commented.

'Yes, Mr. Attorney, if I get any more I shall scarcely know where to put them!'

'Put them where you earned them, General, on your backside!'

Perhaps, because these four men were all so famous, one often forgets their sense of humour: Winston—who would laugh until the tears ran down his cheeks; F.E.—who would tell anecdote after anecdote, not spiteful, bitter ones, which so often made him quite unnecessary enemies at the Bar and in the House of Commons, but gay, amusing stories of people and places, and often against himself; and Max—Max was omnipotent. He seldom told tales, but he laughed, he manipulated the conversation, he could make it gay or sombre at will, and he knew it.

I can see them sitting round the table in that dull beige-coloured room at The Vineyards, with its low ceiling and inadequate lighting from the small windows: F.E. scintillating, sarcastic, devastating; Winston orating sincerely, passionately; Max listening, stimulating, spurring. They would be altering, destroying, controlling the political world.

I would wonder how long they would be. Would there be time when I was sent home in the car to slip out again? Hugo had said he would wait for me. He was blond, blue-eyed, and had been in the Navy, and I thought—yes, I was almost certain—I was falling in love. The old men were still talking, I longed to go dancing!

'I want you to meet Tim Healy—a very old friend of mine,' Max said one evening.

'The first Governor of the Irish Free State?' I asked. 'Wasn't he very revolutionary?'

'He was a great Parliamentarian,' Max corrected, 'a man of fire and vision. Let me tell you a story.'

Max told me how in the war at the time of the retreat from Mons he was walking with Tim Healy from the House of Commons to the Savoy.

'I was oppressed by a foreboding of disaster,' Max said, 'for I had seen a despatch which had just arrived from G.H.Q. in France. But Tim was holding forth about the oppression of the Irish and the awful iniquities of British rule. Suddenly I said to him, "I'm tired of hearing about the grievances of the Irish, let me tell you of the perils of the British Army".'

'What are they?' Tim growled.

'The C.-in-C. has said,' Max replied, ' "I mean to retire to the sea. If the enemy remains in contact, this will be a very difficult operation. I advise you to look to the defences of Le Havre." '

Max told me that for a moment there was complete silence. Then he saw the tears streaming down Tim Healy's cheeks, until in a passionate flow of words he dedicated himself before God to the service of the Allied cause.

'I have known Tim, rebel, agitator, enemy of Great Britain,' Max finished, 'intimately since that hour, but he has never violated the vow he made to me that evening.'

I was naturally curious and interested to meet this remarkable man. Tim Healy was then over seventy, with a white beard and an expression of melancholy gravity; but when he spoke in his broad, warm Irish brogue, I could still hear the fire behind his words.

F.E. wrote of him that year:

'His Parliamentary gifts were individual and extraordinary. He possessed the power of mordant and corrosive sarcasm, the like of which I have never met before. I can still see him standing up to address the House . . . pouring out a long succession of bitter, cruel and wounding insults.'

But F.E. added:

'Concealed within this strange personality by his public ferocity are the heart and the temperament of a warm-hearted child.'

His Excellency, Max and I set off for Templeton, where Jimmy Dunn was giving a party. It was the usual fantastic mixture of the grand, the glamorous, the hangers-on and the hung-on-to. We motored home as dawn was breaking. The old Irishman was full of whisky, and as the Irish always sing in joy or sorrow, sadness or gaiety—he sang.

Most of his songs were, I think, hymns. There were many references to being washed in 'the blood of the Lamb', one about the prodigal son, and a number of dirges about lovers being murdered by the English.

Every so often the Governor of the Irish Free State would turn to Max and me and demand angrily:

'And why don't ye join in, ye heathen?'

Max introduced me to so many celebrities. One was Lloyd George, who had left Downing Street for the last time two years earlier. He was still a buoyant, eloquent personality, enormously energetic, with an uncanny ability to read the public mind almost before it had formed itself. But he had lost all popularity, and it was the fashion at that time to abuse and ridicule everything he said or did. Yet no one could help being fascinated by him.

Margot Asquith had said: 'He could charm the bark off a tree', but this opinion, of course, was mitigated by J. H. Thomas, the Labour leader, who had said: 'You dare not turn your head or blow your nose, or L.G. will trick you.'

I met Lloyd George first at an enormous meeting at which he was speaking to foreign correspondents from all over the world. There was still some fire in his words, still something hypnotic in the way he used his hands and shook his long white hair, but even when we talked, then and on other occasions, I found it hard to credit that people still believed that he was one of the greatest Prime Ministers we had ever had and would make a come-back.

Bob Boothby remembers in 1926 someone in the smoking room of the House of Commons asking about Lloyd George:

'Can you point to one concrete or permanent piece of work he has ever accomplished?'

Lord Balfour, who had appeared to be asleep, suddenly replied:

'He won the greatest war in history, that really was something of an achievement!'

A story which was always told of Lloyd George in the twenties described how during the war someone asked him how soon he wanted something done.

'Tomorrow,' he replied. 'No, today! Better still, yesterday!'

Although the Press was far more discreet in those days than it is now, and although there was still a halo of untouchability about statesmen, Lloyd George's behaviour with women was openly talked about. Typists in Westminster were said to hurry away at his approach, and the new short skirts just coming in in 1924 were an added enticement to his easily aroused interest in a woman, pretty or otherwise.

His friends didn't hesitate to tease him about it. I remember once at a luncheon party Lloyd George saying about some Bill that was coming before the House:

'We mustn't forget it concerns women. It is essential that we should not forget the women.'

There was a guffaw of laughter from everyone present, and someone said:

'That is one thing *you* are never likely to forget.'

Lloyd George took it in good part. He laughed, and I had the feeling he was rather proud of the fact that his friends recognised in him an active masculinity. There was no doubt that a large number of women did like Lloyd George as a man; but in the case of another man his unattractiveness to women was to shape the character of one of the strangest personalities of the period. Leonard Mosley has described him better than anyone else:

'At first glance,' he says, 'I thought Humpty Dumpty had come to our theatre. In the darkened auditorium all I could see was an oval-shaped head, and beneath it a much bigger oval lighter in shade—as if one small brown egg was balancing on top of one large white one. Then I saw the white egg was a silk waistcoat covering an enormous expanse of chest, and that the brown egg was a face cracking open with laughter.'

Viscount Castlerosse was a natural wit but a man so strange to look at, so extraordinary in his habits, that he would have been an eccentric in any age in which he lived.

Max Beaverbrook 'took him up' as he was to take up so many young men, brilliant or otherwise; but his friendship with Castlerosse was to continue all through his life. Valentine's aristocratic flamboyance appealed to him, but I think also that Max of all people saw beneath the flashy façade to the pathetic childlike creature beneath.

Castlerosse was an Irishman and a Catholic, and he loved his estates at Killarney as he was to love nothing else in his life. But, like so many people that I knew, he had had an unhappy childhood. He believed that his mother, whom he adored, preferred his brother Dermot because he was so much better-looking.

'The shock for me,' he told a friend later in life, 'was to discover that my mother loved Dermot much more than me, and to know that she was right in doing so. It was dreadful for me to see my mother looking at both of us and comparing us. I was an ugly, awkward child. My feet were too small for my body, I was frightened of heights, I was slow of speech, and I blushed a lot. I believed that she was always thinking "What a shame Dermot isn't the heir".'

When Dermot was killed in 1915 his mother never recovered. Valentine tried to comfort her, but he was coldly repulsed.

'It was obvious to me,' he said, 'that my mother was thinking "Why should he be alive when Dermot is dead?" '

This started the complexes which were to affect Castlerosse all his life. The fact that he felt himself to be ugly and unwanted made it inevitable that he would believe that women didn't like him.

Because he was ashamed of having no love affairs he invented them, telling wild, improbable tales to his fellow undergraduates at Cambridge of what dashing things he had done in the presence of some entirely mythical young woman.

He hated the Army and its routine, which was perhaps not surprising in an Irishman, but it merely added to his sense of inferiority.

Because he wanted to cut a dash, perhaps as much to himself as anyone else, Castlerosse took to gambling at Deauville. That at the start of the weekend he had £4,000 in the bank, while at the end of it he had to borrow to pay his debts and to get home to England, merely confirmed his sense of failure.

Then fortune came his way. In Paris he met a Canadian called Sir Max Aitken. Later Castlerosse was to write:

'The approach to youth is delicate. Some have a delicate touch, and they alone know how to get response out of mankind . . . Paderewski could do the same with a piano, Max Aitken had this touch . . . I found myself getting on with Max Aitken in great style. Here was a man who laughed with you . . .'

This luncheon, which took place by chance because Lord Birkenhead, who was then still F. E. Smith, happened to ask Castlerosse as one of his guests, was to be a turning-point in his life. When the war was over he and Max became close—and to other people almost incomprehensible—friends.

Castlerosse's loneliness was in some way relieved. With Max he could relax and unburden himself. During the years together they would often have violent rows. Castlerosse got into every sort of trouble, but Max always bailed him out of it. There were endless crises over money, but somehow, with that capacity for friendship which Max had shown in his affection for Bonar Law, their comradeship survived.

But one thing the years of frustration had produced in Valentine was an insatiable appetite for eating and drinking. Today any psychiatrist could explain it by the fact that Castlerosse wanted love, but perhaps he wanted it more greedily than anyone else had done before.

He was a colossal eater. I have watched him, fascinated, eating enough food to satisfy a man and a woman for a week, and at the end he would say he was still hungry.

John Gordon, the great editor of the *Sunday Express*, saw him eat: 'a whole ham at one sitting, loosing the way for it with three large red-peppered vodkas, washing it down with an imperial pint of champagne in a tankard, and topping it off with a bottle of brandy'.

'I don't know how it started,' Valentine said, 'except that suddenly I began to get hungrier and hungrier. I found I needed vast quantities of food to sustain me, and my thirst for alcoholic liquids was practically unquenchable. I do not think that even my worst enemy can say that it has affected the quickness of my mind —just the bloody opposite in fact.'

In 1924 Valentine was easily one of the most spectacular figures in London, his enormous chest enveloped in a purple overcoat, his small feet swathed in spats, the gold watch-chain across the ever-increasing stomach. He would go from Claridges to the Savoy and the Embassy Club, or to one of the hostesses who daily and nightly would besiege him with invitations to their parties.

His uncle, Lord Revelstoke, arranged for him to work with a firm of stockbrokers in the City, but he hated the job and he hated the people. He began to arrive later and later at the office, until finally one of his friends remonstrated with him.

'It is a disgrace how late you come in, Valentine.'

'But think how early I go!' Castlerosse replied.

Shortly after this his uncle, known as an 'Emperor of Finance', told him that his services were no longer needed.

I remember Castlerosse sitting at luncheon stuffing into the food, and making us all roar with laughter as he told the story of how he had gone to the Savoy to lunch with Lord Birkenhead.

'We had an excellent meal,' he said. 'I was on my way to the cloakroom, a cigar in my mouth and my hand in my pocket struggling to get my matches, when my fingers encountered some papers. I pulled them out. Just then somebody bumped into me and they fell to the floor right at the feet of a gentleman whom I recognised as an official of my uncle's firm. He bent down to help me pick up what I had dropped, and handed me back my papers with a knowing and triumphant smile. I recognised them too: they were £20,000 of National War Bonds which I had stuffed into my pocket absent-mindedly and taken with me out to lunch.'

Castlerosse took another huge mouthful of food.

'It did not need the mind of a genius,' he continued, 'to know that once the tale reached my uncle, my career as a stockbroker would be at an end. I went back into the dining room, drank another brandy, while the official of my uncle's firm—a gentleman much given to licking the boots of his superiors—scuttled back to the City with his titbit of scandal. Then with the leisurely calm of a man who has no more to lose I followed.'

Once inside the office Castlerosse went straight to his uncle's room and walked in. He threw the bonds down on Lord Revelstoke's desk.

'Greetings, dear Uncle,' he said genially. 'And how's the old bucket-shop doing today?'

It might have been funny to us, but it was definitely the end of Castlerosse's career in the City, and he fell desperately into debt. Max was to pay his debts and pay them again and again. At the same time he was wise enough to realise that, while Castlerosse was prepared to accept his help, while he was prepared to boast and be excruciatingly funny about his failures, inside he was frustrated and unhappy.

Castlerosse was the Court Jester to the Four Adventurers. He would sit gorging himself with food and drink, apparently not even listening to the conversation, until Max would say:

'What do you think about it, Valentine?'

It was the cue for the song he must sing for his supper: Castlerosse would look up at the ceiling and without a pause give a quick, spontaneous, witty reply. I never knew him fail the challenge.

One of his quickest repartees was at a huge reception given by Lady Astor at St. James's Square. As Valentine came up the stairs to be received, Lady Astor, always audacious, leant forward and patted his enormous stomach, saying:

'If that was on a woman we should know what to think!'

Valentine didn't hesitate before he replied:

'Well, it was last night, so what do you think?'

In 1926 Max had a brain-wave. In April the *Sunday Express* announced a new departure in Sunday journalism.

'The London Log will in future be edited and signed by Viscount Castlerosse.'

Valentine's page was a success from the very moment he started writing. It was clever, witty, indiscreet, and full of names we all knew. Everyone in the social world snatched the *Sunday Express* as soon as it appeared on Sunday morning and read Castlerosse before they even looked at the headlines.

The readers loved the way he lampooned the pompous leaders of society. They liked the impression he gave of always being in the know, of being able to say a great deal more if he dared, but even so, managing to give us spicy human titbits about people who before had just been mere names.

My favourite story of those which Valentine told about himself was when he went to the Arts Ball in Paris dressed like one of Attila's Huns, wearing only a few skins. When he returned half-naked to his hotel he met an elderly maiden lady in the corridor.

'My God!' she ejaculated.

'Yes, madam,' Valentine replied, 'but tonight strictly incognito.'

Then just as it seemed that Valentine had found a special niche for himself, and some of his feelings of insecurity and inadequacy must have been disappearing, he fell in love with the most temperamental, extravagant and beautiful woman in London. Her name was Doris Delavigne.

Doris had been seen round Mayfair for some time before she met Valentine in 1928. Michael Arlen was reputed to have used Doris as a model for the heroine of *The Green Hat*—there were few pretty women he wasn't supposed to have used. Noël Coward certainly copied her in *Private Lives*, using her language, her outlook, her appearance and behaviour.

Elinor Glyn once said, 'She looks like a hungry fox!' But most people compared Doris to a nervous and sensitive deer, possessing the grace and ferocity of a panther.

Doris really was beautiful, and there was not a man who saw her and didn't feel attracted to her. She had perfect legs, a wonderful figure, and a skin which had some strange quality about it—once a man had touched it he never forgot. And yet she had a viper's tongue. She had a vocabulary which left people open-mouthed, and which not unnaturally shocked into silence the majority of those who heard her speak her mind.

Because she was beautiful, because she was outrageous, because she gave the impression of not caring whether people liked her or not, Doris became the rage. Men fought to take her out, and it gave them a certain prestige to be seen dining in her company. She attracted men, from Guards officers to statesmen and politicians, and it was inevitable from the very first that she would marry someone of social importance.

The last thing anyone expected, either for her or for Valentine Castlerosse, was that they would marry each other. They fought from the very beginning. One would see them together at the Embassy Club: Doris's eyes would be flashing and Valentine would be going more crimson in the face than usual. Sometimes she would get up and walk out of the restaurant, leaving him alone, spluttering with fury over his piled plate. After a moment his big fat hand would go out to grasp the neck of a bottle, and he would pour himself another drink.

Valentine lived on the edge of bankruptcy and so did Doris. I remember once going into a well-known jeweller's shop and seeing on the counter twenty or thirty articles of jewellery which I vaguely recognised.

'They belong to Miss Delavigne,' the jeweller told me with a grin. 'When she is down to her last sixpence she sells everything she has and gives an enormous party. Later in the week I expect she will buy them all back again, plus ten per cent of course.'

But Doris could be a good friend—strangely enough a lot of woman liked her. She was always charming to me, going out of her way to do something kind, to say something flattering. She had a slangy way of talking, but what she said was worth listening to, and not only men, but people like Diana Cooper and Venetia Montagu, listened to her and became her friends.

Valentine found it difficult to get dates with her: she was always just going out with someone more important than himself, or on her way to a party to which he hadn't been invited. But he was consumed with a longing to see her, to listen to her, to look at her.

He ran himself into further debt to buy her jewels, furs and pictures. There was nothing new about such attentions, but he could also open those doors of society which were still closed to her by some of the more particular hostesses.

Older men, however, were trying to make Castlerosse see sense.

'You are making a fool of yourself, Valentine!' one of these said in my presence.

'I can't help myself,' Valentine answered in a desperate voice. 'I am not just in love, I'm infatuated, obsessed, bewitched! I can't live without her.'

Everybody in London knew the story of Doris going to see a friend of Castlerosse to tell him how badly she was being treated. She showed him the mass of bruises on her white arms.

'You had better warn him as a friend,' she said, 'that if he behaves like this again I shall inform the police. Meanwhile you can make him return the key of my house; he is not coming in any more.'

The friend found Valentine and gave him the message.

'How dare she say such things,' he exclaimed.

He rolled up his trouser leg and displayed a bandaged calf.

'Look what she has done to me, with her teeth too.'

Everyone agreed that it would be ridiculous and insane for Doris and Valentine to be married. Max Beaverbrook begged Castlerosse to be sensible, and Valentine promised him over and over again that he would leave her alone.

His uncle, Lord Revelstoke, pointed out to him that a trust fund intended for the upkeep and glorification of his beloved

Killarney might be forfeited if he insisted on an alliance with 'this notorious woman'.

Valentine tried to forget his misery in an orgy of drinking and eating. His waistline expanded, and so did his debts. But he had made up his mind. On May 28th, 1928, at 10.30 a.m., he and Doris were married at Hammersmith Register Office.

It was, as everybody had forecast, a disastrous and unhappy marriage. They fought in private, they fought in public. They lived at Doris's house opposite me in Culross Street, and often very early in the morning, if I was awake, I would see an enormous Falstaffian figure in pyjamas walking angrily up and down the pavement, crimson with rage, spluttering with anger, muttering to himself. It was Valentine, having been locked out by Doris after one of their regular rows.

It was pathetic that any man could be so desperately and overwhelmingly jealous as Valentine was, and be married to a woman who must inevitably incite her husband to frantic, agonising, unremitting jealousy.

The story was not to end until World War II, when Doris died of an overdose of sleeping tablets. But the whole drama was first to run through every possible situation, violent, hysterical, incredible, of divorce and reconciliation.

The outward effect on Castlerosse was that he ate and drank more and more until he was over twenty stone. It was a sad ending, but the Castlerosses, like so many others in the twenties, had a bitter-sweet story. At least they gave colour and a certain excitement to living. As far as we the observers were concerned, that was all that mattered.

CHAPTER NINE

There's the famous and notorious,
There's the rich and there's the poor,
There's film-stars, Peers and Peeresses,
All crowded on the floor.
There's the Prince of Wales and Lady F,
And who else do I see?
But every crashing bore I know
In the dear old Embassy!

ON Thursday nights everyone went to the Embassy Club, which the Prince of Wales called 'the Buckingham Palace of night-clubs'. It was in the Piccadilly end of Bond Street, and one found it down a wide, low-ceilinged kind of tunnel, outside which tall, impressive-looking commissionaires adorned with medals stood on duty. Michael Arlen said of them:

'These men have eyes of hawks; for it is their business to sift out the low and vulgar from the fashionable crowds, who perpetually strive for admittance. They are the best shifters of their kind.'

Inside the tunnel at the entrance door of the club there was always a small one-legged man selling gardenias and red carnations for buttonholes. He was there for years, always with a smile and a quip for those he knew, which was pretty nearly everyone.

'Evenin', Captain, got your usual for you.'

'Have a good day at Newmarket, m'lord? Oh! I see you have one, that's disappointin' for me!'

'Well, I suppose I had better have another!'

'Thank you, m'lord, very good of you, m'lord. Got a tip for tomorrow?'

He was almost part of the establishment, and those who weren't greeted by him knew how unimportant they must be.

Downstairs the ladies' cloakroom was a triumph of decorating a cellar to look attractive with fitted carpets, marble basins and gold taps. It was pervaded by a low chatter of well-bred voices and the fragrance of expensive scent. In charge there was a woman dressed in shiny black, looking like a respectable housekeeper from a large country house, who was a friend of all those distinguished enough to be recognised by her.

Once I met in the cloakroom Lady Diana Cooper, whom I hadn't seen since our trip to Deauville several years earlier.

I approached her shyly because she always seemed to me like a goddess far removed from mere models like myself.

'I must thank you, Lady Diana, for saving my life. If you hadn't turned the yacht round that time we were going to Deauville, I am certain it would have gone to the bottom and we should have all been drowned.'

'I was glad to save my own life,' she answered, her blue eyes almost as translucent as the mirror which reflected them, her hair golden as pale corn, her face that of a saint.

'Did you know that the yacht took three days to reach Trouville harbour and that everything on board was smashed?'

'How thankful I am that we turned back!' Lady Diana murmured.

'And did you get to New York safely?' I asked, remembering that that was where she had been going from Deauville to act in *The Miracle*.

'We had a terrible passage,' she answered. 'If only I wasn't so frightened of the sea!'

'Well, thank you once again,' I said a little awkwardly.

I couldn't help being in awe of her, she was so beautiful, so regal. She gave me a smile that was almost a benediction, and with chiffon fluttering around her like angels' wings she went upstairs. How was I to know that in the Second World War she would write:

'Yesterday I bought a seven-year-old cow for twenty-seven pounds. I milked her with speed and success. She gave over a gallon and a half and it only took me twenty minutes!'

How could I guess? And how could I have imagined this:

'The Pig Family Hutchinson is in splendid fatness and should make me a nice profit. . . . I spend a lot of time asphyxiated by the smell and bent double inside the sty shovelling their dung.'

There were sofas all round the walls of the restaurant, which were kept exclusively by Luigi—the most famous *maître d'hôtel* in the whole social world—for the royal, the distinguished and the notorious! Tables packed most of the room, leaving only a small piece of parquet in front of the band—this piece got smaller and smaller as the night progressed and more and more people crowded into the club.

Everyone wore their best clothes; for Thursday night was the night of the week, and all the *habitués* were there, and as many others as could get past the scrutinising eyes of Luigi, who sifted the grain from the chaff with the precision of a Jewish money-lender weighing diamonds.

The restaurant world has always acknowledged that Luigi could 'dress' a room better than anyone else. He knew every scandal, every whisper of a romance, every quarrel, which might make it uncomfortable to put a certain gentleman near a pretty lady who had just rebuffed him, or when he had been recently replaced by a more exciting charmer.

All the young, the gay, the beautiful and those who could afford it went to the Embassy on Thursday evening. No hostess would have been so stupid as to give a party on that night, unless she thought the attractions she offered would completely eclipse those to be found within those softly lit walls, which for no apparent reason had become the smartest place in the whole of Europe.

No one knows why one place becomes smart while another fails. When Luigi died and the Embassy fell on bad times I was asked to bring back the fashionable fold. The proprietors had just spent thousands of pounds on redecoration, which was hard, modern and unbecoming to women.

I made them repaint the club in the soft green of my drawing room, cover the sofas in a pink which matched my bedroom curtains, and remove the ceiling lights and make it warm, cosy and glamorous.

With the help of Ambrose's band and my friends, in three weeks I restored the Embassy to its former glory. But a lot of it was luck!

Let us take any Thursday evening in the late twenties.

As one enters the room seems like a bowl of animated sweet-peas; nearly every woman is wearing a chiffon dress which flutters as she moves and has a long chiffon scarf hanging down from one shoulder. Also on the shoulder is a bunch of real or artificial flowers, and round every thin, graceful left wrist are row upon row of narrow diamond bracelets jokingly known as 'service stripes'.

The faces of the women dancing and sitting round the room have an almost monotonous beauty. They all have large eyes with mascaraed eyelashes, full crimson mouths, narrow aristocratic noses and fine bones. Their hair, cut short and styled close to their well-shaped heads, is like exquisite satin, shiny and neat. Everything about them is neat and the expensive perfection of simplicity.

Their skins are white—very white, the only exception being the warm, golden loveliness of Lady Plunket as she floats by in the arms of Prince George. Dorothé is the first person to be suntanned, and she has whispered to me that in the winter she keeps the same colour by applying diluted iodine to her skin.

Also dancing is the Vicomtesse de Janzé—the great-granddaughter of the beautiful Mrs. Jordan and William IV. She was one of the first society women to wear the very short skirt, and she has a mysterious, haunting beauty, with high cheekbones and pale aquamarine eyes. She is always in love, always surrounded by passionate, ardent lovers. She has a violent temper, when her language becomes Hogarthian and her actions dangerous to those who have annoyed her.

The *habitués* have their special tables. Mrs. Wilfred Ashley arrives wearing her favourite green, and carrying a bigger green ostrich-feather fan than anyone else. She is contemplating building a house in London near the House of Commons, which is to set a new vogue in decoration, having curtains made of mackintosh, a drawing room decorated like a bathroom with jade-green tiles, and the staircase with alternate black and white treads. It is so mentally confusing that the butler falls down and cracks his head open.

Molly Ashley is a compulsive dancer, and she has a list of men who are privileged to partner her night after night. Whether they are amusing or entertaining doesn't matter, the only criterion is that they should be good dancers.

Another well-known *habituée* already on the floor is the Countess of Portarlington. She has a regular dancing-parter. Winnie Portarlington is immensely rich. She is an Australian who married an Irish peer, and is reputedly so wealthy that she lives on the income of her income.

She is the first person in London to have her drawing room done up in the pale oyster colours which were later to become the vogue. Everything is oyster—the walls, furniture, carpets, a background perhaps for herself, or more likely for her scintillating, important guests.

There are lilies everywhere, Winnie's favourite flower. When she takes a shooting party to Stornaway in autumn, lilies are despatched to the Outer Hebrides every day from Fortnum and Mason.

Winnie gives frequent parties for Prince George and will give more later for his wife, the lovely Princess Marina. She also entertains a great number of young men like my brother Ronald, who is the best friend of her (brilliantly clever) son—Lord Carlow. Winnie's teas are famous among those who drop in after a hard day in the House of Commons or the City.

They recall the old Edwardian teas, with every sort of sandwich—watercress, smoked salmon, asparagus, paté and honey—tiny scones with golden butter, made from Jersey cows' milk, and 'Gentleman's Relish' from Fortnum and Mason.

There are fruit cakes, ginger cakes, iced cakes, macaroons, ginger biscuits, éclairs and old fashioned seed cake, and at the right season of the year there are crumpets, muffins or teacakes.

As Winnie pours out cups of tea from the huge Georgian silver tea-pot, she chatters away, knowing all the current social and political intrigues.

Her husband, Lionel Arthur Seymour Dawson-Damer, 6th Earl of Portarlington, as usual arrives at the Embassy Club alone. He doesn't sit at the same table as his wife, who anyway is dancing, but wanders round the room making himself pleasant to all his friends, especially the young, pretty women, which invariably infuriates their escorts.

'Here's that damned cuckoo again,' a man mutters as Lionel descends on them, sitting down at the table unasked, talking and glancing round at the same time just in case there is someone else he would rather be with.

He is fat and wears glasses with enormously enlarged lenses, which gives him the look of a benevolent toad. He is complete teetotal and is the first person I know to use hypnosis to help him remain so.

The Portarlingtons, like many other people, have an old family butler who is a 'character'. His malapropisms are repeated and repeated. The one I like best was when Lionel Portarlington was having a course of massage and his wife asked:

'Who was it who called just now?'

'Oh, it was only his Lordship's messiah, m'lady,' the butler replied.

Although he seems a dilettante, Lord Portarlington is, in fact, a very clever business man. He has done a great deal for the motor trade, and just at this moment has designed a new body for a Rolls-Royce, which has won high praise.

I am to design a new look for a Rolls when my husband buys one in 1927. It was the first Rolls with a white body, black wings and a black hood. The following year the coachbuilders copied my colour scheme and won the 'Concours d'Elégance' at Monte Carlo. I have my daughter's pram painted the same, and in 1929 Raine has the smartest pram in the park.

Alec and Mary Cunningham-Reid arrive in a large party, which includes Charlie Chaplin. The great film star received a very hostile press in 1915 when it was discovered that he was an Englishman living abroad in Hollywood, not doing 'his bit' and with no intention of coming back to fight. But this is all forgotten, and he has now become 'the greatest laughter-maker of our time'.

During the war the troops, while going out to fight, used to sing:

> 'Oh, the moon shines bright on Charlie Chaplin!
> His shoes are cracking
> For want of blacking,
> And his baggy trousers they'd need mending
> Before we send him
> To the Dardanelles.'

But he came back into favour with *Shoulder Arms*, which was anti-German, and in 1919 he was the main reason why half the population went to the cinema. The queues started as early as 6 p.m. for the performance which, like the theatres, was at eight o'clock. The cheapest seats were sixpence.

Charlie Chaplin's counterpart was, of course, the blonde baby-faced Mary Pickford, 'the world's sweetheart'. Mary is very jealous of her husband, the swashbuckling film hero Douglas Fairbanks, and social London is chuckling over the story that Doug had come over from Hollywood alone to stay with a well-known married couple. Mary thought the wife too pretty and Doug too interested. She arrived, there was a 'flaming' row, and she removed him to a hotel.

Off the screen Charlie is short, with iron-grey hair and a twinkle in his eye. He is intensely interested in anything English, and at the beginning of the thirties is to persuade Alec Cunningham-Reid to take him during the election to a meeting which will be broken up.

Rowdyism and broken-up meetings are very much a part of the 1931 election. Charlie Chaplin wants to see for himself. Disguised with a cap and horn-rim spectacles they go down to hear Captain Fin speak at North Dulwich. After three-quarters of an hour a fight begins, and Charlie Chaplin and Alec Cunningham-Reid, and the rest of the party, slip out of a back entrance.

Mary Cunningham-Reid looks beautiful. She has quite a different sort of beauty from her sister, Edwina Mountbatten. Her hair is the perfect Titian red of the Venetian painter, and though she is ecstatically happy she has a kind of wistful fragility about her which reminds one of a Botticelli painting. She has the enormous income of £50,000 a year, but she is completely unspoilt by money—which is later to bring her no happiness but rather a great deal of misery in her life.

At the moment, however, she is radiant, wearing against her white skin enormous aquamarines, and over her shoulders a full-length, priceless chinchilla cape.

She and her husband on their honeymoon 'shot' the first privately made film in England. It was of Africa and native life, places and people we had never seen before, and we found it fascinating.

At a sofa table near to Lady Diana Cooper are two very attractive sisters from America. One is Lady Furness, the other Mrs. Gloria Vanderbilt. The sisters are to make history, both in England and America. It is Thelma Furness who will very shortly be partnering the Prince of Wales and hold his heart until she introduces him to the unknown Wallis Simpson. But at the moment she herself is not yet in the Prince's life, nor has her sister become involved in the endless Vanderbilt litigation, which is to bring her not only deep unhappiness but also poverty.

Thelma and Gloria are so identical that their father can only tell them apart by looking under Thelma's chin for a scar she got roller-skating!

Cecil Beaton said of them:

> 'The Morgan sisters are alike as two magnolias; with their slight lisps and foreign accents, they diffuse, like Lady Howe, an Ouida atmosphere of hot-house elegance and lacy femininity . . . their noses are like begonias, with full blown nostrils, their lips richly carved.'

After Thelma's divorce from her first husband she had been deeply attracted by a charming and talented actor; but the back-stage had shown her, as it had me, the other side of the mystery and glamour of the footlights.

'I could hear Dick's voice on stage,' she says, 'I saw the half-filled jars of cold cream; I saw the boxes of powder and rouge, the tubes of grease-paint, the soiled towels thrown haphazardly on the table below the naked electric bulb. And suddenly all the glamour disappeared. . . . I realised I could never be an actor's wife.'

Lord Furness, always known as 'Duke', is one of the most acute business men in England. The sale of the Furness-Withy Line for £9,000,000 was concluded by him on the back of a menu.

Thelma finds him bold, strong, imaginative, powerful. He swears and curses but is generous and very much in love. It is at the Embassy Club that 'Duke' Furness says to Thelma the first time he takes her there:

'When's that bloody divorce of yours final, anyway?'

Reggie Vanderbilt had asked Gloria to marry him in the Colony Restaurant in New York. Most of our lives were lived in restaurants, so that is where dramatic events mostly took place.

Reggie was comparatively poor, having 'blued' most of his wealth. One day lunching at the Ambassador—another restaurant —Reggie's mother turned to her son and asked:

'Why hasn't Gloria any pearls? Doesn't she like pearls?'

'Indeed she does, Mother,' Reggie replied, 'but the ones I'd like to give her I can't afford.'

Mrs. Vanderbilt was wearing a magnificent rope of pearls wrapped several times round her neck. She beckoned to the *maître d'hôtel*.

'Bring me a pair of scissors,' she said.

She proceeded with great deliberation to untwine the long necklace and put it on the table in front of her. Then she calmly snipped it in half. Handing Gloria more than $50,000 worth of pearls she said:

'There you are, Gloria. All Vanderbilt women wear pearls!'

As Lady Diana moves towards the table next to the sisters, there occurs one of those human, amusing little incidents which are to be repeated and re-repeated around London. In the social treadmill there has for some time been a very rich, very spoilt American, who thinks it rather clever to be over-familiar and casual with the British aristocracy, thus demonstrating that he is not over-impressed by them—which, of course, he really is. As Lady Diana passes his table he puts out his left hand to take hers, making no attempt to get up. She stops for a moment, serenely beautiful.

'I didn't know you had hurt your right hand,' she says. 'I am sorry, I do hope it's not bad.'

There was a moment's startled silence, and then before he can answer she has passed on.

At another table there are some of the Cadogan sisters. There are five of them in all, and four have found husbands among the most distinguished bachelors in the land. No one can believe that this is quite by chance; for their mother is a very domineering character, with great social aspirations for her beautiful girls.

Mary is married to the tall, very young-looking Marquis of Blandford, heir to the Duke of Marlborough. Her eldest sister, Portia, has married a politician, the Rt. Hon. Lord Stanley, Edith is Lady Hillingdon, and Cynthia the wife of racing millionaire Sir Humphrey de Trafford. They are usually all together and are known as 'The Pack'.

I had been friends at Bembridge with number five, Toto. She was quiet, sweet and very shy.

'I don't want to be important like my sisters,' she told me once; but she shivered as she spoke, and I felt it unlikely she would avoid maternal pressure. She married in 1922 and had a divorce in 1929.

An inevitable visitor on a Thursday night is a young man known as 'the Borstal Boy'. He is dark and attractive, and so obviously a 'Michael Arlen' character that one almost feels that he is not real. He has done all the things which are not 'cricket', not 'public school', and not gentlemanly, and yet he has an irresistible attraction for women. When he comes into the Embassy almost every woman looks up with a little glint in her eye. All women love a devil and all women imagine they can reform one.

Later in his career he is to be shot at on a Paris station by a lady who screams 'No other woman shall have what you are taking away from me!' The revolver kicks and the bullet gets him in the shoulder, which is fortunate because otherwise it might have spoilt his attractions.

Another young man who is irresistible to the other sex is dancing very close to a very lovely young woman, who is looking at him with adoring eyes. He is short and dark, but even as he dances one is conscious of his tremendous vitality.

Prince Aly Khan is only eighteen, but he is immeasurably older in his knowledge of life and women. He is reading for the law, but he has recently given a Wild West party with seventeen other young bloods in Lancaster Gate. He has also given wild parties with the top jockey Michael Beary at the Cavendish Hotel, where Rosa Lewis, the cook de luxe of the Edwardians, tells the young about the intrigues and escapades of their fathers and grandfathers and King Edward VII.

But every woman Aly meets thinks the best party is when she is alone with him.

Aly's father, the Aga Khan, has been responsible for his son's education in love. The Aga believes, as do most Moslems, that frequent sexual relations are important to health. He studied the sexual lore of India, and he has been fascinated by the mating of horses which he has studied in his stables.

He has always insisted that there can be no pleasure for a man if the woman is not first passionately awakened. Aly had his first mistress when he was fourteen. Soon after this the Aga sent him to Cairo to an old Arab doctor, a Hakim, who had taught him many years earlier the art of making love.

For centuries a special technique has been known to the physicians of the East, which in Arabic is called *Imsák*. Sir Richard Burton, in his translation of the Ananga Ranga, says:

'This process is called in Arabian medicine *Imsák*, which means "holding" or "retaining".'

The ancient Taoists considered it an extension of man's vital force. Aly has learnt to control himself indefinitely. He can make love for six or seven hours on end; enjoying the effect he has on a woman, content in knowing himself the master.

But there was more to it than that. In bed Aly can make conquests which are begrudged him in the drawing room because of his race.

'They called me a bloody nigger,' he told a friend once, 'and I paid them out by winning all their women.'

In the years ahead Aly is rumoured to have three mistresses at the Ritz at the same time, on different floors. He goes from one to another, and all are completely satisfied and happy, having no idea there is anyone else.

Aly is to be the Casanova of the thirties and forties. He was such a talked-about, much-vaunted lover that someone is to declare:

'You weren't in the swim, and you were really *déclassé, démodé*, nothing, you hardly counted, if you'd not been to bed with Aly.'

Aly gave every woman he loved the memory of a great, if fleeting, love affair. As Elsa Maxwell put it:

'When he fell in love with a woman it was madly and deeply. The only thing, it might last only one night.'

A very different type of young man comes in with a beautiful woman. He is tall, fair and pale, with always a faint air of unhappiness about him. Lord Molyneux is one of the most eligible bachelors in Great Britain. He is the son of the Earl of Sefton, who owns huge estates in the north, and every ambitious mother is casting eyes on him for their daughters. But he won't propose.

'Hello, there's Burghie!'

'How are you, old man?'

'Hi! I want a word with you.'

Everyone in the club seems to be waving or signalling to the tall, fair man with a weather-beaten face, permanently crinkled in a smile. This is Burghie—the most popular sporting figure in society. His full name is Vere Anthony Francis St. Clair Fane, 14th Earl of Westmorland.

He was in the Navy, and there is a story which his shipmates tell that when H.M.S. *Lion* was badly hit at Jutland, and they were ordered to 'abandon ship', Burghie produced a pnemumatic lifebuoy belt which had been sent him by his aunt. He blew it up to such proportions that when he tried to leave the foretop he stuck!

Burghie has done much more than most people. He is one of the three stewards of the committee for the new and popular greyhound racing. He runs a racing stable and it was on his horse Phaco that the Prince of Wales first rode in a public race. Burghie also took the Prince to his first première, which was *Rats* at the Vaudeville Theatre.

More seriously, Burghie has studied business methods in America, has worked in a bank and with a firm of stockbrokers. He is chairman of the Dockland Settlements Board, and is known to make a success of anything he undertakes.

I was walking down Bond Street one day with an elderly Frenchwoman, when Burghie, bowler-hatted and wearing a red carnation, came towards us. She clutched my arm.

'*Alors!*' she exclaimed. 'Why am I not thirty years younger? *Quel homme!* What a beau for a young girl!'

'He is married,' I explained.

'What a beau for a woman!' she substituted.

A fair young man, so beautiful that he looks like a drawing by a Renaissance artist, enters quietly and unobtrusively, but is immediately noticed by most of the women present. He seems shy and joins a small party in a corner. This is Cecil Beaton, the most exciting young photographer, who started by using a Kodak in his mother's drawing room and now has become the 'rage'.

His first sensational portrait was of Edith Sitwell lying flat on the floor looking like a figure from a medieval tomb with a bunch of lilies on her heart, while Cecil snapped her from the top of a rickety stepladder. There was a great deal of criticism.

'Good Lord, can't they even take a decent photograph these days?'

'Sacrilege I call it!'

Margot Asquith just said: 'Sheer blasphemy!'

Cecil also photographed Edith wearing an eighteenth-century

turban and looking like a Zoffany, while in a huge four-poster bed she accepted her morning coffee from a coloured attendant.

'A lady being photographed in bed!'

'A black man in the room!'

'Your grandmother would turn in her grave!'

But the commissions rolled in. Cecil was to write later:

'All at once my life seemed fulfilled. Each week was full of opportunity.'

Cecil invented exciting backgrounds to photographs.

'I discovered materials for photographer's backgrounds,' he says, 'which created an extraordinary atmospheric effect of shimmer, like sunlight on water.'

From the baroque he is the first person to use surrealism in fashion photography and models in angular poses. This causes an uproar at the time. The reactions of Cecil Beaton's sitters are amusing.

Mrs. Asquith says to him:

'You are the only man who can make a plain woman interesting.'

Lady Astor thought he was spending too much time on her:

'Surely that's enough! To take so many pictures is madness.'

Greta Garbo hesitated:

'I wonder . . . if you weren't such a grand and elegant photographer . . .'

She wanted a passport photograph!

The day is to come when Cecil will not only entrance the world with his photographs of royalty, induce tears with those of the war, but also become the most exciting theatrical designer of our generation.

Cecil has two sisters, Nancy and Baba, who are lovely, gentle and liked by everyone. 'Presented' by their brother, they became beautie. without any scratching or clawing to reach that exalted position.

The first time Cecil shows a flair for stage designing is when Nancy and many other lovely people appear at the Galaxy Ball dressed in sequins and shimmering gold and silver-foil as a ballet of the sun, moon and stars.

At one table for two with a very pretty woman sits Michael Arlen, short, dark, debonair and, despite his Savile Row suit and Hawes and Curtis shirt, unmistakably, exotically foreign. Reviews

254

are rude and sarcastic—'Brilliant? Brilliantine', and 'At one bound Michael Arlen has placed himself in the third rank of contemporary novelists'.

But Michael has a yellow Rolls-Royce outside, his bank manager and *maîtres d'hôtel* bow to him, he is pursued by lovely, romantic, insatiable women. Soon, because his literary triumph is short-lived, he will cease to be read. But films and plays have made him very rich. He is to become somewhat of a 'pouncer'; any woman asked to a 'cocktail' at his suite in the Mayfair Hotel is wise to check first on the size of the party. It is often *tête-à-tête*.

A young woman comes in with her handsome husband. They both seem to know everyone. Lady Milbanke is an Australian. She has a serene beauty of which she appears unconscious. She has cool clear eyes, her hair grows in a widow's peak above an exquisitely chiselled nose.

Like most Australians, Sheila is a first-class swimmer, although Bondi Beach is not yet popular with British tourists. She is intelligent and efficient and much later is to be the first of the society owners of a travel agency.

Her husband, Sir John, is also keen on swimming and the new fashioned water-skiing, but he is much better known as 'the Boxing Baronet'. He has the intriguing nickname of 'Buffles', given him because his father, who won the Victoria Cross and was killed at Gallipoli, spent his honeymoon on the Buffells River in South Africa.

Buffles is now an interior decorator; one of his big commissions in the thirties will be Wingfield House, the home of the Woolworth multi-multi millionairess Barbara Hutton.

The table on the left door as one enters is the 'royal box'. Sitting there is Lord Louis Mountbatten and his exquisitely beautiful wife wearing fantastic jewels. Edwina's beauty, because she is so animated, eclipses that of every other woman in the room. She has deep blue eyes which seem to have unexpected tenderness and compassion in them.

Lord Louis never seems to be fully part of the social scene. He is laughing and talking, but one part of his brain is exclusively occupied with his career in the Navy and his insatiable driving ambition. This is to avenge the ungenerous treatment accorded his father Prince Louis of Battenberg at the beginning of the war. It was entirely due to Prince Louis's prescience that the Fleet was fully mobilised the day war broke out. Yet this great service and the fact that he had served for forty-six years in the Royal Navy did not save him from hysterical attacks on those of German birth.

Dickie Mountbatten, who is to become one of the most brilliant and the most acclaimed men of the century, will strive all his life to obliterate the cruelly unjustified sneers which caused his father's resignation.

At Edwina's table is another beauty, the Hon. Mrs. Richard Norton, who has recently tried her hand at running a cinema. Her husband, who is later to be Lord Grantley, is slightly hunch-backed and looks like Richard III.

They have very little money, but Richard Norton is to do a great deal for British films, and as they are both so popular they enjoy widespread hospitality.

Jean Norton is the last of the fabulous beauties whom people would stand up to look at when they came into a restaurant. Unfortunately her huge violet-blue eyes are very short-sighted, and many people think that she is 'cutting' them when she is literally unable to see beyond a few paces.

Her sister Kitty is married to Lord Brownlow. She also is extremely pretty and a very attractive, gentle character, but she is to get thinner and thinner, until in the fifties she is to die of a terrible wasting disease.

Lord Brownlow, whom everybody likes, and who is popular with all sorts and conditions of different people, is to figure in the history books as the man who, utterly loyal to his King, escorts Wallis Simpson secretly to the South of France at the time of his abdication.

Another strikingly beautiful woman joins the Mountbatten party. Paula Gellibrand, who sprang into fame by appearing at the Ritz in a hat covered with wistaria, is now married to the Marquis de Casa Maury. He is slim, pale with large sad eyes, and he has smiled a secret half-smile—the right-hand side of his mouth gently raised—through many difficulties and mis-fortunes.

He is proudly Castilian by ancestry, Cuban by nationality, educated at Beaumont College in England, and he served in the R.F.C. during the war. He was an ace driver, racing in all the Grands Prix driving Bugattis.

256

Now he is married, the lovely Paula has persuaded him to give up racing and take to the sea. His schooner is the first Bermuda-rigged boat in Europe. He has no skipper, he does all his own navigating. Later, when Wall Street crashes, the Marquis is to dream up the idea of the Curzon Cinema.

He spends seven months incognito, using assumed names in other cinemas, learning the trade from the very bottom. He works the projector, books the seats, clears the theatre, and finally, knowing exactly what it is about, he opens the Curzon and it is a huge success.

Bobby, as his friends call him, hates cocktail parties. In fact, he never drinks before eleven o'clock in the evening. He loves animals and has a varied assortment of pets, a cat, a Siamese kitten, an Airdale dog and a mongoose.

He has also sensational ideas on decorating, one of them being that he and Paula should have two baths in one room so that they can talk while they are bathing. Another is to have the curtains which hang in their house in Mayfair covered all over in sequins.

Paula's beauty has become smarter and more sophisticated since she married. Now she has an exoticism about her which makes her outstanding, even in a room filled with other beauties. Yet no one realises as they look at her orchid-like face and vaselined eyelids that she would prefer to be walking windswept and unmade up in the country. One day she is to disappear into the wilds of Ireland.

Lionel Tennyson comes into the room and it is like the sun coming out at Lord's. He is so large, so rubicund, so jovial and smiling. He always reminds me of the words his grandfather— the Poet Laureate—wrote when he was born: 'He glowed like a ruddy shield on the lion's breast'.

Lionel won £2,000 when he captained England at cricket. He was bet £1,000 to £5 that he would not captain the team against Australia in 1921 and another £1,000 to £5 that he would not make 50 runs. He was captain and made 63 runs.

Lionel was wounded twice in the war when he served in the Coldstream Guards, he has broken fingers on both hands and is an excellent golfer. His wife Clare, sister of Lord Glenconner, is with him, looking very lovely, very serene and very much an aristocratic Tennant. But Clare can be very jealous. Once when

Lionel was flirting with a woman at a ball she stalked on to the floor when everyone was clapping at the end of a dance.

Clare slapped the woman hard, first on one side of her face, then on the other, turned and walked away, only saying curtly over her shoulder:

'Come, Lionel!'

He followed her.

Lady Alexandra Metcalfe, always called Baba, the daughter of the Marquis Curzon, arrives looking lovely and ladylike, which is original in itself. She is accompanied by her good-looking husband, 'Fruity'. He has a lean figure, an aquiline nose slightly out of the straight, blond hair, and an indefinable dashingness about him. He is an amusing talker. Valentine Castlerosse once said of him:

'Fruity always takes ninety thousand words to go round a golf course.'

The Prince of Wales first met Fruity in Bombay, then a young Indian Army cavalry officer selected to serve as his A.D.C. He fixed the Prince up with polo ponies, amused him in his Irish brogue and started a friendship which was to last thirty-six years.

Many people were shocked at his informality and familiarity towards the Prince. But H.R.H. was to say himself:

'He behaved towards me, not as though I were a prince, but as though I were an ordinary human being like himself. He always referred to me as "The Little Man".'

Fruity gave up his career in the Army to become an equerry to the Prince, and when the public engagements were finished they would escape together to the Embassy, the Kit-Kat, Quaglinos, the Café de Paris and innumerable other night-spots.

After the opening night of the old Grafton Galleries with Paul Whiteman's band, the Prince wanted to go on dancing. The problem was where? It was impossible to take the whole of Whiteman's band back to York House where he was living.

'Lady Alexandra Curzon made a bold suggestion,' H.R.H. relates, 'that we should go to the house of her father, Lord Curzon, in Carlton House Terrace.'

Lord Curzon was fortunately away, the house was empty and servantless. Baba Curzon rushed ahead, collected some champagne from York House and ripped off the dust-sheets in Carlton House Terrace.

The band followed and the Prince and his party danced until 6 a.m., having to drink champagne out of tooth-glasses from the bedrooms, which were the only glasses Baba could find.

Lord Curzon need never have known of this intrusion had it not been, as the Prince relates, that:

'My brother Harry, a man of some weight, sat casually on his lordship's dining-room table and broke it in two! Baba bravely undertook to tell her father!'

Fruity Metcalfe (who married Baba Curzon) is a dandy or what we call 'a buck'. At White's Club they say that if you follow Fruity down Bond Street he will stop and look into the shop-windows to adjust his tie, hat, handkerchief.

He advises the Prince on his clothes: 'There's something in what the Major says', an expression used by the manager of Hawes and Curtis, has become a joke between them.

Jealous people say:

'Fruity gets the Prince into more trouble than he gets him out of!'

But one thing is obvious: Fruity gives the Prince a companionship he needs very badly. As Fruity is in the club, everyone knows whom they will see in a moment, and sure enough a footman in knee-breeches and a powdered wig pulls aside the velvet curtain, Luigi moves forward—the Heir to the Throne has arrived.

The Prince of Wales, twitching his tie nervously, follows Mrs. Dudley Ward into the room. She is petite, dark, composed, very well dressed and everyone knows he is infatuated with her. Small and birdlike, she is the first of the lovely women to whom he gives his heart.

Freda Dudley Ward has the figure of an adolescent girl, with an allure which is ageless. She is the first person to dress her small daughters like herself in red-and-white-check gingham with a red bow in her hair. Like all seductive, successful women, she has an appealing voice. Hers is high, plaintive and a little sad.

She has, too, that air of needing a man's protection, of being not strong enough to face the world without his strength, of being physically weak, yet spiritually courageous. It is irresistible!

The Prince and Mrs. Dudley Ward join the Mountbattens and their friends, who rise and curtsey or bow smoothly, competently and unobtrusively. They all sit together laughing and talking.

The Prince's entrance seems to accelerate the tempo in the Embassy. More and more people crowd in. The famous black cat, Embassy Jackson, walks along the backs of the sofas bringing luck to the patrons. The dance-floor is crowded, there is a chatter of silver-toned voices.

It is another brilliant evening because the Prince is there, and when the Prince is present everyone in Great Britain and over a quarter of the world's land-surface coloured pink on the map feels that all is well in the British Empire.

The Prince of Wales was in the twenties the most popular young man in Britain and was regarded as the most democratic. We felt that he typified everything that the young felt, especially their desire to overthrow the restriction and conventions of the elderly.

In spite of his natural shyness the Prince of Wales was popular everywhere he went. The *Illustrated London News* summed up the general opinion:

'Surely there has never been so travelled a Prince as ours, and there has never been such a successful Ambassador.'

In 1919 the Prince travelled more than 16,000 miles in four months, from one coast of Canada to the other, from the Atlantic to the Pacific, and into the United States to visit Washington and New York, where he received the Freedom of the City.

It was the first of many Empire tours made in H.M.S. *Renown*, and it was an overwhelming success. In America particularly he caused a furore. When an American magazine ran a competition in which readers were invited to write 'a love-letter to the Prince of Wales', twenty bags of mail arrived in the editor's office.

In 1920 he set off again in *The Renown*, visiting the West Indies, Santiago, Honolulu. Fiji, New Zealand and Australia. In Australia the *Sydney Sun* reported:

'Before the Prince landed the popular idea of Princes was something haughty and removed, but this smiling, appealing, youthful man, so pleased to meet with approval, has shown otherwise to the people of the democratic monarchy of the Empire.'

Of course, they worked him too hard. When he was touring Canada his right hand became so bruised and discoloured that he finally had to use his left.

At home the Prince asked 'to meet the people'. When the

260

students at University College, Southampton, danced round him singing 'Here we go round the Prince of Wales', he stood in the centre, leaning on a walking stick, his bowler hat tilted, and a smile on his lips despite his natural shyness.

What was really pathetic, and was known to quite a number of people, was that the Prince, despite his tremendous success, despite his efforts to uphold the best traditions of the Royal Family, could not gain the approval of his father. Everything he did made headlines in the newspapers, everyone applauded him, copied and praised him, with the exception of George V.

From the very moment the Prince was born the King had very strict rules as to the correct conduct of children.

'Can't you stop that child crying!' he would bark at Lala, the Prince's nanny.

From the moment the Prince could walk, his father never let him forget that he was more or less always on parade. The Prince was dressed in a sailor-suit, as were his brothers.

'If we appeared before him,' H.R.H. said, 'with our Navy lanyards a fraction of an inch out of place, or with our dirks or sporrans awry, there would be an outburst worthy of the quarter-deck aboard ship.'

Once one of the small boys was seen with his hands stuffed into his trouser pockets. Nanny was immediately summoned and ordered to sew up the pockets of all their sailor-suits.

This criticism was to continue all the Prince's life. Once, when he was thirty, after shooting at Sandringham he had gone to the kennels to look after one of his dogs who was sick, and appeared for tea still dressed in his shooting-clothes. King George reprimanded him sharply in front of a number of guests 'for being improperly dressed'. The Prince immediately left the tea-table, hurt and stung by his father's attitude.

There was also a fuss when the Prince first appeared with turn-ups on his trousers, as had become the fashion.

'Is it muddy outside?' King George asked sarcastically.

It was not surprising that there was an outburst of fury when the Prince wore 'Oxford bags', which had become the almost universal fashion, some as wide as thirty inches at the foot. It was also not surprising that when the Prince was alone he would remove his coat, rip off his tie, loosen his collar and roll up his sleeves.

'It was a gesture,' he said, 'not merely for comfort, but in a more symbolic sense for freedom.'

The King drove him hard without quite realising it. When he shot a great deal the King complained:

'You seem to be having too much shooting, and not enough riding or hunting. You must learn to ride and hunt properly, and you have had so many chances this winter at Sandringham. I must say I am disappointed.'

But the King was never satisfied. Later he became equally forcible in his insistence that in the interests of safety the Prince should give up riding in point-to-point races, and in the meantime he wrote to his son at Oxford:

'You have certainly been doing a great deal, hunting two days, out with the beagles twice, golf and shooting one day, besides all your work, which seems a good deal for one week. I only hope you are not overdoing it in the way of exercise.'

In another letter the King says:

'I do not approve of your driving a motor-car and have always said so.'

Even when he was as far away as India, paternal rebukes followed the publication of photographs in the newspaper.

'You and Dicky in the swimming baths together is not decent, you might as well be photographed naked.'

It was not surprising that once he was off duty, the Prince chose the company of people who were gay, amusing and non-critical. He was young, and above all he loved dancing. The Prince of Wales could make any night-club a success once it was known he had visited it.

Martin Poulsen, the perpetually smiling Danish head waiter who had been at the Embassy, opened the Café de Paris near Piccadilly Circus. The large underground restaurant had been built as an exact replica of the Palm Court in the ill-fated *Lusitania*. It was oval-shaped with a balcony all round, from which at one end two curved staircases led down on to the floor to make a natural alcove for the band.

The Café de Paris looked charming, the music was excellent, Poulsen engaged many cabaret acts—among them being a couple of Negroes called Layton and Johnstone—but still the customers didn't come.

The Café de Paris was £10,000 in the red. One evening he said desperately:

'There is nothing for it, I am going to telephone His Royal Highness.'

His partner thought he was joking.

'You can't do that,' he said aghast.

'I can and I shall,' Poulsen replied. 'Things are so bad I have nothing to lose.'

He telephoned the Prince of Wales at York House and was put through to him.

'Your Royal Highness,' said Poulsen, 'you promised me when I was at the Embassy Club that if I ever opened my own place you would visit it.'

'Where are you?' the Prince asked.

'At the Café de Paris.'

'Where's that?'

'In Coventry Street.'

'When do you want me to come?'

'As soon as possible, Your Royal Highness, things are desperate with me.'

'If I am going to be of any use to you,' said the Prince practically, 'you want time to tell people I am coming, and also to let the news get around generally.'

'Yes, Your Royal Highness. Would next Wednesday, the extension night, be convenient?'

'I'll be there.'

Poulsen got to work. He had managed to acquire a closely guarded address book of the Embassy Club clientele without the knowledge of Luigi. He sent four hundred telegrams to the most important members, inviting them to a free evening at the Café de Paris. He also passed the word along to certain newspaper columnists that the Prince was coming.

On Wednesday morning, to his horror and consternation, he found that a water-pipe in the Rialto Cinema immediately above the Café de Paris had broken, and that the water was pouring down the curving staircases on to the dance-floor. It must have happened in the night, for the parquet was already coming up in lumps.

Poulsen used sandbags to stop the water; then he managed to find a large piece of canvas and stretched it over the dance-floor so tightly that it pressed down the bubbles on the floor's surface. The waiters got down to work. They rubbed French chalk into the canvas, and then slid on it to give it a sufficiently slippery surface. It was a question of working against time.

Poulsen was smiling as nearly three hundred of the Embassy Club's distinguished members arrived during the evening. Nevertheless he was a worried man. The champagne, the liqueurs and the supper, he reckoned, was bound to cost him at least £2,000, and there was always the fear that at the very last moment the Prince of Wales would have an official engagement and would not be able to appear.

At last the Prince arrived. With him was Mrs. Dudley Ward, Audrey James, the dark-eyed delight of the gossip-columns, Brigadier-General Trotter, who had only one arm, and Lord Graves, the first gentleman bookmaker. The Prince and his party were bowed to a table, which was afterwards known as 'the royal box', and Poulsen prayed that the Prince would be content to watch and not take to the dance-floor.

The Prince, quite unaware that the *maître d'hôtel* was holding his breath, got up to dance, and stayed on the floor for nearly twenty minutes. There is an unwritten law that for however long a prince dances the band continues to play. Once Jack Harris's band at the Embassy Club had to play for one hour and fifty-five minutes without stopping.

When the Prince sat down he sent for Poulsen.

'You have the best floor on which I have ever danced,' he said.

After this the Café de Paris was established as the smartest place in London after the Embassy Club. Sometimes the Prince arrived with Mrs. Dudley Ward, but soon he began to appear with Lady Furness, nearly always in a party, with Brigadier-General Trotter or Fruity Metcalfe in attendance.

Others of the Royal Family followed in due course. The Duke and Duchess of York were occasionally seen there, Prince George came frequently, Prince Henry occasionally, and naturally the gossip columnists were to be there every night in search of new material and new faces.

At the far end of the restaurant there was a table reserved for Viscount Castlerosse. Sometimes his wife Doris would be with him, but more frequently he would be surrounded by members of the Prince of Wales's set.

Charles Graves, the tall, keen-eyed prolific writer, who shrewdly and acutely chronicled current events and current people, was to write a most amusing and informative book called *Champagne and Chandeliers* about the Café de Paris. He was to be seen there almost every night.

He was an unshakably loyal friend, but a dangerous enemy. His pretty dark wife Peggy, whom I loved, was born into the frothy social world, but not only wrote extremely well for innumerable magazines and newspapers, but quietly and effectively did a part-time daily job at Paddington Green Children's Hospital from the time she 'came out' until she died.

The millionaire stockbroker Sir Mackay Edgar and the fraudulent financier Jimmy White had a special telephone installed from their office to a table on the right-hand side of the balcony. This meant they could sell in New York after the London Stock Exchange had closed. At one time they were trying to corner Mexican Eagles and a stock called Waste Food Products.

Jack Harris, who was now the band-leader at the Café de Paris, took their tips and made thousands. But Jimmy White committed suicide in 1927 at the age of forty-nine to avoid a spectacular financial crash. He had started life as a bricklayer in Rochdale and became a legendary gambler, backer of many theatrical shows and a racehorse owner. The '43' lost its best customer.

The Café de Paris was different from the Embassy in that it employed dance hostesses. There were only a few of them, selected for their dancing ability and their looks. They received £2 a week and their supper, but naturally they made a great deal more than that.

One dance hostess I remember was very pretty, with her fair hair swept back off her oval forehead, and with a marvellous pink and white complexion. Her name was Nora Turner, and whenever the Duke of Marlborough appeared, which was very frequently, he would dance for hours with her. She was later to be one of the most publicised women in London when she married Sir Bernard Docker.

The Duke of Marlborough never to my mind looked like a duke. He was very short, slight and frail. He was an excellent dancer and always wore black suède shoes. He had a strange mannerism of emptying his pockets and placing the contents on the table. His possessions were not much to look at—a box of matches, his keys and some small change. He never seemed to have a great deal to say, and I often thought that Nora Turner had a bored look on her face.

But the Duke's close friends found him sensitive, deeply religious and interested in the mystical. He was a sad and lonely man and became a Catholic. In 1926 he wished to marry again, and in consequence there was world-wide commotion because the Protestants were furious at the Roman Rota for annulling his episcopal marriage to Consuelo.

When the Duke's conversion to Catholicism was announced, his mother—an Ulster Hamilton—telegraphed him: 'To hell with the Pope!'

It was at the Café de Paris that a very beautiful girl, who looked oriental with her dark skin and slanted eyes, danced with Morris Elbey, the bearded film director. He gave her three days' work as an extra in his current film.

It was against all the rules that a dance hostess should be absent without leave. Poulsen was furious, and on Merle Oberon's return she was informed that next time she did it she would be fired.

The next time was when she became a film extra in Alexander Korda's film *The Private Life of Henry VIII*. She was so outstanding that Korda spotted her and gave her the part of Anne Boleyn. When Merle Oberon next visited the Café de Paris it was as Mrs. Alexander Korda.

A tail-coat was, at first, absolutely compulsory at the Café de Paris, although later dinner-jackets crept in. But even when things got still more relaxed no one was allowed on the dance-floor except in evening dress.

After a time Members of Parliament used to come from the House of Commons, and other people, distinguished enough to be admitted despite their day-clothes, were allowed to eat on the balcony. Oswald Mosley frequently supped there, often with Hilary Charles, who with her sister, Pat, resembled pretty, fragile butterflies.

Oswald Mosley, tall, dark, with almost black eyes which never seemed to smile, always seemed a rather frightening figure to me. When he was elected to Parliament he was acclaimed as being absolutely brilliant, and his first speeches commanded universal admiration in the House. He stood as an Independent, and all three parties wooed him. As it was obvious that his leanings were towards the left, it was said confidently by everyone that sooner or later he would lead the Labour Party.

Sir Robert Throgmorton was a very eligible bachelor, who was frequently to be found at the Café de Paris. He was usually referred to as 'The Sleeping Baronet' or 'The Dormouse' because he had an enigmatic expression of face. Actually he suffered from insomnia. He was adored by his mother, a Catholic, who lived, as my own mother did, in Worcestershire.

Robert Throgmorton rather played at being the fool, but actually he had a first-class brain. He was lazy because he liked being lazy. He hated making plans, he didn't want to take anything seriously. He loathed inventions, cocktails and women who tried to reform him. He was a curious phenomenon with a great deal of charm.

One of the most interesting men who seemed to be permanently at the Café de Paris—at least I never went there without seeing him—was Sir Louis Greig. He was perhaps the most versatile man of the period. He had been adulated as an international rugger player, he was a sailor, airman, a stockbroker, a brilliant tennis player, an extra Gentleman Usher to the King, Comptroller to the Duke of York and his partner in the men's doubles at Wimbledon.

He had joined the Navy at the age of twenty and became a surgeon-lieutenant, but when the authorities learnt how good he was at rugger he was posted to Osborne. Within a few years he found himself attached to the Duke of York, and went with him to Malaya. There they were both transferred to the Royal Air Force.

Only when the Duke married the fascinatingly sweet little Lady Elizabeth Bowes-Lyon, who became the most loved person in the land, did Louis Greig join a firm of stockbrokers. But this didn't stop him from keeping himself one of the fittest men of his age in the country, and being continually asked for 'a game of tennis' when it could be fitted in amongst his other activities.

But above all things he enjoyed dancing, and while the band played he was seldom off the floor.

One very popular person at the Café de Paris and everywhere else he went was the Maharajah of Rajpipla, who was always known as 'Pip'. He had an income of £200,000 a year, and lived a double life because in England he was democratic, unassuming and unceasingly gay. In India he was very much the dignified ruler over the millions of his people who revered him.

Over here Pip won the Irish Derby and the Irish Two Thousand Guineas, and his Sunday afternoon parties at his house at Old Windsor were legendary.

In the East, Pip entertained in his enormous palace those who enjoyed big game hunting, like the Duke of Sutherland, polo players and anyone who wanted to gape at his state army, his vast fleet of motor-cars and the royal ceremonial by which he was surrounded.

One of the most elegant visitors to the Café de Paris was the Marquis of Milford Haven, elder brother of Lord Louis Mountbatten. He had been in the Navy, like his father and brother, for twenty-seven years and always carried a silver cigarette case—which held fifty—engraved with his rank and actions during those years. He had been trained at Osborne and had been present at the Battles of Heligoland, Jutland and Dogger Bank.

Like so many men of the period he had a passion for model railways—Jack Hulbert was another devotee—and had two miles of track in a barn in the grounds of his home near Maidenhead.

Lord Milford Haven was brilliantly intelligent and had been decorated by the Swedes, the Italians, the Spanish and the Russians. He married Nada, the daughter of the Grand Duke Michael of Russia, and there was something exotic and intriguing about them both.

Later Nada Milford Haven accompanied her sister-in-law, Edwina Mountbatten, on many of her restless travels around the world.

'Nada is the perfect companion,' Edwina told me, 'she enjoys everything, never fusses, never complains and always has something new and unexpected to say. It is impossible to be bored when one is with her.'

The two of them were to go to many strange places, including an archaeological tour in Persia. In Damascus they bought an ancient motor-car which carried them safely over six hundred miles of open desert to Bagdad. The route to Teheran lay over a mountain range and through wild and hostile country through which no unescorted women had ever journeyed before.

On they went again, despite the British Ambassador's warnings against the Kurds, and they eventually reached Persepolis, the buried city discovered by Professor Herzfield with its Elamite, Achaemenian and Sassanian rock carvings.

'It was disappointingly quiet!' Edwina said later, and made light of what was really a notable feat.

'But,' she went on, 'it was the most exciting place we had ever seen . . . we stepped back into history. It made us feel of very little consequence.'

The Prince of Wales sometimes visited the Café de Paris in the morning or the afternoon to practise the Charleston when it first became the rage. He would bring Mrs. Dudley Ward and have the whole polished parquet floor to himself.

The Charleston arrived in London from the United States in the summer of 1925, and was received in state by sixty dancing instructors assembled by the *Dancing Times* at the Carnival Club in Dean Street. Then it swept the country, but not without a great deal of criticism and opposition. It was banned by hotels and in public halls as 'a Negro dance'.

'I set my face absolutely against the Charleston,' Mrs. Wilfred Ashley said. 'I think acrobatics in the ballroom are in the worst of taste.'

This was followed by my own remarks, which sound now very pompous, and I can't think why I ever made them.

'It is only the very objectional Oxford-trousered, tight-waisted kind of young man,' I said, 'who is to be seen doing the Charleston, and the girls who dance it will wear ultra-short frocks, ultra tight, and use make-up to excess. It is all hideously vulgar.'

Naturally nobody paid any attention, any more than they listened to the Vicar of St. Adrian's, Bristol, who declared:

'Any lover of the beautiful would die rather than be associated with the Charleston. It is neurotic! It is rotten! It stinks! Phew! Open the windows!'

But the fact that the Prince of Wales was seen doing it extremely well in every night-club naturally took the sting out of such opposition.

Santos Casani, a well-known dance instructor, demonstrated the steps of the Charleston on the roof of a taxi moving down Regent Street. He and his staff gave as many as 280 lessons a day.

269

Millions of people took their ballroom dancing very seriously. By now the dancing craze was widely popular on the radio, and listeners were invited to roll back the carpet and take a few steps. 'Tea for Two' was sung, whistled and played morning, noon and night, and 'The Indian Love Call' made a great number of people practise yodelling in their bath, and at other times when it was well calculated to annoy their neighbours.

But one could still talk in night-clubs, gossip across the table or murmur sweet nothings to one's companion.

New night-clubs opened almost every week, and closed as quickly. Smart society, or by now it was almost Café society, stuck to their favourites. 'The Not', a small oblong room under-neath the Café Anglais in Leicester Square, was also bought by Poulsen and his partner.

'The Not' became a forcing ground for new talent. Hutch started there, the most delightful as well as the most talented of all the coloured performers of the twenties; so did Elsa Lanchester, Terry-Thomas, Florence Desmond and Douglas Byng.

Douglas Byng, who was witty both on and off the stage, was the first female-impersonator that I ever knew. He was a charming, intelligent man, and in the thirties I was to perform at a charity matinée with him, in which I was dressed as a débutante, and he was my tiara-ed dowager of a mother.

The Duchess of York, as well as Prince George, were two of his admirers. Douglas wrote all his own songs, one of his most famous being 'Flora MacDonald', which he sang wearing a Scottish plaid and a red wig. The words were:

'Flora MacDonald, Flora MacDonald,
Happy with haggis and dripping with dew,
Many's the time she's been out in the heather,
Bending the bracken with young Charlie Stew.

'Flora MacDonald, Flora MacDonald,
'Twas she, when Charles called her and bade her
come forth,
Clung to his kilt and went over the border
(Yes, right over the border),
Old Flora MacDonald, the hen of the north.'

270

Douglas was often asked to write songs on some particular theme. Prince George suggested the idea of 'Argentine Annie', which was a great favourite, but Douglas really had quite enough ideas of his own. He always made me laugh, and once when I asked him where he was going for a holiday, he conjured up a perfect picture when he replied:

'I am off, dear, to be among the beaded bodices of Bournemouth.'

In the very early twenties there was a night-club in Leicester Square called 'Lamb's', where there was a magnificent pianist. I and my friends used to go night after night just to hear him play. It wasn't surprising that we found him good, for his name was Charlie Kunz, and later he was to sell millions of his records.

There were to be two night-clubs called 'The Bat'. The first, the old 'Bat', was in Frith Street. It was narrow, dark, overcrowded, noisy and irrepressibly gay. I remember Teddy Gerard, panther-like, with her hard-bright eyes turned up at the corners, a perpetual tomboy, playing the drums and singing at the top of her voice!

When one of my husband's friends was at Eton at the beginning of the war he used to sneak up to London to see Teddy in *Bric-à-Brac*. She always met him in her dressing room stark naked.

The new 'Bat' in Albemarle Street had balloons attached to the ceiling, which was low and smoky. One evening when I went there a cartoonist was drawing a red-headed, bediamonded woman with too low a dress and too loud a voice, while an Egyptian was telling fortunes.

A very pretty young woman in the process of divorcing her gay racing-driver husband arrived to find him talking earnestly to an unhappily married beauty.

She marched up to the table, picked up a glass of champagne and threw it in his face. He didn't even flinch.

'I say, old girl, you must be over-tired!' he said quietly. 'It's the heat, I expect.'

His wife smashed the empty glass on the ground and with tears running down her face rushed out of the club followed by the man who had brought her. He paused long enough to say:

'Sorry, old man!'

The racing-driver waved an acknowledgment.

No one took the slightest notice.

The Café de Paris closed for redecorations in April 1929. When it reopened it had been painted red, green and gold and was very glamorous. This was in keeping with the new fashion. Short dresses had disappeared, women with plucked eyebrows wore their dresses to the ground. Among those dancing, in a long gown and wearing a necklace of magnificent black pearls, was Lady Furness, partnered by the Prince of Wales.

'I found in him what at that time I most wanted and needed,' Thelma said. 'Not only was he fascinating to me in terms of his own personality, but he was the perfect compensation for my emotional heart. "Duke" was rugged, blustering, carelessly self-indulgent, the Prince was shy, gracious, meticulously considerate.'

It was the beginning of a great romance.

How many romances started and ended in night-clubs? Love was born—and died—to the music of the band. We lived a lifetime of emotion from the moment we stepped on to the floor until with surprise we found the room was nearly empty, and reluctantly we knew we must leave. Another night was over.

Was the happiness, the closeness, the understanding we felt as we danced real, or was the cold wind blowing pieces of paper along the deserted streets and the pale grey dawn over the wet roof-tops reality? It was hard to know. One thing I vowed to myself over and over again:

> 'I'll follow my secret heart
> My whole life through.
> I'll keep all my dreams apart
> 'Till one comes true.
> No matter what price is paid
> What stars may fade above,
> I'll follow my secret heart,
> 'Till I find love.'

CHAPTER TEN

Even when the darkest clouds are in the sky,
You mustn't sigh
And you mustn't cry:
Just spread a little happiness as you go by,
Please try!
What's the use of worrying and feeling blue?
When days are long
Keep on smiling through;
And spread a little happiness
Till dreams come true.

ON Monday, 3rd May 1926, I, like the majority of the public, learnt with astonishment that we faced the unknown dangers of a General Strike at midnight.

The astonishment was very real, for communications between Parliament and the public were not good, and neither the papers nor the wireless had prepared us for what a number of people feared was the beginning of a revolution.

Although there were all sorts of alarming rumours of what might happen, at the same time the British tradition of facing things calmly was very evident. On the first morning public transport ceased abruptly in a strange, almost eerie silence, but non-union workers were determined to get to their jobs, and my brother Ronald was one of them.

The previous March he had started work in Leadenhall Street, and he accepted a lift from a friend of his on the carrier of his motor-bicycle. They started off gaily from Royal Avenue in Chelsea, where we then lived. I remember waving them goodbye, feeling a kind of irrepressible excitement that something unusual was happening. I watched them disappear down King's Road and went back into the house.

An hour or so later we learnt there had been an accident. In crossing Westminster Bridge a car had swerved unpleasantly near them. Instinctively Ronald had drawn in his long legs. His foot touched the wheel of the motor-bicycle, and the spokes cut through the leather of his shoe and sliced the back of his heel from his foot.

He was carried into Westminster Hospital, where they sewed on his heel and sent him home in a taxi.

For two weeks he was in bed, suffering acute agony, after which my mother took him to Eastbourne to convalesce before he returned to work on crutches.

I got in touch with my friends and found that everybody was volunteering to help in any way they could, and that centres had been set up in different parts of London where volunteers could apply. I discovered that my nearest centre was at Hyde Park Corner.

I didn't, of course, learn until later the reasons for the strike. What I did sense, and what had been obvious from my brother's attitude, was that the majority of Londoners resented being held to ransom by the strikers, and it was felt to be an adventure to fight back by carrying on as usual.

A shop assistant thrilled to Sir John Simon's affirmation that 'You can wear out the shoes of a working girl, but you cannot wear out her spirit'. There were certainly some very tired feet in the processions of exhausted men and women tramping home-ward in the evening from the City and the West End.

What the strikers didn't envisage was the defensive solidarity of what they called 'the bourgeoisie'. It was the bulldog deter-mination 'not to give in' which had not been known since the autumn of 1914.

Long before the recruiting centre at the Foreign Office opened on the day before the strike, the courtyard had been filled with men and women waiting to enrol. Three hundred thousand were enlisted in the Volunteer Service Corps within a few days, and the strike-breaking machinery of the Government was to prove brilliantly effective.

Hyde Park was transformed, between midnight on Sunday and Monday afternoon, into a vast centre for the distribution of milk; in fact two million gallons were handled every day. Huts, sentry boxes, telephone systems were quickly erected to cope with the five hundred lorries which had been commandeered.

On the third day of the strike my mother said:

'It is an extraordinary thing, but there seems to be no increase in food prices.'

With Ronald's accident, I was too busy the first day of the strike to offer to do anything. The following morning we learnt there had been violent demonstrations. A motor convoy passing through Poplar had been surrounced by a mob which destroyed one of the cars. Police had made a baton charge on the crowd, and several men had been arrested. But these outbreaks, and those that followed on the second day, only angered, instead of frightening, the majority of people.

There were no newspapers, with the exception of *The Times* in a very abbreviated form. I didn't know until later that Lady Diana Cooper had been sitting up all night to help fold *The Times*, and that it was being produced by the non-union members of the staff.

What was more important was that the *British Gazette*, a newssheet edited by Mr. Winston Churchill, began to appear on the streets, and by the ninth and last day of its publication achieved a sale of more than two million copies.

Viscount Hambledon, the head of W. H. Smith, with three or four of his friends, kept the printing machines going for the *British Gazette*, and 'the Bentley boys', and every other man I knew who had a fast car, were engaged in carrying the newssheets all over the country.

By the third day seventeen hundred trains were run, wholly by volunteer labour. Motor launches took office workers up the Thames to the City. All private cars offered lifts, and were packed to capacity.

The young men who had been laughed at as effeminate, and decried as being limp and purposeless, now came into their own. Nearly the whole of Buck's Club and White's were enrolled as special constables, among them the Duke of Rutland and Lord Tennyson.

Sir 'Buffles' Milbanke was a police sergeant, and Sir Anthony Lindsay-Hogg, who had been spoken of so often as the playboy of the period, carried the *British Gazette* backwards and forwards to Manchester day after day, with hardly two hours' sleep before he was back on the road.

It was not known at the time, but the Prince of Wales lent his car and his chauffeur to carry the *British Gazette* to Wales.

Lady Louis Mountbatten and her friend, the Hon. Mrs. Richard Norton, were on the switchboard of the *Daily Express*, and the Universities enrolled to a man, most of them longing to drive a train.

One request at Oxford from the undergraduates to Lord Winterton when he was there was that he would allow them to kidnap the Master of Balliol, Lord Lindsay, a prominent Socialist, who they alleged, without any solid evidence to support the accusation, was trying to impede the smooth working of the volunteer organisation.

Hundreds of undergraduates came to London from Oxford and Cambridge to enrol as special constables, and Lady Howard de Walden was asked if she would put some of them up. She decided that by sleeping them on the floor of the ballroom and the other big rooms in her house she could take about two hundred, and she also offered to feed them. When asked how soon she could begin, she replied:

'Now, today, and I will give them lunch.'

This sounded optimistic, but she had remembered that there would be a great many cancellations of receptions and dances arranged for the summer season, and that the caterers would be only too pleased to sell their now unwanted food.

In two days' time Lady Howard de Walden had organised a canteen in her garage and was feeding not only all her own visitors, but all the other youths who had been put up in different houses in Belgrave Square.

'The night-shift young men,' she recalls, 'played bridge to keep themselves awake in a passage which was near the telephone and a small side door into the stable yard. Then, after a telephone call, and a grinding and rumbling of engines, they would be off in lorries to the trouble spots with truncheons in their belts.'

On the third day of the strike the headquarters at Hyde Park gave me a message to take to the Harrow Road. Someone in the office with a car was going that way, so I got a lift in the right direction, and then set off to walk. It was a cold, wet day.

Not used to this part of London, I looked about me with interest and a little apprehension. The dirty streets, the dilapidated, mean little houses badly in need of repair, the ragged children

276

running about with insufficient clothes and bare feet and the general air of poverty and depression struck me with surprise.

My mother had in 1922 worked in Bermondsey at a Mothers' Centre. She had told me then of the sufferings of the very poor, how a large percentage of children she cared for were suffering from gathered ears and noses, partial blindness and many other complaints, which indicated syphilitic parents.

She told me, too, of the dirt and lack of sanitation, of children covered in lice, which they looked on as being a commonplace of life, not at all extraordinary or in need of being cured. But to see such conditions for myself was a very different thing.

For the first time since the strike began I wondered if the miners were not justified in refusing a cut in their wages. Were they, anyway, earning a living wage? And could it really be true that the British workmen wanted to overthrow the country just because they had been indoctrinated with Communism?

The streets got dirtier and more depressing. There were miserable, bedraggled dogs with their ribs showing, cats lurking round overflowing, stinking dustbins, and men standing at the street corners and in doorways, surly and unsmiling, who I thought must be strikers.

I began to remember the tales of areas where there was severe unemployment—of mining villages where the children stayed away from school because they had no clothes; of mothers fainting from lack of food as they waited in queues; of half-derelict houses where the rain dripped through the ceiling, and overcrowding meant ten or more people sharing a room.

I hadn't listened, hadn't believed it—but now I began to think of all I had heard.

I wondered if I was lost, and then, to my relief, saw a special constable. He was a pale-faced, very thin young Jew. He was wearing a special constable's armband over a threadbare overcoat, which seemed an inadequate protection against the rain and wind.

I told him I was looking for the vicarage, and he replied that I was only two streets away from it.

'Is everything all right down here?' I asked him.

'Like a morgue,' he answered. 'I shall be glad when my beat's finished and I can get off to work.'

'What do you do?' I asked.

'Pianist in a dance band,' he replied.

I laughed.

'I doubt if I shall be able to go dancing tonight, all the men are too busy.'

'There was quite a good crowd where I was playing last night,' he answered.

I left him and found my way to the vicarage. It was an ugly, Victorian building with the inevitable smell of cabbage, worn linoleum on the floors, and a clutter of children's prams, bicycles and prayer books in the hall.

There seemed to be no one about, but a hand-printed piece of paper pinned to the door told me that the volunteer office was upstairs.

I climbed the staircase, and as I reached a turn a woman carrying a shopping-bag was coming down. I stood aside to let her pass as the stairs were narrow, but as she seemed in a hurry she bumped against me. The impact made her loosen her hold on the shopping-bag, and it rolled down the stairs. Out of it fell a loaf of bread, a tired-looking cabbage, half a dozen dirty potatoes.

'I'm so sorry!' I exclaimed, and to my consternation she burst into tears.

She was not a young woman, she was wearing a shabby black suit, a scarf round her neck, and she had no hat. She stood there crying for a moment without putting up her hands. In dismay I went down the stairs again, picked up the bag and put back into it the bread, the cabbage and the potatoes.

'I'm so sorry,' I repeated, 'it was clumsy of me, but I don't think anything is damaged.'

'It isn't that,' she muttered, pulling out a torn handkerchief, 'it isn't that, miss, and you 'aven't done any 'arm.'

'Is anything the matter?' I asked, thinking that as this was the vicarage she might have come for consolation in a bereavement.

'It's this strike,' she said, blowing her nose fiercely and coming down the stairs towards me. 'I came 'ere to see if they could give me any work—paid work. But they says everyone is a-doing it for nothing.'

I hesitated.

'Is your husband on strike?' I asked.

She looked over her shoulder.

'Don't tell 'em upstairs,' she pleaded, 'and 'e'd kill me if 'e

278

knew, but I've got to get some money somehow. I've got a baby at home with bronchitis, and there's not a thing to eat except what's in the bag. What good is that to a man and five kids.'

'Five?' I exclaimed.

She nodded.

'What does your husband do?' I asked.

'' 'E's a tram-driver,' she replied. 'The wages aren't bad, but we've got behind with the rent, owing to the little one being so ill—a-coughing all night she's been. Out in sympathy they calls it. To my mind sympathy begins at 'ome.'

'I am sorry,' I said.

'That's all right, miss,' she said, taking the bag from me. 'I don't want to worrit you with our troubles. I'd no right to come 'ere. We'll manage, only I prays God it don't go on too long.'

'Can't you ask the vicar for help?' I enquired. 'Perhaps he has a fund for something like this.'

'I tried 'im before,' she answered, 'and 'e couldn't give us money. 'Tisn't as though we're church-goers. I 'aven't the time on a Sunday, that's a fact.'

I groped for my purse.

'I'm afraid I haven't got much money with me,' I said, 'but let me help.'

'No, miss,' she replied, 'there's no call for you to do that. I'm not begging.'

'Of course you aren't,' I agreed, 'but it's for the baby who is ill.'

I opened my purse. Fortunately I had 22s. 3d. with me. It seemed quite a large sum to me, and the woman was almost speechless.

'I can't take all this, miss.'

'Yes, you can,' I answered. 'Remember, it's for the children.'

'God bless you, miss,' she said, the tears starting to her eyes again.

At the sound of someone coming down the stairs, I thrust the money quickly into her hand.

'I am sure it will all be over soon,' I said comfortingly, and ran up the stairs to deliver my message.

But going home I knew that 22s. 3d. had not salved my conscience. How long would it last to feed a family of five children? And how many families were there without help, without hope?

London's worst disorders on the second day were at Camberwell, when motor-cars were attacked and two policemen seriously injured. We also learnt of the ugly incidents in the north, riots in Edinburgh, and at Leeds passengers in emergency cars were wounded by lumps of coal and flying glass.

By now ships were being unloaded in the docks by undergraduates, their amateur efforts giving great amusement to the regular dockers. Middle-aged men and women worked in canteens, kept open day and night in town halls, to serve the needs of the emergency lorry-drivers.

Troops were moved into London in large numbers. A hundred lorries, escorted by twenty armoured cars and a detachment from two regiments of the Brigade of Guards, drove from Hyde Park to the docks and returned by noon. This was a show of strength and produced a certain amount of hostile booing, but there was no real trouble.

Sometimes the strikers formed defence corps under ex-N.C.O.s, which prevented police charges on picket-lines, but by the end of the strike 260,000 special constables had been enrolled, and their families were promised allowances and pensions in the event of injury or death.

The *Daily Mirror News Bulletin* for Wednesday, 5th May 1926, a single sheet which cost a penny, said:

'THE DAILY MIRROR calls upon its readers to do all in their power to support the Government. Its message to all is "Stand Fast".'

Strike Brevities
Milk will be dearer tomorrow to the extent of 2d. a quart.
Clyde shipyards are still carrying on.

Sport
All racing, with the exception of Chester Races, is cancelled.
First-class cricket continued yesterday:
The Australians made 336, of which Gregory scored 120, and got Leicester out for 96.

Stock Exchange
The London Stock Exchange carried on business as usual.

On the second day of the strike, when I was walking back down King's Road to Royal Avenue, I met a young man called

Brian Buchel, an actor, who was the frequent dance-partner of one of my friends.

'Do you know anywhere I could stay?' he asked me. 'I've volunteered to drive a bus, but I've got to find a bed for the night.'

I took him home, and my mother offered to put him up. The next three days he would come in from work so tired that we had to keep him awake while he ate.

On the Friday Brian said at breakfast:

'I've got to find someone to go with me on the front of my bus today. The chap who came yesterday is driving himself, and we have to take someone with us in case there is trouble.'

I suggested one or two men whom we both knew, and Brian made several telephone calls. But our friends were all busy with their own jobs. One had realised his lifelong ambition in being allowed to drive a train, another was on duty in Hyde Park, a third thought that as there was rioting at the docks it would be more exciting down there.

'Well, I'll go with you,' I offered at length.

Brian didn't make very much protest, he was so keen to be off.

We went to collect his bus, an old and rickety one, and, of course, open at the top.

Most buses travelled with two men in front and a policeman beside them. There was no policeman available in the bus station, but the supervisor handed me a large truncheon.

'What am I supposed to do with this?' I asked.

'Hit someone with it if there's any trouble,' I was told.

The truncheon was so heavy I could hardly lift it, and I felt it was unlikely to be much use in an emergency. But there was no time to argue. Brian got the bus started and I climbed into the front seat beside him.

Our route was Cromwell Road, Hammersmith Broadway, and on to Richmond. At Hammersmith there had already been trouble, and we were told one bus had been set on fire. However, it seemed fairly quiet, until the bus broke down.

'What a place to choose!' I said to Brian.

He jumped out and opened the bonnet. At the best of times he wasn't much of a mechanic. He was looking at it rather helplessly when a man in a cloth cap came up and spoke to him.

I listened apprehensively. The man looked just the type of person to be aggressive.

' 'Aving trouble, sonny?' I heard him ask Brian.

'I can't think what's wrong,' Brian replied dismally.

' 'Ere, let me 'ave a look.'

The man bent over the engine, did something magical, then nodded to Brian to get back into the driver's seat. He swung the handle and the engine spluttered into life.

'Thank you very much,' Brian shouted, and I thanked him, too.

The man grinned.

'I'll be driving one myself in a day or two.'

He winked at me, and we set off.

'Do you realise that must be one of the strikers?' I said in awestruck tones to Brian.

'Jolly good chap,' Brian replied.

When we got to Richmond our last passenger descended. Our conductor—a boy about seventeen—came round and said:

'I don't know about you two, but I could do with a cup of tea.'

'Let's go to the Star and Garter,' I suggested.

It was then a hotel and had not yet become the magnificent hospital for plastic surgery which was to be known all over the world in the years to come.

Brian drove the bus with difficulty and much coaxing up the hill to the Star and Garter. We drove into the car-park amongst a number of smart shining private cars. The attendant looked at us in surprise.

'Mind my car,' Brian said haughtily as we disappeared into the hotel.

It was said afterwards that Sir John Simon's intervention on Thursday, 6th May, when he gave his opinion that the strike was illegal, 'profoundly influenced public opinion'. But it was not until 12.20 p.m. on Wednesday, 12th May, that a deputation of the T.U.C. met the Prime Minister, Mr. Baldwin, at No. 10 Downing Street. The news was at once broadcast that the strike had ended, and Mr. Baldwin said firmly:

'I am not out to smash trade unions and I will not allow the strike to be made a pretext for the imposition of worse conditions.'

Never in the wildest dreams of the ordinary public, or in those of gossamer, fun-seeking young Mayfair, would there seem to be any likely connection between Osbert Sitwell and the grim, explosive near-revolution taking place between the trade unions and the coal-owners.

Osbert Sitwell, the eldest of a sensational much-publicised trio, was not only poet, writer, musician, humorist, practical joker and satirist, he was also closely and traditionally concerned with politics, knowing intimately the coal country and the miners near his home at Renishaw.

Osbert saw clearly the desperate peril into which the nation had drifted without its being fully realised either by the Government or by the leaders of the trade unions.

While the miners were claiming 'Not a penny off the pay, not a second off the day', and the rest of the country backing the Government were crying 'Aren't we splendid? Look how we are coping with the situation!', the greatest asset of the British race stood in jeopardy—our long-established civil peace.

Osbert felt that to force the strikers and the whole Labour Party to extremes by not giving them an opportunity to save their faces was to invite disaster. As things were, the most trifling incident might precipitate fighting.

'Who wanted such a struggle?' Osbert asked in his account of the crisis. 'Some pickets were in a militant mood, not less bellicose was the Thug Militia of St. James's Street, the bands of young steel-helmeted clubmen. But no one, not even these strikers or strike-crushers, desired this particular outbreak.'

But events were rushing along at too swift a rate. The attitude of both sides was hardening, and each half of the nation was growing tired and angry.

Arnold Bennett reflects the feeling at the Reform Club in his diary:

'General opinion that the fight would be short but violent. Bloodshed anticipated next week.'

Duff Cooper relates on Wednesday, 5th May:

'Diana asked me this morning how soon we could with honour leave the country. I said not until the massacres begin.'

On Friday Osbert was asked by Lady Wimborne to luncheon. As there was no transport he had to walk from King's Road to

Wimborne House in Arlington Street in the pouring rain. He then drove with Lady Wimborne in her Rolls-Royce to the Embassy Club. Here Osbert burst into flame.

'Why,' he demanded, 'does no one do anything to stop the strike? Why does no one even try?'

'What can be done?' Lady Wimborne asked gently. 'What could we do?'

'You know every sort of politician,' Osbert replied, 'you ask them all to luncheon in ordinary times. Make use of the habit now.'

'Yes, but how?'

'It is obvious,' Osbert answered, 'that the trade unions have drifted into a false position, one which they hate in their hearts. Try to get them to meet the coal-owners privately.'

Lady Wimborne wasted no time. The following day at luncheon at Wimborne House the guests included Lord Londonderry and Lord Gainford, both great coal-owners; the Rt. Hon. J. H. Thomas, Chairman of the Trade Union Council; J. A. Spender, editor of the Liberal *Westminster Gazette*; Lord Reading; Mrs. Snowden representing her husband; and, of course, Osbert with the Wimbornes.

J. H. Thomas, always known as the 'Rt. Hon. Dress Shirt', the last to arrive, was obviously worried and tired almost beyond breaking-point. The achievement of the Wimborne luncheon which lasted nearly four hours, was the admission by J. H. Thomas that the miners were now in the mood to accept the controversial Report of the Coal Commission. This was so important that Lord Reading wrote down a formula, and Lord Wimborne left with it immediately for the House of Commons, to see Lord Birkenhead and Winston Churchill.

The ball had been set rolling, but there were many obstacles still ahead. Lord Birkenhead said in a private letter to the Viceroy of India:

'It would be possible to say without exaggeration of the miners' leaders that they were the stupidest men in England, if we had not had frequent occasion to meet the owners.'

On 11th May the two ex-Viceroys, Lord Wimborne and Lord Reading, made sustained and impassioned appeals to J. H. Thomas to call off the strike immediately. At first it appeared as if he would not yield.

'It was with my pen at my writing-table,' Lord Wimborne told me, 'that Birkenhead drafted a formula, together with Thomas, which was exactly what was wanted. J.H. turned to me and said "If you will get this to the P.M. tonight, and if he puts it out tomorrow morning early without altering a comma, the strike will be off by midday". My secretary went off with it to Downing Street in the middle of the night—I told him he was to give it to Baldwin whether he was asleep or not! He had the dickens of a job to force his way into Baldwin's bedroom—but he did it!'

Lady Wimborne telephoned the news to Osbert at 2.15 a.m.

'So great was my relief and joy,' he recounts, 'that I couldn't sleep.'

At no time during the General Strike was feeling so bitter on the men's side as in the days immediately following its conclusion. There had been riots, picketing had been far from peaceful, many people had been injured while the struggle was actually in progress, but not one life had been lost.

The first fatal casualty occurred three days after peace was declared, when a volunteer worker named 'Peachy' was attacked as he was going home through Rotherhithe Tunnel and was so brutally knocked about that he died.

On the whole, however, physical violence was the lesser evil of the conflict. Broken heads could be patched, but broken wills and damaged faith took far longer to heal. The men felt betrayed.

The loss to trade was, we were told, to be in the neighbourhood of £30,000,000, but what seemed so utterly senseless was that the miners who had started the strike gained nothing, and were to continue their fight pointlessly and hopelessly for another six months.

For the majority of young people in the twenties the strike seemed at the time an adventurous exercise; and yet looking back it meant far more than that. It was for me, and a great number of my contemporaries, a milestone. It was a moment when we ceased to be young and carefree and thoughtless, when we began to think. In fact, what really happened was that we began to grow up.

We had always known that because we were born into a certain stratum of society we had a responsibility for those less fortunate. For those who had lived in great castles on country estates it had been automatic that they should look after their tenants and the people who worked on their land, that they should visit them when they were ill and help them in their difficulties.

For those like myself, who were poor, there was still the idea that by the accident of birth one was, with or without money, the 'Lady Bountiful', someone to whom less-fortunate people could turn when they were in trouble, and who would always be willing to help.

My mother had no money to give away after my paternal grandfather's financial crash in 1902, but all through the years we had lived at Pershore she had been what was called a district visitor. The worst slums in the small town had been under her care. She visited them once or twice a week, she went down dirty stinking alleys, where one pump in the centre of a courtyard provided the water for forty people. She helped the mothers when they were pregnant, she saw that the children went to Sunday School, and that a doctor was called when someone was dying.

I took this all as a matter of course, just as once or twice a week I would walk beside my brother's pram and go with Nanny to a cottage to hand over soup or outworn clothing for those in need.

But in London, as I danced day and night, it seemed as if I had no responsibility. Yet after the strike I began to think about those dirty, mean streets, those ragged children, and those men who had struck because they were denied what they believed was just for themselves and their families.

Now that my brother was living at home I began to learn about things that I had only vaguely heard my father discussing before he was killed—the political implications of poverty, the right of everyone, whoever he might be, for his voice to be heard in the running of the nation.

Two years earlier, while still at Charterhouse, Ronald had written a long and passionate letter on the injustices suffered by Labour.

'I have been talking to some of the men working on the roads there,' he said, 'and they have almost convinced me that Socialism is the right policy. Every man should give to society as a whole more than he takes from it, and until that is brought about England cannot be saved. Peace will never come, nor prosperity.

I believe that every man should have a living wage, not the paltry dole of 18s., for which while in employment he has paid 1s. 2d. a week. It is wrong for boys of fourteen to be cast into this world with no future and less education. I am fearfully worried about England's state, and we do need a broad policy.'

But when we talked about Socialism, Ronald could not reconcile himself to the overthrow of tradition. He believed in Private Enterprise and in the freedom of the individual. He thought that Socialism would not only prove restrictive in industry, but that their centralisation of bureaucracy would prove impractical and expensive.

At the beginning of the General Strike we had talked of all the things that should be done so that the social structure could be made fair and just for everyone.

'The extremes of wealth and poverty in this country are unjust,' Ronald said. 'How can we reconcile the fact that the Government has asked the men toiling for a pittance in the mines to take a cut in their wages while they are given no hope of security in the future, or even a promise that it will not be done again and again'.

I would argue with him because I wanted to crystallise my own thoughts on the matter, but when I told him about the woman I had met on the stairs down the Harrow Road, Ronald exploded.

'Can't you see that it's wrong that a man should be starved into submission? The miners believe in what they are fighting for. To hit them through their families is to make them nothing but slaves and serfs. A man, even if his convictions are wrong, must be allowed to express them. Fight him if you will, but not with the weapon of starvation.'

Three years later Ronald was to work in Shoreditch in support of Viscount Knebworth, who was standing as a Conservative candidate. By this time Ronald had moved to the Conservative Central Office, having decided that his career must lie in politics because only by becoming a Member of Parliament could he help people and put forward his ideas for the betterment of the country.

Anthony Knebworth was the son of the Earl of Lytton. He was a good-looking, lovable person, tremendously idealistic, and he and Ronald argued and disagreed and agreed with each other, each firmly convinced that 'something must be done'.

Shoreditch was a Labour stronghold: Anthony had no hope of winning the seat, but it was considered good experience. Ronald was shocked beyond words at the conditions he found in Shoreditch—the same type of shock that I had experienced that damp, wet day during the General Strike.

The desire he already had within him to improve the lot of the working people burst into a blaze of anger. His hatred of injustice was something which had been with him ever since he was a child; now it became a crusade. Having seen how people were living in Shoreditch, he knew he would never rest until he could bring hope and faith to the people who most needed it.

'For all men,' he said, 'there must be security for their old age, and freedom while they are young from the terror of unemployment.'

It was what he saw in those mean, dismal streets which made him fight for what later, after he was killed, were to become the foundation planks of Conservative Party policy—no unemployment, family allowances, holidays with pay, social security, location of industry, and above all national planning so that the Distressed Areas would have work. At the time these ideas were revolutionary, but they were conceived in Ronald's mind at the end of the twenties, when he convinced me, as he did so many of his friends, that that was what we too had to fight to bring about.

Of course most people said:

'These high ideals are impossible to put into practice. Anyway, what can I do, personally, about it? It's the responsibility of the Government.'

Ronald replied in a political article:

'Ideals must be related to the world in which we live. We live in the world. We strive to better ourselves. We strive to better the conditions of the world around us as a development of ourselves. No government can change men's souls; the souls of men change governments.'

To me he said simply:

'You and I must every day give more to the world than we take out. Money is not the answer. The most expensive and the most valuable thing we can give is ourselves.'

I tried then because he asked me to do so. I still go on trying. Anthony Knebworth became the Member of Parliament for

Hitchin. He felt he must also serve his country and joined the Auxiliary Air Force. On 30th April 1933 he crashed when practising a formation flight with his squadron at Hendon. He was obeying an order when the aeroplane struck a rise in the ground.

Ronald was the first Member of Parliament to be killed at Dunkirk in 1940. He represented the King's Norton Division of Birmingham and had become the only Tory champion of the Distressed Areas.

After the General Strike we ostensibly went on dancing, yet some of the gaiety and spontaneity seemed to have gone out of it. Noël Coward, as usual sensitive to the mood of the moment, sang:

> 'I'm getting tired of Jazz tunes
> Monotonous
> They've gotten us
> Crazy now.
> Tho' they're amusing as tunes
> Music has gone somehow.'

We developed a social conscience and became aware of the charities which needed our help, not just because it was an excuse for dressing up, but because something had to be done, and it was extremely difficult to raise money.

Lady Howard de Walden had been appalled at the conditions in Queen Charlotte's Hospital, which was then more or less dedicated to unmarried mothers who had priority for their first lying-in. She set about finding out how many maternity beds there were after the war in the whole of London. Doctors helped her, and she went from hospital to hospital. There were no more than five hundred beds for a population of eight million.

She learnt all she could about the running of Queen Charlotte's. She noticed that the women were never allowed to have their babies beside them, and were kept in for only five days. Then, weak and often far too ill to cope with a young baby, they were turned out into the streets to make room for another mother.

Sanitary arrangements were pitifully old-fashioned: in fact Lady Howard de Walden complained:

'Nothing much seemed to have been done since good Queen Charlotte's day.'

It was obvious that what was wanted was a big new hospital with everything up to date, but, of course, it all came down to one thing—lack of money.

The largest financial crash of the decade—when Clarence Hatry was arrested—took place in September 1929. In October the Wall Street Stock Market collapsed. The repercussions of these two disasters not only bankrupted a lot of people, but caused slumps in industry everywhere. Unemployment soared in every country in the world.

There was a despairing song from the penniless and the workless:

'Brother, can you spare a dime?'

While for the once well-to-do, the wealthy and the social hangers-on, there were some plaintive lines from Noël Coward, which were too near to the truth to be really funny:

'Children of the Ritz
Children of the Ritz
Sleek and civilised
Fretfully surprised
Though Mr. Molyneux has gowned us
The world is tumbling around us
Without a sou
What can we do?
We'll soon be begging for a crust
We can't survive
And keep alive
Without the darling Bankers' Trust.'

All the same, Lady Howard de Walden was determined she would build a new hospital, and she asked Mr. Seymour Leslie, a little man with a big heart who was to promote so many appeals in the thirties, if he would help her. He came to see me.

'Barbara, do think of some way we can make money for Queen Charlotte's Maternity Hospital—they need it desperately.'

'What had you in mind?'

'A dinner-dance was suggested by the committee. We can get the Kit-Kat.'

'That's good; people love going there, and it's big.'

'Yes, but if we are going to sell the tickets at a fancy price, we must have an attraction.'

'You would have to pay for a cabaret. . . . Wait, I've got an idea, why not a pageant?'

'A pageant! At a dinner-dance! It's never been done!'

'Then we'll do it. And as it's for the hospital, why not "Queen Charlotte's Birthday Dinner".'

'How do you mean?'

'With beauties dressed up as the dinner. We'll start with Oysters! Think how lovely that dress will be! And we'll end with Plum Pudding!'

We didn't, we ended with Champagne, a fabulous breathtaking dress made in a new, sensational, transparent material manufactured from wood pulp. In a few years it was to be used for wrapping everything from sausages to cigarettes—it was called Cellophane. I wore it!

I asked Lady Curzon, who had been the Queen of Beauty in the Elizabethan Tourney arranged by Lady Randolph Churchill before the war, if she would be Queen Charlotte.

'But she was hideous!' Mary protested.

'No one remembers that! Besides I want a lovely queen, so we have to take artistic licence!'

'I couldn't play anyone so ugly!'

So Binnie Hale was Queen Charlotte, and looked quite inaccurately ravishing. We also made a lot of money. The hospital committee was thrilled.

I was to go on to design a dozen pageants in the threadbare thirties, when it got more and more difficult to raise money. Sometimes I used to feel cynical when I saw how much women were prepared to pay for the fun of dressing up. But they would never have given it direct to the charity, so it had to be enticed out of them.

The young, like myself, had no money to give or to lose, so we found the song of the moment very appropriate. And our young men sang it with gusto!

'I can't give you anything but love, Baby.'

Other things changed and contributed to our feeling of growing older, one of these being a change in our figures. In 1929 C. B. Cochran put his famous Young Ladies on a diet for *Wake Up and Dream*—not to slim but to give them feminine curves.

'Girls between the ages of eighteen and twenty-two are unable to stand the strain,' he said, 'they seem to live on nothing but ginger ale, orange juice and cigarettes. I am determined to revive the natural figure.'

Mr. Cochran's Young Ladies were scientifically weighed and measured. They stopped fainting during rehearsals, and the slender, wraith-like figure was doomed. Cochran's diet consisted of cream soup, a boiled egg or an omelette with cheese, wholemeal bread and butter, salad, fresh fruit and honey.

What was momentous was that the bra was invented. Mrs. Kennedy of Kesto borrowed two silk handkerchiefs from her husband, folded them to form triangles and sewed them together. After years of being flat-chested, our busts were uplifted and we had 'it'.

This was the new name for a new sex appeal, invented by Elinor Glyn, after seeing Clara Bow who was slinky, catlike, seductive, yet full of vitality and verve. We were *women* again, so Noël Coward made us sing:

'Teach me to dance like Grandma used to dance
    I refuse to dance—Blues,
  Black Bottoms, Charlestons, What wind blew them in?
    Monkeys do them in Zoos. . . .'

How often people write of the twenties as a stupid phase, not realising that it was a tremendously exciting time of transition. It was the growing up of a new generation into a new era; and while adolescence is always difficult and tempestuous, it is also the foundation for the future.

So much was discovered, invented and developed in the twenties from which the world has benefited and been profoundly thankful. It was not really until World War II that the general public became aware of the miracles that penicillin could perform, but it was the twenties which should be thanked for its conception.

What was so fantastic about the discovery of penicillin was

that it was accidental, and due initially to the untidiness of Professor Fleming.

In 1928 he placed in a glass dish a culture of bacteria which cause blood-poisoning. He watched its growth under a microscope, then pushed it on one side. Today the bacteria can still be seen as a scattering of yellow blobs, but on one side of the saucer only. On the other side there is a patch of green mould and no yellow blobs. Looking at it Fleming noticed these.

'This mould,' he said, 'seems to produce a substance which kills bacteria.'

Spores, minute particles floating in the air, had alighted on the dish, multiplied, and set to work to kill the bacteria. This would never have happened if Fleming hadn't been so casual as to leave the dish lying about after use. What we owe to him is his perspicacity in noticing what had happened and in a flash of insight realising its significance.

'The crude penicillin I made in those days,' Sir Alexander Fleming said later, 'was weak, and much too impure for injecting into the body.'

But in 1941 its efficacy in the treatment of human infections was developed, and saved thousand upon thousand lives.

Another exciting medical discovery of tremendous benefit to mankind was the insulin treatment of diabetes, developed by Frederick Grant Banting, the Canadian doctor. The first patients to receive insulin were in Toronto General Hospital in 1922.

Constance Collier the actress was desperately ill, suffering from diabetes, and thought that she was dying. Mrs. Robinson the fortune-teller told her she would be cured by a new invention only known 'far across the water'.

Constance Collier went to Switzerland where the doctors told her there was no hope. Then she heard insulin had been discovered in Canada. She went there and was cured. Banting later received the Nobel Prize.

At Cambridge University Ernest Rutherford made one of the most profound discoveries of the twentieth century. This was announced in 1919 as 'the first artificial transmutation of matter'. Rutherford believed that the vast energy trapped in the atomic mucleus would never find practical appreciation, but his theory of the atom gave rise at the time to thousands of atom jokes!

Max Planck's revolutionary ideas on energy made possible the calculation of the orbits of electrons inside an atom, which became the foundation of new physics from 1925 onwards.

A scientist friend sent me this little verse:

> 'Planck has a plan-k
> Entirely new.
> Thanks to Planck,
> My mind is blank,
> Of all I knew.'

We began to believe after the war that science had debunked religion.

'How can there be a God and the evolution of the species?'

'Where is heaven? Science shows it isn't above us!'

Sir Arthur Eddington developed a new conception of the Universe, its galaxies, nebulae and stars. He explained it in his book *The Nature of the Physical World* in 1928. He and his scientists arrived at the astonishing conclusion that the world finally resolves itself into terms of 'abstract mathematics'.

'The external world of physics,' he said, 'has become a world of shadows.'

But Sir Arthur was not content to leave it at that. He was a mystic and deeply convinced that there was something more 'beyond the things that physics and astronomy can reveal, something in human experience that cannot be accounted for by scientific symbolism because it belongs to another world.'

Scientists were astonished when he announced:

'I believe in the in-dwelling of the Divine Spirit in the mind of man.'

In 1921 Ronald, home for the holidays from Charterhouse, showed me a newspaper heading which read:

'*Hun Professor Catches Light Bending.*'

'Whatever does that mean?' I asked.

'Einstein has proved that light does not travel in a straight line!'

'I never thought it did, I thought it "smoogged" about the place!'

I still think that is rather a good word for it!

There was a verse which we all quoted, and thought ourselves very clever:

'I don't like the family Stein!
There's Gert,[1] there is Ep,[2] there is Ein.[3]
Gert's writings are punk,
Ep's statues are junk,
And no one can understand Ein.'

When Einstein heard of the first atom bomb being dropped, his peace of mind vanished. After Hiroshima he said:

'If only I had known, I'd have been a locksmith.'

In the twenties there were also wonderful physical achievements.

In 1921 there began a series of British attacks on Mount Everest. The first was a reconnaissance party which attained 23,000 feet. In 1922 they came to within 1,700 feet of the summit, which is calculated to 29,002 feet.

We were sure that the spirits of Everest, somehow linked with the Tibetan Mahatmas—implicitly believed in by the followers of Madame Blavatsky—would never permit man to reach the top. Sir Edmund Hillary proved us wrong on the day of the Coronation of Elizabeth II in 1953.

In 1922 Sir Ernest Shackleton died of heart failure. He had left London in the ship *Quest* for a three years' tour of Antarctica. During his polar journeys he had found the gigantic Beardmore glacier, discovered the Antarctic plateau of frozen desert a thousand square miles in extent, surveyed 1,300 miles of new land so accurately that all succeeding travellers have relied upon his maps.

Shackleton was not only an adventurer and an explorer; he had, someone said, 'the curiosity of a scientist—and the sensibility of a poet'.

When in 1921 he sailed in *The Quest* the whole nation thrilled to his daring. He was, however, forty-seven, and he wrote in his diary:

'Ah me, the years that have gone since in the pride of young manhood I first went forth to the fight! I grow old and tired, but must always lead on.'

Shackleton's last entry read:

[1] Gertrude Stein, American *avant-garde* writer.
[2] Jacob Epstein, sculptor, creator of 'Rima'.
[3] Professor Albert Einstein, mathematician and physicist.

'In the darkening twilight I saw a lone star hover gem-like above the sky.'

He was a lone star. Thirty-six years were to pass before the Trans-Antarctic Overland Journey was attempted again and achieved by Sir Vivian Fuchs.

When I flew over the North Pole in 1969 and looked down on the endless desolation of snow and ice, I marvelled how human beings could brave the terrible loneliness and immensity of either Pole and live.

In 1925 Mr. J. L. Baird was working in his attic in Soho when he called to an office-boy, William Taynton, working in the room below.[1] William entered Baird's attic and saw a strange assembly of soap boxes, bicycle-sprockets, sealing-wax and bull's-eye lenses, with a ventriloquist's doll sitting in front of the contraption.

'What are you doing?' William asked.

'I'm trying to see this doll through that brick wall,' Baird replied.

William thought he was mad!

Another day Baird asked William to sit in front of the machine. Powerful lights with tin reflectors were nearly touching his face, it was very hot. He was fed up and rising to leave when Baird shouted from the next room.

'Hang on, hang on a second longer! Put your tongue out, William!'

William was sure he was crazy.

'Shake your head!' Baird shouted. 'Open your mouth! Shut your eyes!'—then suddenly he yelled, 'I can see you, William! I can see you!'

That was how a London office-boy became the first person in the world to be seen on television.

Other exciting events and 'first times' to remember were:

1922—An Act of Parliament ended the employment of children in factories. It seems incredible that it should have lasted so long.

1925—The first electric record players were marketed. I wonder we had not developed bulging muscles in our right arms from the everlasting winding of the old gramophones. The running-

[1] From *Scrap-book of the 20's* by Leslie Bailey.

down of the record was also disrupting, and produced many an anticlimax. One would be dancing to:

> 'I'll leave you never
> Love you for ever . . .'

'This is wonderful, being able to dance with you like this!'
'Yes, isn't it?'
'There's something I've been wanting to ask you—something which means everything in the world to me—darling, will you . . . ?'

> 'Sa . . . y you will . . . lo . . . v . . . e . . .
> me . . . t . . . o . . . o.'

'Oh, damn the gramophone!'

1927—On October 6th, in the film *The Jazz Singer*, Al Jolson sang the song 'Mammy'. It killed silent pictures.

The same year Alan Cobham flew to Cape Town and back, then to Australia, 28,000 miles and back. He landed in his D.H.50 on the Thames in front of the House of Commons, where he was received by a huge crowd and members of the Government. He was knighted and in 1929 his 'Air Circus', as it was called, toured the country and gave five-shilling trips to forty thousand passengers without a single mishap.

Also in 1926 the first transatlantic public telephone service. The first time I spoke across the Atlantic was to Sir James Dunn. I was flabbergasted.

'Hello, Barbara, this is Jimmy calling you from New York.'
'From New York?'
'Yes!'
'Oh . . . what's the weather like?'
At £15 for three minutes!

1928—Kingsford Smith made the first Pacific flight from America to Australia, and Squadron-Leader Bert Hinkler did the first solo flight in an Avro Avian from Croydon to Australia in fifteen and a half days.

I thought of Hinkler last year when flying home from

Australia by Qantas. They told me that when they have their jet planes they expect to make the journey in nine hours!

1929—Whittle's first patent for the jet engine. Everything was getting faster and faster, life was moving quicker and quicker. A lovers' lament for the future went prophetically:

> 'We travelled slowly when we met,
> By horse and cart or bicyclet.
> Your arms were shelter when 'twas wet,
> Soon you'll flash past me in a jet.'

So many 'firsts' were achieved, so many risks taken, so many lives lost, was it surprising that in 1929 women, worried and apprehensive, sang with feeling:

> 'Button up your overcoat
> When the wind is free,
> Take good care of yourself,
> You belong to me.'

Whatever the writers, satirists and some songs of the period may suggest, the twenties were not a period of diffidence, apathy or mental sluggishness. British adventurers and dreamers, men who had guts to see beyond the horizon and behind the impossible, whether it was on Everest or in the workshop or the laboratory, were all struggling to make themselves heard.

We were young, we were ignorant, we were careless, we were thoughtless; but at the same time in every one of us there was a feeling that we were going forward, and sooner or later we would do something worth while.

It takes time to grow up, but it happens to every one of us. We didn't develop without a great deal of personal suffering. We got a lot of hard knocks, a lot of snubs, but we learnt never to whine. It was a form of pride and an obstinate, rather splendid courage.

Cecil Beaton was ducked in the river during Lord Herbert's coming-of-age party at Wilton. He says:

'Out of the darkness a group of tail-coated young men surrounded me and, without a word of explanation, high-jacked me across the lawns at an enormous pace towards the river. . . . In the panic that assailed me, the emotions of humiliation and shame were stronger than fear. . . .

'I was determined not to leave the ball. While the water ran down my legs and oozed out of my shoes, I remained by a window . . . making conversation. . . . Later I danced. . . . About one thing I was determined, the incident would never be mentioned by me. So far as I was concerned, it had never taken place.'

I, too, never spoke of the times I was hurt. I, too, pretended that they had never happened. Today, when I receive an offensive or anonymous letter, I tear it up immediately. When someone is rude to me I never speak of it. I will not admit such a thing has happened.

Sirocco, a play by Noël Coward, was a catastrophe. The audience booed Ivor Novello and Noël was spat on as he left the theatre.

Eddie Marsh related:

'I supped with them both that night at Ivor's flat, and have seldom been more impressed than by the dispassionate courage, free from all trace of self-pity, with which these two routed aspirants, neither of whom would have been surprised to be told that he was irreparably done-for, discussed the failure and its causes.'

We were hurt and wounded, but we would never surrender.

We didn't want sympathy—as Noël Coward said many years later:

'One's real inside self is a private place and should always stay like that. It is no one else's business.'

I found in the twenties that anything that was original, anything that was outside the ordinary, the hum-drum, was at first to be misunderstood, decried and condemned.

It is hard when you're young to do something from an entirely idealistic point of view, and be told you're seeking publicity, and wanting only to promote yourself entirely from selfish motives.

Everyone resents being snubbed or sneered at: but for all of us, I think, the opposition from those who fought us, who criticised us, who alleged that we were everything that was bad and stupid, only made us more determined than ever that we would show them they were wrong.

Looking back I can see how the General Strike affected so

many of us. After it was over, Edwina Mountbatten, rich and beautiful, began her travels all over the world. She was not yet dedicated to a life of service and to alleviating suffering—that was to come in the 1940's—but she now began her preparation for it—unconsciously perhaps—but who is to know how we are guided in these things?

She got to know people of all nations and of all classes. She learnt to travel without comfort, to endure hardship without noticing it, to understand what other people were feeling. It was to make her perhaps the most celebrated woman of our generation—a woman for whom the two Houses of the Indian Parliament stood in silence for two minutes when she died.

But for others, in not perhaps such a spectacular way, there were changes. They got married and settled down, they took up new interests outside the murmur of dance bands and the confines of dark, smoky night-clubs.

For the beautiful Jean Norton the General Strike was a moment when she realised something of the sufferings of those who toiled manually for long hours on low wages. When the Second World War came she was to work in a factory, under such gruelling circumstances that it affected her health and eventually killed her.

But for all of us, however much we changed later, however wiser and more stable we became, the beginning of the twenties will always remain in our minds a period of irrepressible gaiety, when we snatched at the wings of happiness and, for a short while, felt they lifted us towards the stars; when we declared with Peter Pan:

'I am youth, I am joy, I am the little bird which has broken out of the egg.'

We were young, we were alive, we could laugh and love, and our feet could dance. That was ecstasy, that was youth, and it can never come again.

Index